CRIMES OF THE SCENE

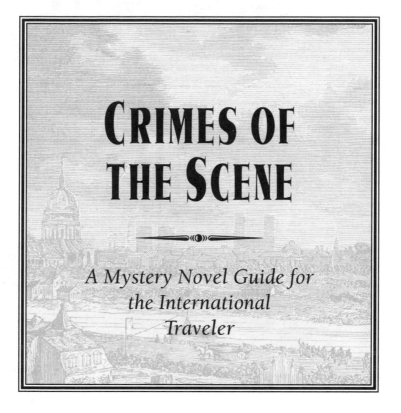

CRIMES OF THE SCENE

A Mystery Novel Guide for the International Traveler

NINA KING
WITH ROBIN WINKS
AND OTHER CONTRIBUTORS

ST. MARTIN'S PRESS ❧ NEW YORK

Production Editor: David Stanford Burr

Book design by Ellen R. Sasahara

Library of Congress Cataloging-in-Publication Data

King, Nina.
    Crimes of the scene : a mystery novel guide for the international traveler / Nina King with Robin Winks and other contributors.—1st ed.
        p.   cm.
    "A Thomas Dunne book."
    Includes index.
    ISBN 0-312-15174-8
    1. Detective and mystery stories—History and criticism. 2. Setting (Literature) I. Winks, Robin W. II. Title.
PN3448.D4K56   1997
809.3'872—dc21   96-44225
                                                          CIP

First edition: April 1997

10 9 8 7 6 5 4 3 2 1

CONTENTS

NOTE: UNATTRIBUTED CHAPTERS AND
CLOSE-UPS ARE BY NINA KING.

ACKNOWLEDGMENTS

Crimes of the Scene began in the summer of 1992 when I as editor of the *Washington Post Book World*, asked Robin Winks, distinguished historian and mystery aficionado, to write a three-part series on mysteries as travel literature. Readers were enthusiastic; they wanted more, and I did, too. Later that year I suggested to Robin that we collaborate on a book-length version.

While working on *Crimes of the Scene,* I consulted many secondary sources. From the start, one was indispensable: Allen J. Hubin's two-volume *Crime Fiction II: A Comprehensive Bibliography 1749–1990* (New York & London, Garland, 1994), which meticulously cross-indexes thousands of mystery novels by their settings.

Robin Winks's other commitments eventually forced him to limit his contributions to *Crimes,* so I recruited other talented writers to cover areas of the world I knew little about. And I hit the road myself—at least metaphorically—on every possible occasion. I am grateful to my bosses at the *Post,* Managing Editor Robert Kaiser and Executive Editor Leonard Downie, for their generosity and encouragement, and to my colleagues at *Book World* for their critical skills, their knowledge of many things, and their patience with my constant chatter about the perils of travel and of authorship.

I am grateful, too, to my editors at St. Martin's Press, Tom Dunne and the peerless Ruth Cavin. It was Ruth who introduced me to the international organization of mystery writers known as AIEP (Asociación Internacional de Escritores Policiacos) and to the always helpful Mary Frisque, executive director of its North American branch. At AIEP gatherings in Gijòn, Spain, in Prague, and in Havana, I found comrades and contributors, and a wealth of facts and ideas. I owe special thanks to my AIEP friends and to my other hard-reading companions on trips abroad during the years I've been working on this book: Suzanne Curley, Dianne Donovan, Wendy Law-Yone, Peggy Manring, and Eleni Meleagrou.

Crimes of the Scene is dedicated to my very first traveling companions: my father, the late Rear Adm. James W. Davis, and my mother, Ruth Steele Davis, who taught me how to pack a suitcase and encouraged me—by her example—to bring along an open mind.

And something to read, just in case.

CRIMES OF THE SCENE

INTRODUCTION

By Nina King

> All tourists cherish an illusion, of which no amount of experience
> can ever completely cure them; they imagine that they will find
> time, in the course of their travels, to do a lot of reading. They see
> themselves, at the end of a day's sightseeing or motoring . . . stu-
> diously turning over the pages of all the vast and serious works
> which, at ordinary seasons, they never find time to read. . . . They
> come home to make the discovery that they have read something
> less than half a chapter of the *Golden Bough* and the first fifty-two
> lines of the *Inferno*.
>
> —Aldous Huxley, *Along the Road*

I'M A LONGTIME cherisher of the touristic illusion described by Huxley.
My version of it is that I will read the great works of the country I'm
visiting on their home ground: Proust in Paris, Joyce in Dublin, Gibbon
in Rome. Inevitably I return home none the wiser, having fallen asleep
for ten nights running on the third page of *Swann's Way*.

Huxley's solution was a book that could be read in snippets before
sleep prevailed (La Rochefoucauld's *Maximes*, for example). Mine is a book
that will defy sleepiness while painlessly imparting local information: a
mystery or crime novel set in the place I'm visiting.

Though in its formative years the mystery novel tended to stay put in
the drawing rooms of English country houses, only venturing forth to
wander the mean streets of Los Angeles or New York, it is now a worldwide phenomenon. There are mysteries set in Beirut and Belize, Calcutta
and Casablanca. Not all are of high quality, either as fiction or as travel
writing. But the best of them offer valuable information about a place and

insight into its people in the guise of entertainment. What more could the weary tourist—or the armchair traveler—ask?

Though there are distinctions to be drawn between mysteries and thrillers, detective and spy novels, we ignore them here. The spy novel is, most often, also a mystery, and some of the best travel writing is by the likes of John Buchan, Graham Greene, John le Carré, and Adam Hall. In fact, as Robin Winks has written elsewhere, the spy novel—with its protagonist sometimes on the run and sometimes fading into the background to avoid discovery—probably set the standard for accuracy of setting for all popular crime fiction. "The first law for a secret agent," writes Ian Fleming in *The Man with the Golden Gun* (NY, 1965), "is to get his geography right, his means of access and exit, and assure his communications with the outside world."

Crimes of the Scene is a guide to the world of the mystery. It includes mysteries set in almost every part of the world, with two major exceptions: the United States and Great Britain. So numerous are the mysteries set in those two countries that each needs a guidebook of its own.

At the heart of the book are annotated reading lists—comprising hundreds of brief reviews of crime novels grouped by setting. In most areas, the annotated reading list is prefaced by a short essay on some aspect of that region's mysteries—for example, the shadow cast by Franco in mysteries set in Spain. Whenever possible the lists include novels written by natives of the region, though we are limited to those that have been translated into English. As a result, this book is weighted toward novels by English and American writers—and, inevitably, to the outsiders' viewpoints that they bring to "foreign lands."

Both outsiders and insiders have things to tell us, but there is no doubt that we can learn more from the best of the translated local writers than from the English and American visitors. Their models may have been Chandler and Hammett and McBain, but Simenon and Sjowall/Wahloo and van de Wetering and Vásquez Montalbán and Taibo have changed and enriched the American hard-boiled tradition and made it their own, *le roman noir* or *la novela negra*.

One of the most obvious changes: in the hands of Europeans and Latin Americans, the mystery is much more apt to be a vehicle for systematic social criticism—particularly from a leftist point of view—than it was even for Dashiell Hammett, the sometime Communist.

Unlike the hard-boiled mystery, the spy novel—from Buchan to Bond and Buckley—has inclined to political conservatism. The great villains of the Cold War thriller are the Soviets, the Red Chinese, and *los barbudos* of Castro's Cuba. However, in the works of the very best spy novelists—Eric Ambler, Graham Greene, John le Carré—irony and ambiguity, not ideology, reign supreme.

Another generalization, this one based on content rather than point of view: for most Americans it is difficult to realize how large and vivid and *recent* World War II looms in the European imagination (and here "European" includes British). It is amazing how often the solution of a mystery plot is the unveiling of a secret from that war—an act of altruism or betrayal, a treasure or a tattoo. Related to this is the stubborn curse of anti-Semitism, which surfaces in many books by English and French writers in particular.

The selection of books included in each section of this guide obviously reflects the taste and interests of the writer of that section. The general criteria considered by all the contributors include the quality of the writing; the authenticity and/or evocativeness of the setting; an effort at variety (different subgenres, times, social milieux, etc.).

For places where there are many titles to choose from (e.g., Paris or Moscow), all these criteria can be applied. But for places where there are few choices, routine or even inferior mysteries may be listed for the sake of geographical completeness.

Accuracy of detail is particularly important to the reader on the spot, or indeed to anyone who knows the place well. On the one hand there is the thrill of recognition ("I've eaten in that café!"), on the other, there is the equally thrilling irritation provoked by an author's mistakes ("Doesn't Tony Hillerman *know* that Washington, D.C., cabs don't have meters?").

But to the vicarious traveler, authenticity is much less important. What matters is that the place *feel* right, that the novel be convincingly evocative of a *genius loci*. With the masters of setting and atmosphere, in fact, there is always a risk that the fictional version will overwhelm the real and distort the reader's image of a place. The damp, smoky Paris of Inspector Maigret may remain vivid in the reader's imagination long after the snapshots of last year's French vacation have faded.

Though *Crimes of the Scene*'s primary purpose is to serve as a guide to the best and/or the most characteristic mysteries of each destination, it is our hope and our intention that the essays, brief reviews, quotes, and

"close-up" features will be interesting and entertaining reading in themselves, and that the book as a whole will make a modest contribution to
the history of the genre.

ON INTERPRETING THE LISTS: The Reading Lists feature short reviews of
the best and/or most representative books available for each country or
region. Most are followed by even briefer listings labeled "Noted But Not
Reviewed." Some of the latter may be inferior books; others may simply
have surfaced too late to be read in their entirety.

In all the listings we include in parentheses the place and date of first
publication followed by that of the edition used (if different). For example, "(NY, 1941, 1989)" indicates the book was first published in New
York in 1941, and that the reviewer used a 1989 reissue. In the case of
translated books we also try to include the date of first foreign publication in brackets.

THE HONOR ROLL: All the contributors to *Crimes* were given the option
of designating one or more books with the old Michelin tag *vaut le voyage,* suggesting (tongue slightly in cheek) that it would be worth the trip
just to read this book on location. The six books so designated are:

> Mexico: *The Shadow of the Shadow* by Paco Ignacio Taibo II
> Cuba: *Our Man in Havana* by Graham Greene
> Belize: *High Adventure* by Donald E. Westlake
> Eritrea: *To Asmara* by Thomas Keneally
> Russia: *USSA* by David Madsen
> Holland: *Auprès de ma blonde* by Nicolas Freeling

ON FINDING THE BOOKS: This can be difficult and we ask your indulgence
for frustrations you may encounter. Like all books today, mysteries have
a short shelf life. And they tend to go in and out of print very quickly.
Books that are in print are no problem. Any decent bookstore can tell you
if a title is available and then order it for you. Most specialty mystery bookstores will, in fact, have most of the titles in print at any given time on
their shelves. There are dozens of such stores all over the country. Two of
the most famous are New York's Mysterious Bookshop, 129 West 56th St.,
New York, NY 10019, (212) 765-0900, (800) 352-2840; and Murder Ink,
2486 Broadway, New York, NY 10025, (212) 362-8905, (800) 488-8123.

My local favorites are MysteryBooks, 1715 Connecticut Avenue NW, Washington, DC 20009, (202) 483-1600, (800) 955-2279; and Mystery Bookshop Bethesda, 7700 Old Georgetown Rd., Bethesda, MD 20814, (301) 657-2665, (800) 572-8533.

Sources for more obscure titles include rare-book stores (though these can be pricey) and the book-sale rooms of mystery fan conventions—such as the annual Malice Domestic and Bouchercon meetings. (Mystery bookshops should have information on these events. See also the listings in such publications as *The Armchair Detective*.) For British editions not in print in this country, try London's Murder One bookstore, 71–73 Charing Cross Road WC2H 0AA, ph. (011) 44-171-734-3483, or Crime in Store, 14 Bedford Street, Covent Garden, London WC2E 9HE. Their phone number is (011) 44–171–379–3795. This store, which is new in 1996, has as some of its shareholders seven well-known British mystery authors, and the wife of another. Used bookstores—especially those specializing in paperbacks, can be treasure troves. A good mail-order source is Mysteries by Mail, which issues frequent catalogs with a fine selection of titles and good bargains: Write Mysteries by Mail, 171-C Brush St., P.O. Box 8515, Ukiah, CA 95482-8515, (800) 722-0726. And keep an eye on the World Wide Web if you're so inclined. Resources for mystery and travel fans are growing apace.

Your ultimate resource is the public library, especially old, big-city libraries that have not been totally taken over by computer terminals and still have that public-library smell of incipient paper decay.

If you're not near one of those, your local interlibrary loan system can work wonders.

The best strategy for accumulating a good traveling reader library, however, is to keep your eyes peeled at all times and to be flexible. Go ahead, buy that used Peter Corris paperback for a dollar, even if you're not heading for Australia this year. Maybe next.

I

———— ≈((◉))≈ ————

FRANCE

MONTMARTRE IN THE TWENTIES: *The Boulevard de Clichy, Montmartre. Pivot and pulse of night life, centre of all the tiny streets on which famous night clubs cling to the hill. Rue Pigalle, rue Fontaine, rue Blanche, rue de Clichy, all revolve on a glowing hub, and startled visitors are tilted into them down cobble-stoned ways. Your brain whirls with the bang of jazz. You are drunk, or you mean to get drunk. You have a woman or you will have one shortly. Certainly unthinking people will tell you that Paris at night has lost its lure. In Berlin, in Rome, in New York (they will say), great, shining temples of hilarity have made Paris haunts seem cheap and dingy. As though efficiency were the object in drinking, or making love, or humanly acting the fool . . . if this is your object . . . , this childish mystery, this roar, this damp smell of fresh trees and old sawdust, this do-as-you-please easiness, this splattering of coloured lights, will never turn your head: but memories will be lost to your old age.* (John Dickson Carr, *The Corpse in the Waxworks*)

DAWN IN PARIS: *Having crossed Place de la Bastille, he was passing a little bistro on his way down Boulevard Henri IV. The door, like the door of most cafés on this cold morning, was shut for the first time for months. As he went past, someone opened it, and Maigret's nostrils were asssailed by a gust of fragrance which was forever to remain with him as the very quintessence of Paris at daybreak: the fragrance of frothy coffee and hot croissants, spiced with a hint of rum. . . .* (Georges Simenon, *Maigret and the Spinster*)

FRENCH COUNTRY (THE PAS DE CALAIS): *He drove past lonely stone farmhouses, sleeping in the benediction of the afternoon sun, with their orchards bowed as if under the burden not only of fruit but the vast curve of the dappled sky, past the rolling heave of rich brown earth and the soft silky ripple of ripening corn, between low stone walls whose foundations had heard the tramp of leather boots marching to Agincourt, over swiftly rushing streams and a broad placid river—and always beneath the*

*great sweep of the sky which in that part of the country seemed to bear
down in benediction and forgiveness on the bold earth that always thrust
and arched so arrogantly to meet it.* (Pierre Audemars, *A Woven Web*)

*Alas, no more shall I find
the absurd and magnificent lyricism of Fantômas,
the naive enchantment of Arsène Lupin,
the melancholy tenderness of Rouletabille*

(Jean Cocteau, cited in Benvenuti
and Rizzoni, *The Whodunit*)

The French Connection:
Leblanc, Leroux, and le Noir

IN THE BEGINNING, the detective novel spoke French as often as it did
English. Though various critics have found the granddaddy of all
gumshoes in the eighth-century Chinese Judge Dee, or Voltaire's *Zadig*
(1748), or William Godwin's *Caleb Williams* (1794), Dickens's Inspector
Bucket (*Bleak House,* 1853), or Wilkie Collins's Sergeant Cuff (*The Moon-
stone,* 1868), the conventional genealogy honors the American Edgar Allan
Poe as the creator of the first true detective story, "The Murders in the Rue
Morgue" (1841), starring the great French ratiocinator Chevalier C. Auguste Dupin. But Poe was influenced to some extent by the *Mémoires* of a
real-life French detective, François Eugene Vidocq (1775–1857), a bizarre
character whose career comprised stints as a thief, a police informer, the
first chief of the Sûreté (the criminal investigation branch of the national
police), and the founder of the first modern detective agency. (In "The Murders in the Rue Morgue," however, Dupin dismisses Vidocq as "a good
guesser, and a persevering man," but one lacking in "educated thought."*)

---

*This sketch of the history of the detective novel in France is chiefly based on the
following sources: Stefano Benvenuti and Gianni Rizzoni, *The Whodunit: An Informal
History of Detective Fiction,* translated by Anthony Eyre (NY: Macmillan, 1980);
François Rivière, *Les couleurs du noir: Biographie d'un genre* ([Paris]: Chêne, 1989);
T. J. Hale, editor, *Great French Detective Stories* (NY: Vanguard, 1984); Julian Symons,
Bloody Murder: From the Detective Story to the Crime Novel, 3d ed. (NY: Mysterious,
1992); T. J. Binyon, *"Murder Will Out" The Detective in Fiction* (NY: Oxford, 1989);
Patrick Marnham, *The Man Who Wasn't Maigret: A Portrait of Georges Simenon*
(NY: Harcourt Brace, 1994).

Both Vidocq and Poe influenced Arthur Conan Doyle, the second giant of the genre, whose first Sherlock Holmes adventure, *A Study in Scarlet*, was published in 1887. So, too, did another Frenchman, Emile Gaboriau, who is widely regarded as the inventor of both the full-length *roman policier* (*L'Affaire Lerouge*, 1873) and of "the first modern police detective" (Lecoq of the Sûreté). Doyle and his British colleagues, in their turn, influenced the French writers Gaston Leroux, author of an archetypal locked-room mystery, *"Le mystère de la chambre jaune"* ("The Mystery of the Yellow Room," 1907–1908), and other puzzlers which are solved by a young reporter known as "Rouletabille"; and Maurice Leblanc, inventor in 1905 of the raffish Arsene Lupin, *"gentleman-cambrioleur"*—thief, master of disguise, protector of widows and orphans, and "outlaw detective." The works of both Gaboriau and Leroux were once very popular in English translation as well as in France, though they are little read today.

Thus, from its invention by Poe, an American writing of a Paris he had never seen, the mystery was a cross-Channel and a transatlantic phenomenon—"multicultural," we'd say today. In this century, the most famous "French" detective (Jules Maigret) was the creation of a Belgian (Simenon). The most famous "Belgian" detective (Hercule Poirot) was created by an Englishwoman (Agatha Christie), modeled in part on a "French" detective (Inspector Hannaud) invented by an Englishman (A. E. W. Mason).

Though the twenties and thirties are usually regarded as the Golden Age of the British mystery, France in the thirties also produced some original voices—Georges Simenon chief among them. Pierre Véry wrote poetic puzzle novels that have been described as "fairy tales for grown-ups"; Claude Aveline, a "serious" literary novelist, wrote *"une suite policière"* of five psychological thrillers starting in 1932 with *The Double Death of Frédéric Belot*.

Though Maigret has a huge English and American following, most of the publishing traffic in mysteries and detectives from the thirties on has been from west to east, from America to France. A French imp of the perverse has caused the French not only to embrace such homegrown antiheroes as Marcel Allain and Pierre Souvestre's Fantômas, master criminal and "angel of evil," but also to import some of the most violent and vulgar American crime writers and their British imitators—and to intellectualize their significance out of all proportion. Just as Fantômas, who lives on the roofs of Paris and loves to kill, became the darling of the Surrealists and other intellectuals from his first appearance in 1911, Lemmy Caution became a cult figure in France in the forties.

This was due in part to Marcel Duhamel, a major figure in the transatlantic traffic in tough-guy fiction, who, in 1945, founded a publishing imprint called Série Noire. Duhamel published not only Dashiell Hammett and Raymond Chandler in translation but also their English imitators James Hadley Chase, whose blood-drenched *No Orchids for Miss Blandish* (1939) was compared by besotted French critics to Dostoyevsky and Céline, and Peter Cheyney, author of the cruel and ultraviolent Caution novels. (At his peak, according to Julian Symons, Cheyney sold 300,000 copies a year in the United States and 900,000 in France.) The Série Noire and similar imprints also encouraged many French imitations of the hardest-boiled Americans, as well as producing what one history of the genre calls a genuine "poet of the underworld," the anarchistic Le Breton (Auguste Monfort), and a Rabelaisian master of slang, Sanantonio (Frédéric Dard).

Overlooked in the transatlantic commerce in mysteries was another French original, Leo Malet, whose books only recently have appeared in translation in England. Malet began his Chandleresque Nestor Burma series in 1943, with *120 rue de la Gare,* while Chandler himself was still publishing. Though Malet, a poet and member of the Surrealist group, is sometimes dismissed as an imitator of the hard-boiled Americans, both by date and style he more accurately is described as a precursor of the French *roman noir.* His novels are still intriguing—both as mysteries and for their portrait of Paris in the forties and fifties.

Malet and his private eye, tough, sardonic Nestor Burma—*"l'homme qui met le mystère K.O."* (the man who knocks out the mystery)—know their mean streets so well that in the fifties Malet undertook to write one Burma novel set in each of Paris's twenty arrondissements, under the general title of *Les nouveaux mystères de Paris.* (Only fifteen were completed.) A serious student of Paris might well consider using them as a guide.

In the fifties and sixties, the team of Pierre Boileau and Thomas Narcejac wrote important criticism of the genre, as well as psychological thrillers including those that became the movies *Vertigo* and *Les diaboliques.* Sometimes grouped with them are the sophisticated and unsettling thrillers written in the sixties by Jean-Baptiste Rossi under the pseudonym Sebastien Japrisot.

More recently, the work of Didier Daeninckx has achieved popular and critical acclaim in France. The first two Daeninckx novels available in English offer dark visions of a corrupt and unjust society. His preferred settings are the working-class inner suburbs/slums of Paris—the Porte d'Italie area of the Thirteenth Arrondissement, for example (also the 1880 scene of the crime in Gaboriau's *Monsieur LeCoq*). Daeninckx's point of view is strongly left-wing, and social criticism sometimes overwhelms entertainment in his novels. Though he shares their political orientation, he lacks the craftsmanship of Maj Sjowall and Per Wahloo and the sense of humor of Paco Ignacio Taibo and Manuel Vásquez Montalbán.

Meanwhile, English and American writers have used France as the setting for numerous books—especially naughty Paris and the sunny Riviera, which the English used to treat like a sort of upscale suburb of Brighton. Among the first English mysteries featuring French settings and characters are A. E. W. Mason's five novels about Inspector Hannaud; in the forties and fifties, Marten Cumberland produced more than thirty Commissaire Saturnin Dax mysteries; and Pierre Audemars's two-dozen-plus novels about M. Pinaud of the Sûreté appeared from the late fifties to the mid-eighties. In recent years, there are Mark Hebden's novels, set in Burgundy, featuring Chief Insp. Evariste Pel, and Nicholas Freeling's Inspector Castang series. Two new series are Mickey Friedman's novels about Paris-based journalist Georgia Lee Maxwell and Dean Fuller's books featuring Alex Grismolet of the Sûreté. Since Patricia Highsmith's psychopathic rogue, Tom Ripley, has settled in the country near Fontainebleau, there has been plenty of work for the police.

Thanks in part to American and English writers, France is well represented in crime novels for all tastes: the cosy and the hard-boiled, romantic suspense, psychological thrillers, academic puzzles and spy adventures. But every reading traveler to France should bring along a few of the short novels devoted to the most original and influential creation of the continental mystery, Inspector Jules Maigret of the Sûreté, protagonist of seventy-five novels by the Belgian-born Georges Simenon. By one account, Simenon's books have sold 500 million copies in fifty-five languages, making him the world's best-selling novelist. He is also the only French detective novelist to achieve major success in the English-speaking world.

Maigret bestrides the world of European crime fiction like a colossus in a bowler hat, and the metaphoric Sons of Simenon ply their trade in many lands. Amsterdam's Van der Valk, Stockholm's Martin Beck, Florence's Guarnaccia, Majorca's Alvarez, Burgundy's Pel: all these fictional cops and many others share, to some degree, Maigret's sensitivity to atmosphere and to place, his curiosity, his grasp of the dark side of human nature and his tendency to identify with the criminal, his bourgeois home life, his fondness for food and drink, his vulnerability to colds and flu, his idiosyncratic methods of detection, and his willingness to break the rules.

READING LIST

AMES, Delano. *Corpse Diplomatique* (London, 1950, 1953). This is one of an endearing (but difficult to find) series featuring a lighthearted young couple named Dagobert and Jane Brown. Though usually short on money, the Browns manage to travel a lot. In this outing, Dagobert, a man of intense if short-lived enthusiasms, has decided to learn Provençal in order to translate the poems of a heretofore neglected twelfth-century troubadour, so they settle into a pension in Nice. When one of the other guests, a low-key blackmailer, is killed, the Browns get involved in seeking the murderer. The Browns drink a lot (Dagobert is intent on trying every available French aperitif), go to nightclubs, have witty conversations, and in general come across like a young English version of the roughly contemporaneous "Mr. and Mrs. North." The novel celebrates the Côte d'Azur at its most playful.

AUDEMARS, Pierre. *A Woven Web* (NY, 1965). M. Pinaud of the Paris Sûreté, the *soi-disant* "greatest detective in the world," has a nice wife and two young daughters, a bit of a midlife crisis, and a roving eye. He falls drastically in love with Josette, a schoolgirl he meets regularly on a bus. Then one day Josette's not there. This is the first of several plots that gradually converge through a combination of coincidence and intuitive leaps on Pinaud's part. Raiding the house of a big-time black marketeer, Pinaud finds his teenage beloved drugged and degraded. He rescues her but not soon enough. Then someone starts attacking English tourists by ramming their cars with a truck. Is it the black marketeer? Or Josette's grieving father? The plot's overwrought, but Audemars, who is British, writes well in a mock-heroic style. The scenery is fine—especially the French countryside in the northern region called the Pas de Calais and glorious Lac Leman as described in a side trip to Switzerland. One critic has noted "inexplicable geographical dislocations" in some of Audemars's dozens of books, however; so be warned.

————. *Gone to Her Death* (NY, 1981). An unexpected bequest has made it possible for Pinaud and his wife to buy their dream country house in the fictional village of Vervion in Normandy. Then an equally unexpected political shakeup in the Sûreté forces Pinaud into early retirement. Plus, there's a young female corpse in the woodshed of his new home, and Pinaud is a suspect. Naturally, he starts his own investigation (the alert reader will be ahead of him), as well as trying a new career as a traveling salesman. The latter is rather tediously chronicled, but the village local color is appealing.

AVELINE, Claude. *The Double Death of Frédéric Belot* [Paris, 1932], translated by Ann Lindsay (Garden City, NY, 1974); an earlier translation appeared in 1940. Usually described as a psychological thriller, this novel also has strong elements of the classic puzzle—with as much emphasis on the how as on the who or why. M. Belot, a high-ranking police official, is found shot in his Paris apartment by his godson, who is also in the police. But there are not one but two bodies in the apartment (one dead, one barely alive) and they are identical. Belot, it turns out, has been using his double to double his own capacity for work. An enticing premise, but a novel in which the most interesting and relevant setting is the floor-plan of the victim's apartment.

BELLAIRS, George [Harold Blundell]. *All Roads to Sospel* (GB, 1976; NY, 1981). Inspector Thomas Littlejohn presides over this longtime semi-comic series, which began in 1941. Most of the novels are set on the Isle of Man, though perhaps ten take place in the South of France where Littlejohn often visits his pal Commissaire Dorange of the Nice Sûreté. That's what he's doing when the conductor of an English tour bus and his girlfriend are murdered on the treacherous road to Sospel, a tiny scenic village in the mountains north of Menton. (A clue: If you keep on the road north of Sospel you'll end up in Torino, Italy, a drug-smuggling center.) There's not much to this novel; let's hope the author was just having a bad day, since there are at least sixty more titles in the series.

BOND, Michael. *Monsieur Pamplemousse and the Secret Mission* (NY, 1984, NY, 1987). Accompanied by his faithful bloodhound, Pommes Frites, M. Aristide Pamplemousse—once a policeman, now an inspector for a gastronomic guidebook—is dispatched to try to save his boss's aunt's dreadful hotel in a village near Saumur in the département of Maine-et-Loire. There he finds that someone is spiking the horrid cuisine with a powerful aphrodisiac. "A bawdy romp," says the cover blurb. Well, at least the scenery (including stops at Monet's gardens at Giverny and Proust's childhood town, Illiers-Combray) is agreeable. Pommes Frites is the most attractive character, perhaps to be expected from a writer better known as the author of the "Paddington Bear" books. The second of a many-volumed series.

CARR, John Dickson. *The Corpse in the Waxworks* (NY, 1932, 1990). In this florid evocation of Paris in the twenties, a corpse turns up in the arms of a star display—"the Satyr of the Seine"—in a wax museum's Gallery of Horrors. But the really naughty stuff is going on next door in a private club whose members—respectable *citoyens* and *citoyennes* by day—don masks to indulge in illicit rendezvous by night. Though Carr is the acknowledged master of the locked-room mystery, in this early novel he seems equally interested in the *louche* atmosphere of Bohemian Paris—black jazz at the Moulin Rouge, "the fleshy beat of a tango," hints of unspeakable depravity. His detective is Henri Bencolin, a high police official, a bit of a decadent and a dandy, all world-weariness and late-Romantic posturing. Richly atmospheric, this is the Paris that appalled and enthralled our great-grandparents. (See also Carr's other Bencolin novels with Parisian settings, *It Walks by Night* [1930] and *The Four False Weapons* [1937].)

CUMBERLAND, Marten. *Hate for Sale* (London, 1957). Fat but highly effective Special Commissaire Saturnin Dax and handsome Brigadier Felix Norman, a former boxer, are called in when a journalist is killed by professional hitmen. Leading suspects include the journalist's former employer, a sleazy tabloid magnate; blackmail seems a likely motive. The case takes Dax and Norman from Paris to "Laville-sur-Mer," a fictional seaside resort. This is the twenty-fifth in a series that Jacques Barzun and Wendell Taylor, in their *Catalogue of Crime*, consistently rated higher than the Maigret novels. They were wrong, but this book is indeed sharply written and witty. Cumberland's trademark style consists of very short chapters, each topped with a well-chosen literary quote.

DAENINCKX, Didier. *Murder in Memoriam* [Paris, 1984], translated by Liz Heron (London, 1991). A young history teacher is shot and killed during a 1961 Algerian demonstration in Paris, a demonstration he has no part in. Twenty years later, his son—also a history teacher—is murdered in a similar fashion while in Toulouse doing research in the municipal archives. Inspector Cadin of the Toulouse police suspects a connection. His investigation reveals a cover-up of a police massacre of the '61 demonstrators, plus a government plot to assassinate leaders on both sides of the Algerian conflict.

He also learns that the research Bernard Thiraud was doing in Toulouse was a continuation of his father's research on his hometown, the suburb of Drancy. Following in their paths, Cadin discovers that the Thirauds' research implicates some highly placed people as eager collaborators in the Vichy government's deportation of Jewish children to the death camps. These multiple strands of past evils make for a very tangled plot indeed, and Daeninckx's skill as a novelist is not always up to the challenge. But the book has been credited with helping bring some Nazi collaborators to trial and with having made public the '61 massacre and cover-up.

————. *A Very Profitable War* [Paris, 1984], translated by Sarah Martin (NY and London, 1994). Like its predecessor, this novel is also dominated by the pressure of the horrific past. Set in Paris a few years after the end of World War I, it stars René Griffon, a veteran of the trenches turned hard-boiled private eye. He is hired by a war-hero colonel to track down the colonel's blackmailers. Daeninckx is full of interesting Paris anecdotes. he introduces, for example, a prewar anarchist group that specialized in appropriating housing for the poor by means of such antic gestures as a day " 'against the Tyranny of the Concierges,' during which the . . . commandos put fleas, bugs and cockroaches through the keyholes of the concierges' doors!" But here again Daeninckx's social and political passions exceed his ability to express them novelistically. And a different translator has produced a text bristling with unnecessary and annoying exclamation points!

ELKINS, Aaron. *Old Bones* (NY; 1987, 1988). Set in Brittany and Normandy, this installment of a popular series begins spectacularly with an old man's losing struggle with the freak tides of Mont-Saint-Michel. Elkins's series character is a much-traveled American anthropologist, Gideon Oliver, known as "the skeleton detective" for his skill in reading the odd femur or tibia (see also Chapter XVIII, "Mexico"). Gideon's at a cop conference in St. Malo when an acquaintance, the most obnoxious member of a generally obnoxious family who has gathered to quarrel on their nearby family estate, is poisoned.

The bones of the title turn up in the cellar of the manor where they, and an SS officer's uniform, have been languishing since the war. A third murder also comes to light, when it turns out the drowning death of the family patriarch that began the novel was no accident. When not detecting, Gideon takes in the sights of St. Malo, Dinan, and of course Mont-Saint-Michel itself, where he eats the famed local *agneau de pré salé* (salt-meadow lamb) at the (real) Restaurant Mouton Blanc and comes close to drowning. Thoroughly enjoyable, and the meal sounds delicious.

FREELING, Nicolas. *The Night Lords* (London and NY, 1978; NY, 1980). This is the fourth of the Henri Castang novels that Freeling began after he had killed off his most famous series character, Van der Valk of Amsterdam (see Chapter VI). Castang, an inspector of the Police Judiciaire in an unnamed provincial city, is a much more stolid character than Van der Valk, less intuitive, more a creature of procedure. He is also the vehicle for Freeling's observations on matters political and social.

This long and slow-moving novel shows little of the sensitivity to place and atmosphere that characterized Freeling's Amsterdam novels. Though the plot takes Castang on a tour of Normandy—Rouen, Caen, Bayeux, Deauville—it's a brisk and not very colorful one. In his "foreword" to the next installment in the series, *Castang's City* (1980), Freeling insists that the city in question is imaginary, based neither on Toulouse nor Strasbourg—intended to be representative, not specific.

In *The Night Lords,* Castang and his colleagues are preoccupied with three corpses (in descending order of political importance): the naked female stuffed in the trunk of a Rolls-Royce that was transporting a British High Court judge on vacation; the hanged brother of Castang's landlady; the *clochard* found stabbed near Castang's apartment building. But Freeling seems to lose interest in his mystery; he has bigger fish to fry, and Castang fries them in long conversations about the sociopathic personality, individual versus state responsibility, the differences between the French and the English legal systems, the reality of evil, and much more. (Starting with *Dressing of Diamond* in 1974, through *A Dwarf Kingdom,* 1996, there are seventeen Castang novels. See, also, Chapter IV, "Eastern Europe").

FRIEDMAN, Mickey. *Magic Mirror* (NY, 1988; in Britain, published as *Deadly Reflections,* 1989). In this first of a series, Friedman's detective is Georgia Lee Maxwell, an updated version of a tradition of perky heroines that dates at least to Nancy Drew and her chums. Maxwell is a journalist who quits her job as society editor for the *Bay City* (Fla.) *Sun* to live and write in Paris. A freelance assignment puts her on the scene when a museum security guard is murdered by two masked men who steal only one thing: the mirror in which the sixteenth-century prophet Nostradamus supposedly saw his visions of the future. It turns out that a group of psychics called the Speculatori also have an unseemly interest in the mirror. It's Nancy Drew in Umberto Eco Land, but Georgia Lee has an agreeable, self-deprecating sense of humor and Friedman a nice sense of place. Paris is in the details, and Friedman gets a lot of them right. But there are a few false notes. It's been a long time since I've sat regularly in Parisian cafés, but surely even today the beverage to sip at the Deux Magots is *un grand crème*—not a cappuccino. (See also Friedman's other Georgia Lee novel: *A Temporary Ghost* [1989].)

GABORIAU, Emile. *Monsieur LeCoq* ([Paris, 1880]; NY, 1901). "Without hesitation, LeCoq threw himself upon his knees in the snow, in order to examine [some footprints]; he rose again almost immediately. 'These indentations were not made by the feet of men,' said he. 'There have been women here.' " Generally considered to be the best of Gaboriau's seven detective novels, this classic thriller begins with the sensational murder of three in a lowlife dive in a Paris slum. Young police detective LeCoq applies Poe's ratiocinative techniques, and he is the first fictional detective to take a plaster cast of footprints. Still readable but just barely.

HEBDEN, Mark [John Harris]. *Pel and the Predators* (NY, 1984). This is one of fifteen or so police procedurals set in an unidentified city in Burgundy and featuring Insp. Clovis Pel and his team. Pel is meant to be a comic creation, but his eccentricities quickly hardened into shtick. Chief among them, his antipathy to anything non-Burgundian. When he is ordered to go to Brittany on a case, Pel is upset: "Concarneau was not only outside Burgundy—and to Pel anything beyond the frontiers of his native province was a wilderness—it was almost outside France, beyond which, to Pel, a Frenchman if ever there was one, there was only darkness." Though there's some local color, Hebden makes a point of not naming the city where Pel is based. The other sites in the novel, including several in Brittany, are a mixture of the real and the invented. The plot, however, is clever. The discovery of a Burgundian corpse on a Breton beach is followed by the discovery of a forty-year-old corpse preserved in a cave. Both turn out to be young women of independent mind and dubious morals, and a connection between the two ultimately emerges. Meanwhile, someone has sent Pel a letter-bomb, and he gets a bad cold. (One of the other novels in the series is discussed in Chapter XVIII, "Mexico").

HIGHSMITH, Patricia. *Ripley's Game* (London, 1974; NY, 1993). Highsmith's infamous rogue (see *The Talented Mr. Ripley,* Chapter III, "Italy") is all grown up and living with his wealthy wife in a beautiful house in "Villeperce" near Fontainebleau. Ripley dabbles in art as painter, forger, fence, and thief; he detests murder "unless it's absolutely necessary." He has mellowed but remains socially sensitive. When a neighbor, Jonathan Trevanny, snubs him at a party, Ripley takes a most insidious revenge: A crook friend is trying to hire someone unsuspicious to kill two Mafiosi; Tom suggests he approach Trevanny (who has leukemia), amused by the thought of his reaction—and his possible vulnerability because of his illness and his family's need for money. Trevanny is indeed vulnerable, and Ripley himself gets a lot more involved than he intended as the bodies pile up. The novel is a stunning mixture of suspense, both physical and psychological. (There are three other Ripley novels set in Villeperce: *Ripley Under Ground* [1970], *The Boy Who Followed Ripley* [1980], and *Ripley Under Water* [1991]).

JAPRISOT, Sebastien [Jean-Baptiste Rossi]. *The Lady in the Car with Glasses and a Gun* [1966], translated by Helen Weaver (NY, 1967, 1980). Having accompanied her boss to the airport, Dany Longo is supposed to return his white Thunderbird to Paris. Instead Dany, a troubled young woman, succumbs to a longing to see the sea and points the car toward the Riviera. When she stops at a gas station near Avallon, someone or something crushes her hand and two people claim to have met her traveling the opposite direction earlier that same day—complete with glasses, T-bird, and bandaged hand. This is just the first of a series of bizarre and frightening encounters that plunge Dany into a nightmare of self-doubt. Is she mad—or the victim of an impossibly complex conspiracy? And what about the dead body in the T-bird's trunk?

The big mystery in this truly creepy tale is not Who but What—as in "What the hell is going on here?" Though one can plot Dany's nightmare route from Orly to Villeneuve-lès-Avignon on a map, only a twisted soul would want to follow it in real life. Japrisot's delineation of Dany's plight is so effective and so troubling that no solution could live up to it—though the one he offers is not bad. (See also Japrisot's *The 10:30 from Marseilles*

[*The Sleeping-Car Murders*] [NY, 1963], *Trap for Cinderella* [NY, 1964], *Goodbye, Friend* [NY, 1969], and *One Deadly Summer* [NY, 1980].)

MALCOLM, John. *The Gwen John Sculpture* (NY, 1986). One of a series of well-written novels about art investment adviser Tim Simpson, this one includes scenes in the Dordogne and the Paris suburb of Meudon, both settings associated with the sculptor Rodin. Simpson is trying to track down a previously unknown Rodin sculpture of the British painter Gwen John. It quickly becomes evident that he has some tough, violent competition.

MALET, Leo. *Dynamite Versus Q.E.D.* [Paris, 1945]; translated by Peter Hudson (GB, 1991). The setting is occupied Paris in 1942; the style is hard-boiled American (though the translation mixes English and American slang in a sometimes unnerving fashion). Private eye Nestor "Dynamite" Burma goes out in search of tobacco; gets caught in an air raid; meets a beautiful but very suspicious dame, follows her on a whim and runs into a murder victim. "Two bullets had made their way into his stomach to see what he was made of, and decided not to come out again." Burma has a shady past, an individualistic code of honor, a loyal and lovely secretary, and bad taste in other women. The plotting is unmemorable but the portrait of daily life in wartime France is fascinating. (*Q.E.D.*, incidentally, is the name of a sleazy tabloid.)

————. *Mayhem in the Marais* [Paris, 1958], translated by Alex Buchet (GB, 1991). When, on the morning after a drunken party, an artist finds a murdered "Jewess" on his studio couch, he calls his friend Nestor Burma for help. ("You don't usually do still-lifes," cracks Burma.) The focus of the novel soon shifts to the old Jewish community of Paris, centered on the rue des Rosiers northeast of the Hotel de Ville, in the Fourth Arrondissement. The plot involves a big-time gangster named Bramovici, who during the war was a particularly nasty Jewish collaborator with the Nazi occupiers of Paris. Bramovici is being tracked by some smaller-time crooks who believe he has a fortune secreted in Paris and by an Israeli commando seeking revenge for his sister's betrayal and death. The book's most interesting and disturbing aspect is the complex attitudes toward Jews that it reflects. Burma seems to embody liberal tolerance, but Malet's descriptions of Jewish characters include every stereotype imaginable, from large noses and "greasy locks" to greed and chicanery. (See also *Mission to Marseilles* [Paris, 1947; GB, 1991], which takes Burma to the unoccupied area of France in 1942.)

MASON, A. E. W. *Murder at the Villa Rose* (GB, 1910; NY, n.d.). Though the word *quaint* does occur to a contemporary reader of this once-famous novel, no less an authority than Howard Haycraft called Mason's protagonist, M. Hanaud of the Sûreté, "one of the indisputable 'greats' among fictional sleuths." In this first outing, the "elephantinely elfish" Hanaud is vacationing at Aix-les-Bains—the waters in the morning, baccarat at night—when a rich, elderly Englishwoman is brutally murdered and her beautiful protégée, a young woman of dubious background, becomes the prime suspect. The plot, which involves séances, drugs, and other melodrama, is clumsy. But there are some oddly revealing period touches, as in this comment on an embarrassingly anti-Semitic judge: "he has that bee in his bonnet, like so many others. Everywhere he must see l'affaire Dreyfus . . . There are thousands like that—good, kindly, just people in the ordinary ways of life, but behind every crime they see the Jew." The novel is rich in atmosphere, and both clever Hanaud—who may have been a model for Hercule Poirot—and his dopey sidekick, M. Ricardo, are entertaining. (See also Mason's other Hanaud novels: *The House of the Arrow* [1924], which is set in Dijon; *The Prisoner in the Opal* [1928], Bordeaux; *They Wouldn't Be Chessmen* [1935], Trouville; and *The House in Lordship Lane* [1946], Brittany.)

PAUL, Elliot. *The Mysterious Mickey Finn* (NY, 1939, 1984). "Philo Vance / Needs a kick in the pance." The words are Ogden Nash's, but the sentiment apparently was shared by many familiar with the S. S. Van Dine series featuring fatuous polymath and man-of-the-world Vance. Among them, Elliot Paul reportedly sought to deliver the necessary kick in the form of this high-spirited, satiric tale about an American amateur detective, Homer Evans, who not only knows more than Vance, but exceeds him in languid affectation. Homer, however, proved to have a life of his own, and eight other comic mystery novels featuring him followed.

Like this one, most of them are set in France, among expatriate artists whose lives center on the *terrasses* of the *grands cafés* of Montparnasse: the Dôme, the Coupole, the Rotonde, the Select, and "possibly the Falstaff or the Dingo."

The crimes Homer is called upon to solve involve art-forging, tax evasion, kidnapping, and, of course, murder. Among his useful skills: the ability to detect a forged El Greco, to make a Mickey Finn, and to render harmless a contact mine. His chief comrade is his sharpshooting western girlfriend, Miriam. Most of the minor characters have silly names: M. Paty de Pussy, Miss Hydrangea Palmerstone Waite, Barnabé Vieuxchamps, Prefect Gaston Honoré Crayon de Crayon, Dr. Hyacinthe Toudoux. There is a lot of farcical action as well as wordplay, and some splendid local color of the *entre-deuxs guerre* period in Montparnasse, when "mankind was dancing without thought of the fiddler's recompense." (The other Homer Evans mysteries with French settings include: *Hugger-Mugger in the Louvre* [NY, 1940]; *Mayhem in B-Flat* [NY, 1940]; *Murder on the Left Bank* [NY and London, 1951].)

SAUL, John Ralston. *The Birds of Prey* (NY, 1977, 1980). Journalist Charles Stone's investigation of the suspicious death of the French army chief of staff leads to dangerous discoveries of intrigue and power-grabbing in the highest ranks of the French government and military. This first thriller by a distinguished Canadian intellectual (author of *Voltaire's Bastards: The Dictatorship of Reason in the West*) assumes considerable knowledge of post–World War II French history, especially the Gaullist period and the trauma of Algeria, and may frustrate some readers as a result.

NOTED BUT NOT REVIEWED

AMBLER, Eric. *Epitaph for a Spy* (NY, 1938, 1991). Set in the fictional village of St. Gatien on the Riviera in the late thirties, this is a classic "wrong man" adventure. A Hungarian-born language teacher is accused of espionage. To prove his innocence, he must find the guilty.

FULLER, Dean. *A Death in Paris* (NY, 1992). Chief-Inspector Alex Grismolet of the Sûreté and his Lithuanian sidekick Vrnas probe the death of an aging American aristocrat in the Parc de Monceau.

———. *Death of a Critic* (NY, 1996). A detested theater critic bows out.

MacINNES, Helen. *Assignment in Brittany* (NY, 1942, 1969). A British soldier parachutes into occupied French territory to take the place of a French look-alike and to spy on the Germans.

MONBRUN, Estelle [Elyane Dezon-Jones]. *Murder chez Proust* [Paris, 1994], translated by David Martyn (NY, 1995). Just as the Proust Association is gathering for its annual meeting at Illiers-Combray, someone kills its unpopular president. This satire of academics and their foibles caused a stir in France.

CLOSE-UP: THE MAIGRET FILE

Maigret: A Tribute

By Jim Lehrer

To read a Maigret novel is to be in Paris with the master detective. It is also to smell pipe smoke and calvados. To eat sandwiches from the Brasserie Dauphine. To know Maigret's detectives Lucas, Lapointe, Janvier, and Torrance. And to know pimps, piano players, magistrates, concierges, killers, deputies, dancers, and shopgirls.

Maigret is the chief superintendent and head of the criminal investigation division of the Paris police, having worked his way up from patrolman. His Paris is one of small cafés and mostly small people committing small murders and other crimes. It is a Paris where the snow falls gently, the rain pours softly, the air is alive with the smell of food and drink.

Maigret is a celebrity in Paris and France and even in the rest of Europe and in America among law enforcement officers. He is known and revered because he almost always gets his man—or woman—but also because he does it with calm and understanding and perseverance. He is a simple man with simple techniques that work with the most complicated of criminals and their crimes. Physical evidence is important to Maigret, but not as important as the psychological. He is a nice man, a good man, who understands and empathizes with the criminals as he pursues them.

Maigret's creator was Georges Simenon, who died in 1989 at the age of eighty-six. He was not a very nice or good man. That is by most accounts, at least, including some of his own. He made modest gossip-column headlines in 1977, for instance, by claiming to have slept with more than ten thousand women.

Whatever his sexual statistics, Simenon could correctly claim to be one of the most prolific writers of all time. Of the hundreds of novels he wrote, seventy-six were "Maigrets." Most have been translated into English, and new editions appear frequently. They do not have to be read in chronological order. *Maigret and the Hundred Gibbets,* which was published in 1931, is as alive and fresh as *Maigret and the Killer,* published in

1969. Most are set in Paris, but there are also a few from the provinces, from Belgium, Holland, and from the United States, where he went on special assignments.

They are superb examples of clean, spare writing. With a simple phrase the room is stifling, a shirt collar tightens unbearably, a terrified soul trembles, a glass of beer soothes. Most are between 115 and 150 pages. That makes them perfect for airplane flights in the two-to-three-hour category. But be careful. I found myself once on landing with twenty pages still to go in a Maigret. I had the taxi take a longer way into the town so I could finish it before I had to do what I had come to that particular city to do. On another occasion, I lied to my escort when we got to the hotel, claiming I had "some calls to make" before we went about our business. I raced to my hotel room and finished my Maigret. It could not wait.

Finishing a Maigret can never wait.

Four Decades of Maigret: A Sampling

1931: Maigret and the Enigmatic Lett [*Pietr-le-Letton*], translated by Daphne Woodward (London, 1963, 1970). Though no fewer than eleven Maigret titles were published in 1931, Simenon contended, and his biographer, Patrick Marnham, is convinced, that this was the first Maigret "written in the full sense, not just with the character but in the style." Already in place at police headquarters on the Quai des Orfèvres is the superannuated office stove, to which Maigret—always susceptible to colds—clings. In place, too, are the glasses of beer and the pipes that fuel his working hours; at home his long-suffering wife waits to serve him a plate of "savory stew" at any hour of the day or night.

Set in Paris and Fécamp on the Norman coast, the plot pits Maigret against a master criminal, the puzzling Latvian of the title, who variously appears to be a friend and colleague of millionaire businessmen, a Norwegian ship captain, a Russian drunk, or the corpse found on a train. By the time he solves the mystery, Maigret has come to empathize with his prey—as he will in numerous cases to come.

1940: Maigret on the Riviera [*Liberty Bar*], translated by Geoffrey Sainsbury (NY, 1940, 1988):

When Maigret got off the train at Antibes, half the station was bathed
in a blaze of sunlight, through which people moved like shadows—
shadows in straw hats and white trousers, with tennis rackets in their
hands. Spring had burst out suddenly, and the air hummed with the heat.
On the other side of the platform were cactuses and palm trees and, far-
ther off, a strip of blue sea. . . .

1942: Maigret and the Spinster [*Cécile est morte*], translated by Eileen Ellenbogen (NY, 1977, 1982). Maigret's enjoyment of the first Parisian fog
of the year, "a milky haze interspersed with haloes of light," is curtailed
by the disappearance of Cécile Pardon, the spinster of the title, who has
been bothering him for months with complaints of mysteriously moved
furniture in the apartment she shares with an invalid aunt. When both
women are murdered, Maigret must deal with his own sense of guilt as
well as the enigmas of the case. He finds some solace in beer and a ham
sandwich at La Coupole and in an excellent coq au vin at a bistro near
the Porte d'Orleans.

1951: Maigret and the Burglar's Wife [*Maigret et la grande perche*], translated
by J. Maclaren-Ross (NY, 1990, 1991). A former prostitute whom Maigret
once arrested comes to him with a problem: Her safe-cracker husband has
disappeared after finding a corpse in a house he was burglarizing in suburban Neuilly. The owners of the house, a dentist and his mother, deny
the existence of both corpse and burglary. But the dentist's wife is nowhere
to be found. Meanwhile, Paris is steaming in an August heat wave, and
Maigret and his wife take an evening walk and sit on a café terrace:

> *The sun had set. It was getting cooler, though gusts of warm air still*
> *seemed to rise from the sidewalk. The windows of the brasserie were*
> *open, and a depleted orchestra was playing inside. Most of the customers*
> *sat without talking, just as they, at their table, did, watching the passers-*
> *by. Their faces gradually melted into the dusk. Soon the streetlight made*
> *them look quite different.*
>
> *Like other couples, they turned toward home, Madame Maigret's*
> *hand tucked in her husband's arm.*

1951: Maigret's Memoirs [*Les mémoires de Maigret*, translated by Jean Stewart ([London, 1963]; NY, 1985). Maigret—writing in the first person
here—meets Georges Simenon, who becomes his unauthorized histor-

ian, creating what Simenon calls "semiliterature" out of Maigret's much more complicated reality. Here we learn the truth about such defining myths as Maigret's bowler hat, his old coat with the velvet collar, his office stove. We also learn more about Maigret's attitudes—toward Paris's immigrant populations, for example. But the myths survive this dose of reality.

1964: *Maigret and the Apparition* [*Maigret et le fantôme*], translated by Eileen Ellenbogen (NY, 1976, 1980). One of Maigret's men is shot while staking out a prosperous art collector's home in Montmartre. Investigating, Maigret finds an art forgery ring, a rather *louche* domestic arrangement . . . and a fabulous view.

> *The view on one side was of rooftops stretching as far as Saint-Ouen; on the other, with the sails of the Moulin de la Galette in the foreground, almost the whole of Paris could be seen, including the layout of the boulevards, the large open space of the Champs-Elysées, the windings of the River Seine, and the gilded dome of the Invalides.*

Maigret's Places

THOUGH MAIGRET IS eternally identified with Paris, he strayed from its precincts on a number of occasions, traveling as far afield as Tucson, Arizona. The following list identifies the settings of each of Simenon's seventy-six Maigret mysteries, and gives their English titles. If there is major action in more than one province or country, the book will be listed under both locations.

Paris and Its Suburbs
Cécile est morte (Maigret and the Spinster), 1942
L'écluse no. 1 (The Lock at Charenton), 1933
La guinguette à deux sous (The Guinguette by the Seine), 1931
Maigret (Maigret Returns), 1934
Maigret au 'Picratt's' (Maigret in Montmarte), 1951
Maigret en meublé (Maigret Takes a Room), 1951

Maigret et la grande perche (Maigret and the Burglar's Wife), 1951
Maigret et l'homme du banc (Maigret and the Man on the Boulevard; Maigret and the Man on the Bench), 1953
Maigret et la jeune morte (Maigret and the Young Girl), 1954
Maigret chez le ministre (Maigret and the Minister), 1955
Maigret et le corps sans tête (Maigret and the Headless Corpse), 1955
Maigret tend un piège (Maigret Sets a Trap), 1955
Un échec de Maigret (Maigret's Failure), 1956
Maigret et son mort (Maigret's Special Murder), 1948
Maigret et les viellards (Maigret in Society), 1960
Maigret et les braves gens (Maigret and the Black Sheep), 1962
Maigret et le client de Samedi (Maigret and the Saturday Caller), 1962
Maigret et le clochard (Maigret and the Dosser; Maigret and the Bum), 1963
Le colère de Maigret (Maigret Loses His Temper), 1963
Maigret et le fantôme (Maigret and the Ghost; Maigret and the Apparition), 1964
Maigret se défend (Maigret on the Defensive), 1964
La patience de Maigret (The Patience of Maigret; Maigret Bides His Time), 1965
Maigret se trompe (Maigret's Mistake), 1953
La première enquête de Maigret (Maigret's First Case), 1949
Un noël de Maigret (Maigret's Christmas), 1951
La nuit du carrefour (The Crossroad Murders), 1931
Signé Picpus (To Any Lengths), 1944
Les scruples de Maigret (Maigret Has Scruples), 1958
La tête d'un homme (A Battle of Nerves; Maigret's War of Nerves), 1931
Le voleur de Maigret (Maigret's Pickpocket; Maigret and the Pickpocket), 1967
Maigret hésite (Maigret Hesitates), 1968
L'ami d'enfance de Maigret (Maigret's Boyhood Friend), 1968
Maigret et le marchand du vin (Maigret and the Wine Merchant), 1970
Maigret et M. Charles (Maigret and Monsieur Charles), 1972

Berry/Bourbonnais
L'affaire Saint-Fiacre (The Saint-Fiacre Affair; Maigret and the Countess; Maigret Goes Home): Moulins, 1932
Les mémoires de Maigret (Maigret's Memoirs): Moulins, 1951

M. Gallet, décédé (The Death of Monsieur Gallet): Sancerre, 1931
Maigret à Vichy (Maigret Takes the Waters; Maigret in Vichy), Vichy, 1968

Brittany
Maigret et l'homme tout seul (Maigret and the Loner): La Baule, 1971
Le chien jaune (A Face for a Clue; Maigret and the Yellow Dog): Concarneau, 1931
L'amie de Mme. Maigret (Madame Maigret's Own Case): Concarneau, 1950
Maigret s'amuse (Maigret's Little Joke): Concarneau, 1957
Les mémoires de Maigret (Maigret's Memoirs): Nantes, 1951
L'affaire Saint-Fiacre (The Saint-Fiacre Affair; Maigret and the Countess; Maigret Goes Home): Saint Fiacre, 1932

Burgundy
M. Gallet, décédé (The Death of Monsieur Gallet): Saint-Fargeau, 1931

Champagne/Ardennes
Chez les Flamands (The Flemish Shop): Givet, 1932

Charentes
Maigret à l'école (Maigret Goes to School): Saint André-sur-mer, 1954

Dordogne
Le fou de Bergerac (The Madman of Bergerac; Maigret Travels South): Bergerac, 1932

Île-de-France
Maigret aux Assises (Maigret in Court): Chelles, 1960
Maigret et le voleur paresseux (Maigret and the Lazy Burglar): Corbeil, 1961
Maigret et le tueur (Maigret and the Killer): Jouy-en-Josas, 1969
Maigret, Lognon et les gangsters (Maigret and the Gangsters): Maisons-Lafitte, 1952
Félicie est là (Maigret and the Toy Village): Poissy, 1944
La maison du juge (Maigret in Exile): Versailles, 1942

Loire/Centre
Maigret se fâche (Maigret in Retirement): Meung-sur-Loire, 1944
Maigret à New York (Inspector Maigret in New York's Underworld): Meung-sur-Loire, 1947

Marne

Le Charretier de 'La Providence' (The Crime at Lock 14): Vitry-la-François, 1931

Normandy

Le port des brumes (Death of a Harbor Master): Caen and Ouistreham, 1932

Maigret et la vieille dame (Maigret and the Old Lady): Étretat, 1950

Pietr-le-Letton (The Case of Peter the Lett; Maigret and the Enigmatic Lett): Fécamp, 1931

Au rendez-vous des Terre-Neuvas (The Sailors' Rendez-vous): Fécamp, 1931

Maigret et les témoins récalcitrants (Maigret and the Reluctant Witnesses): Ivry, 1959

Pitou

L'inspecteur cadavre (Maigret's Rival): Saint-Aubin-les-Marais, 1944

Provence

'Liberty Bar' (Liberty Bar; Maigret on the Riviera): Antibes, Cannes, and Nice, 1932

Maigret et l'indicateur (Maigret and the Flea): Bandol, 1971

Les caves du Majestic (Maigret and the Hotel Majestic): Cannes, 1942

Maigret s'amuse (Maigret's Little Joke): Cannes, 1957

Mon ami Maigret (My Friend Maigret): Porquerolles, 1949

Maigret voyage (Maigret and the Millionaires): Nice, 1958

La folle de Maigret (Maigret and the Madwoman): Toulon, 1970

Maigret aux Assises (Maigret in Court): Toulon, 1960

Vendée

La Maison du juge (Maigret in Exile): L'Aiguillon-sur-mer and Lucon, 1942

Une confidence de Maigret (Maigret Has Doubts): Fontenay-le-Comte, 1959

Maigret a peur (Maigret Afraid): Fontenay-le-Comte, 1953

Les vacances de Maigret (A Summer Holiday): Les Sables d'Olonne, 1948

Belgium
L'ombre chinoise (The Shadow in the Courtyard): Jeumont, Flanders, 1932
Le Pendu de St. Pholien (Maigret and the Hundred Gibbets): Liege, 1931
La danseuse du Gai-Moulin (At the Gai-Moulin; Maigret at the Gai-Moulin): Liège, 1931

England
Le revolver de Maigret (Maigret's Revolver): London, 1952

Germany
Le Pendu de St. Pholien (Maigret and the Hundred Gibbets): Bremen, 1931

Holland
Maigret et l'affaire Nahour (Maigret and the Nahour Case): Amsterdam, 1966
Un crime en Hollande (A Crime in Holland; Maigret in Holland): Delfzijl, 1931

Monaco
Maigret voyage (Maigret and the Millionaires): Monte Carlo, 1958

Switzerland
Maigret voyage (Maigret and the Millionaires): Lausanne, 1958

United States
Maigret à New York (Inspector Maigret in New York's Underworld): New York City, 1947
Maigret chez le coroner (Maigret and the Coroner): Tucson, Arizona, 1949

II

SPAIN

BARCELONA, 1975: *Up and down the Ramblas young and old people alike had expelled the fear that was left in them, on the day that the Dictator died. Happiness in their hearts—but silence on their lips. The shops ran out of bottles of cheap champagne that day; the streets and terraces were full of people enjoying the pleasure of being together without the great crushing shadow hanging over them. But still in silence, still with that cautiousness with words that they had learned in the years of the Terror. . . .* (Manuel Vázquez Montalbán, The Angst-Ridden Executive)

WHEN IN SPAIN IN EARLY JULY, head for Gijón and the annual Semana Negra fête. The brainchild of Mexican novelist Paco Ignacio Taibo II (who was born in Gijón), "Black Week" brings together mystery writers from around the world to talk about their craft in the middle of a large and lively carnival—complete with Ferris wheels, shooting galleries, and nonstop eating and drinking. (For information, contact Semana Negra, Apto de Correos 271, 33280 Gijon, Asturias, Spain, (011) 34–85–35–36–63.

After the Dictator

THE MYSTERY WAS late coming of age in Spain. In a 1991 essay on the *novela negra** (the Spanish term for the preferred, socially critical, hard-boiled variety), novelist Manuel Quinto suggests a number of reasons. The most obvious is the unhappy influence of the Franco govern-

---

*Manuel Quinto's essay is the introduction to *Negro como la noche: Manuel Vázquez Montalbán presenta Juan Antonio de Blas, et al.,* an anthology of Spanish writers published as a volume in the uniform edition of Montalbán's work (Madrid: Júcar, 1991).

ment, which censored the discussion of what Quinto considers to be basic elements of the genre: "Freudian analysis of the characters, political corruption, economic tentacles of power."

In the sixties, at least two English series made use of Spanish local color and Spanish police detectives, but social criticism was not the forte of either. The novels of John and Emery Bonett are classic tourist tales set on the Costa Brava, with casts of characters that are predominantly English except for the detective and a hotel employee or two. The plots have little to do with the setting; the English bring their own crimes with them. The detective, Inspector Salvador Borges of the Civil Guard, is praised for his sympathetic interviewing technique and his "violet eyes"; he is Spanish but tastefully so. The constraints of Franco's Spain are nowhere in evidence.

Delano Ames's Juan Llorca novels are more ambitious—and better. Not only is the detective Spanish; he is also the first-person narrator, an engaging and not very efficient character who is given to passionate crushes on expatriate English women. The main setting of the five Llorca novels is the fictional village of Madrigal del Mar on the Costa Blanca somewhere between Alicante and Valencia. The locals are believable types. Franco's government is represented by a secret police agent who is always on the lookout for signs of disrespect toward "the regime" and who seems quite prepared to beat a confession out of a stubborn suspect. The villagers take this philosophically; the tone of the novels is almost lighthearted.

Following Franco's death in 1975, the Spanish crime novel changed rapidly. In two very different series from the late seventies and eighties, Englishman David Serafin's Inspector Bernal novels and Manuel Vázquez Montalbán's Pepe Carvalho adventures, the drama of Spanish politics is often in the foreground.

In the 1980s, according to Quinto, the *novela negra* flourished, with writers such as Juan Madrid and Andreu Martin making names for themselves in the Spanish-reading world. The vagaries of translation are such, however, that only Montalbán's novels have been translated into English at this writing—and only four of them, in small-press editions. They are excellent and deserve wider notice.

The translation situation in Spain is further complicated by the fact that a number of interesting mystery novelists write in Catalan, rather than Castilian. Among them are Jaume Fuster, whose popular Lluis Arquer mysteries have *not* been published in English, and Maria-Antònia Oliver, two of whose hard-boiled feminist novels recently have.

In the first of Oliver's translated novels, *Study in Lilac,* the author pays a sort of backhanded homage to Fuster by introducing Lluis Arquer, "the best snoop in Barcelona," as a character, then subjecting him to a lecture on rape and its appropriate punishment. (Montalbán's Carvalho also appears but only in a walk-on.) Such self-conscious references to one's fictional antecedents or contemporaries are almost a standard feature of the Spanish mystery. Fuster's Arquer owes his name to Ross MacDonald's Lew Archer, for example, and Pepe Carvalho's neighbor and pal is Enric Fuster. Carvalho amuses himself in *The Angst-Ridden Executive* trying to pick a professional role model: "Bogart playing Chandler? [sic] Alan Ladd doing Hammett? Paul Newman as Harper?"

READING LIST

AMES, Delano. *The Man in the Tricorn Hat* ([London, 1960]; Chicago, 1966). First in the series featuring Juan Llorca, corporal of the Guardia Civil in the fictional seaside town of Madrigal, the "unspoiled Pearl of the Costa Blanca." (In several important details Madrigal sounds like the real town of Alcoy.) Murder comes late in this book. For most of the first half, Llorca is dealing with the mysteries in the background of his lady love, an expatriate English painter; her contemporary relationships with two other men, one an American millionaire, the other an English blackmailer; and the booming business of a local aristocrat who keeps "finding" unknown masterpieces by El Greco and Goya in his castle's lumber room and selling them at bargain prices. There is a lot of local color. For example, the millionaire gets murdered during the town's annual bacchanal, the Moros y Cristianos festival, in which the townspeople reenact that historic enmity.

———. *The Man with Three Jaguars* ([London, 1961]; Chicago, 1967). In this episode, Llorca has been transferred to the booming tourist town of Alcalá. Again he gets involved with a rich lady tourist; this one has a millionaire husband who plays with toy soldiers. (See also the two other Llorca novels: *The Man with Three Chins* [1965] and *The Man with Three Passports* [1967]. Delano Ames also wrote the Jane and Dagobert Brown novels (see Chapter I, "France"), which, though very different in perspective, reflect the same good nature and wit.)

BONETT, John and Emery [pseudonyms for John and Felicity Coulson]. *Murder on the Costa Brava* (in England, *This Side Murder,* 1967; (NY, 1968). Though the authors try hard to give a Spanish flavor to their tale—going so far as to include a recipe for paella—it could have happened anywhere. The guests gathered at a super-luxurious resort hotel, la Cristina (perhaps based on Hostal la Gavina in S'Agaró), include a sleazy journalist who is about to publish a book smearing the reputation of a great Victorian novelist, a scholar of the novelist, the novelist's great-grandchildren, a number of people the journalist has calumnied in his weekly column, the journalist's abused wife, etc. Need I add that the journalist bites the dust? (There are four other Inspector Borges tales, all involving literary crimes and misdemeanors.)

DAVIDSEN, Leif. *The Sardine Deception* [Copenhagen, 1984], translated from the Danish by Tiina Nunnally and Steve Murray (Seattle, 1986). This is a fine thriller that deserves to be better known. In the beautiful seaside town of San Sebastián in the Basque country, star Danish TV journalist Charlotte Damsborg is blown to bits in what is thought to be an ETA terrorist bombing. Her thoroughly domesticated husband (who works part-time and cares for the kids while she pursues her glamorous career) travels to Spain to collect his wife's remains. There he becomes involved with a cocky Swedish journalist (one of his wife's many ex-lovers) and two Basque nationalists who have renounced violence in the new political climate of the early eighties. There are plenty of violent types around, however, including some in the "democratic" Spanish government. There is also a plot afoot among supporters of the late dictator to overthrow the regime. This short, very readable book crams in a good deal of information about Spanish national politics in the post-Franco period, as well as about the Basque separatist movement. It also makes vivid use of chaotic and hallucinatory scenes of carnival in San Sebastián. (The weird title refers to a carnival rite; the original Danish title, which translates as "Unholy Alliance," makes more sense.)

JEFFRIES, Roderic. *Murder's Long Memory* (GB, 1991; NY, 1992). The detective in this prolific English series set in Mallorca (eighteen books at last count, starting in 1974) is Inspector Enrique Alvarez of the Cuerpo General de Policía, a native Mallorquin with a fondness for brandy and good food, who lives with his brother and shrewish sister-in-law and hankers after the rural life. The underlying theme of this novel and the series as a whole is the deterioration of his "lotus island" as a result of the tourist boom: "Once there had been fields, trees, sheep, goats, pigs, birds, space and solitude; now there was Cala Forsaya. Large hotels and blocks of apartments, restaurants, cafés, liquor and memento stores, lined and stretched back from the sandy beach."

As a cop, Alvarez is part sophisticated investigator (DNA tests and such) and part canny peasant, who follows his intuitions in defiance of his superior. In this case he solves a couple of current murders, plus a fifty-year-old one dating from World War II, when Spain, still dazed from its own civil war, maintained a precarious neutrality. The plot's implausible, to say the least, but there's some great scenery. Unfortunately, some place-names have been changed—to protect the cognoscenti?—so the book is not much help to a visitor seeking the few, but spectacular, unspoiled spots that remain.

————. *A Fatal Fleece* (GB and US, 1992). Here the underlying argument of the series—the evils of unchecked development versus the prosperity that tourism has brought to many Mallorquins—rises to the surface when Alvarez suspects that the sudden wealth of an odd assortment of natives and foreigners could only be the result of a shady land deal.

Jeffries is an amiable writer, but this series is formulaic in the extreme. Alvarez is lazy, slow to move, but incredibly stubborn once a case has piqued his curiosity. He's always at odds with his unimaginative boss. His food and booze consumption rivals Pepe Carvalho's, and his most characteristic gesture is to reach for the bottle of *coñac* in the bottom right-hand drawer of his desk. The other characters invariably include snobbish British expats, who disdain both the "unreliable" natives and the vulgar German package-tourists. It's all a bit claustrophobic.

OLIVER, Maria-Antònia. *Study in Lilac,* [Barcelona, 1985], translated by Kathleen McNerney (Seattle, 1987). Written and first published in Catalan, this fiercely feminist book pays tribute to Dashiell Hammett while turning the macho conventions of his work upside down. Oliver's detective is Appolònia Guiu, a wise-cracking Mallorquin now living in Barcelona. In the book's opening pages she takes on two cases: the search for a seventeen-year-old runaway and rape victim and the less routine case of a beautiful, elegant antique dealer, who—with a glance at Barcelona's famous architect—calls herself "Ms. Gaudí" and who claims to have been defrauded of a unique wooden statue by three men. (Neither client nor crime is as originally described.) The city of Barcelona is not a vivid player in this violent tale. As for the title: "Haven't you ever noticed," Guiu asks Lluis Arquer, "the graffiti done in lilac saying 'Against rape, castration'?" (Also available in English: Oliver's *Antipodes* [Barcelona, 1987; Seattle, 1989], which continues Lònia Guiu's adventures in Australia and Mallorca.)

O'MARIE, Sister Carol Anne. *Murder Makes a Pilgrimage* (NY, 1993, 1994). A novel featuring a pair of wise old nuns as amateur sleuths (and written by such another) sounds both anachronistic and, well, dreadfully cosy. But this fifth in the series about the "old dears" has its charms, and the setting of Santiago de Compostela, one of the great pilgrimage destinations of the Middle Ages, is evoked in awestruck detail. Sister Mary Helen and Sister Eileen have won a free vacation in Santiago. On their first morning, Mary Helen can't resist poking around in the cathedral. "Before I settle down to morning prayer," she thinks, "I'll just pop in for a quick visit to the shrine of St. James." There, behind the casket of St. James the Greater, apostle of Christ, she finds the brutally murdered body of a member of their tour group.

PÉREZ-REVERTE, Arturo. *The Flanders Panel* [Spain, 1990], translated by Margaret Jull Costa (NY, 1994). Julia, a Spanish art restorer, is working on a fifteenth-century painting by a fictional Flemish master, Pieter van Huys (not to be confused with the historical sixteenth-century painter Pieter Huys of Antwerp). Called *The Game of Chess,* the painting depicts a duke and a knight intent on the chessboard, while a beautiful woman sits reading in the background. It's a priceless masterpiece made even more so when an X ray reveals a Latin inscription, variously translated as "Who killed the knight?" or "Who took the knight?"

With the help of a chess genius' "retrograde analysis" of the game in the painting, Julia and her friends solve a five hundred-year-old murder mystery—only to discover that there's also a contemporary murderer at work, who's playing a deadly game of his own.

This is a very clever and literate novel of the genre book critic Michael Dirda calls "the antiquarian romance." The Madrid setting plays only a minor role, however—except for one scary after-hours scene in the Prado gallery dominated by Bosch's *Garden of Earthly Delights*. The real foreign land in this novel is the chessboard, and it helps if you already speak the language.

SERAFIN, David. *Madrid Underground* (GB, 1982; NY, 1984). One of a series featuring Superintendent Luis Bernal of the Madrid police, written by Oxford professor Ian Michael under a pseudonym. Set in May

1977, as Spain prepares for its first general election post-Franco, the novel is full of historical and political observations, plus some tidbits for tourists—for example, the correct term for draft beer (*una caña*).

The plot concerns the race to catch a psychopath who keeps leaving bizarre mementos on subway seats—first a dummy who emits real blood, later a real body, then pieces of another. Each of the short chapters is named after a Metro station and Serafin provides a map of the subway system. The result is an odd cross between a modern police procedural and an old-fashioned railway timetable mystery.

————. *Christmas Rising* (GB, 1982; NY, 1983). Serafin uses the ecclesiastical calendar from the first Sunday in Advent through the Feast of the Epiphany as a kind of organizing device. (The colors of the traditional vestments also provide clues.) The novel begins in December 1981, when Bernal—and his team—is called in by the royal palace to stave off a possible rightist coup against the government. (In real life, King Juan Carlos himself helped prevent such a coup in February of 1981.) Again, lots of historical and scenic background but little charm. Except for his physical resemblance to the "late Caudillo," Bernal is not a very memorable character. Nor is he an engaging one. He has a pious, penny-pinching peasant wife and keeps a complacent mistress on the side. Serafin's writing is often clunky, sometimes sounding like a translation. (See also *Saturday of Glory* [1979], and three other titles.)

VÁZQUEZ MONTALBÁN, Manuel. *The Angst-Ridden Executive* [Barcelona, 1977], translated by Ed Emery (GB, 1990). Pepe Carvalho, a small-time Barcelona private eye with a colorful past (ex-Communist, ex-CIA "treble agent") may be in over his head this time. The year is 1976. Franco is dead but Spain's political future is still very much up in the air. Nightly demonstrations and riots in the streets parallel the high-level jockeying for position by political parties of all stripes and by apolitical multinational corporations interested in stable markets. The "angst-ridden executive" of the title, Antonio Juama, holds a high position in one such corporation. When he is found murdered with a pair of women's "knickers" in his pocket, the company and the police are eager to write it off as the consequence of an overly adventurous sex life. Carvalho is called in by an unsatisfied friend of Juama's to look into the case more closely.

Plotting is not Montalbán's strong suit, and he has trouble with endings. But the political and historical background are brought to vivid life through the stories of Juama and six college friends—all Marxists then,

one known as "the 'first red student' of the post-War period"—and what
has become of them a quarter-century later. He is good, too, on the
sounds, smells, and—above all—tastes of Barcelona. Pepe Carvalho eats
and drinks as much and as enthusiastically as any detective in literary
history (Nero Wolfe included). Consider this early-morning snack (he's
on his way to lunch): "spidercrab with snails," followed by "kidney beans
and *butifarra* [sausage], with a side-dish of garlic mayonnaise." And bread
and wine and almond pastry. (Montalbán has published a cookbook
called *Las recetas de Carvalho*.)

Carvalho's sidekicks include a former car thief, Biscuter, who serves
as his secretary and cook, and Carvalho's girlfriend Charo, a good-natured
prostitute (oh well, nobody's perfect). His disillusioned romanticism is
summed up in his habit of using books as kindling for the fireplace—
especially those books he labels "transcendental": "The more a book has
pretensions to being transcendental, the more guilty it is. At some point
in its life it must have conned someone."

————. *Murder in the Central Committee* [Barcelona, 1981], translated
from the Spanish (London and Sydney, 1984). Former Communist Carvalho is hired by former cohorts when the general secretary of the newly
legal Spanish Communist Party is assassinated. Having eliminated the legendary Trilateral Commission, Pepe quickly narrows the suspects down
to a handful, all important or representative figures in the party's history
from the Spanish Civil War to Eurocommunism. The investigation inevitably brings back a lot of Pepe's past. In the present, however, he manages to see a bit of Madrid, while staying in the Opera Hotel, eating Iranian
caviar and Madrid-style tripe at the old and esteemed restaurant Lhardys,
hanging out in seedy Malsaña bars and coming close to being murdered
himself. This is a meaty political novel as well as a puzzle.

————. *An Olympic Death* [Barcelona, 1991], translated by Ed Emery
(NY and GB, 1992). The Berlin Wall has fallen, and Barcelona is in a frenzy
of building and boosterism in preparation for the '92 Olympics. Melancholy times for an old radical like Carvalho, who's feeling his age though
he's kept his sense of irony. Then a beautiful French woman walks into
his office and adds the pain of unrequited love to his other woes. She
wants his help in finding the great love of her life, a young Greek named
Aleksos. The quest takes them through a labyrinth of abandoned factories and warehouses in the proletarian areas of Barcelona known as Poble
Nou and Icaria—ruins temporarily occupied by photographers and sculp-

tors, but soon to be torn down to make way for the Olympic Village. (In Spain this book is called "The Greek Labyrinth," and Montalbán certainly doesn't stint on the classical allusions.) By novel's end, Carvalho has burned copies of *Zorba the Greek, The Four Horsemen of the Apocalypse,* and *Peter Pan.* (The fourth translated title in the Carvalho series is *Southern Seas* [1979].)

WILSON, Barbara. *Gaudí Afternoon* (Seattle, 1990). The title pays homonymic homage to Dorothy Sayers's classic *Gaudy Night* (1936), and the two novels do have in common a mostly feminine (and feminist) cast. But Sayers's title refers to an Oxford college alumni fête and Wilson's to Antoni Gaudí, the modernist architect whose fantastic, playful creations— the mansion Palau Güell, the apartment building known as La Pedrera, the church of the Sagrada Família, etc.) make Barcelona's cityscape unique. All are skillfully introduced by Wilson in this lively and unconventional tale.

The narrator is Spanish translator and amateur detective Cassandra Reilly, who is hired by a jaunty young lesbian named Frankie to find her gay ex-husband somewhere in Barcelona. It transpires, however, that Frankie is a transsexual, and that she/he's really looking for his ex-*wife,* an extremely butch lesbian called Ben, who has run off to Spain with her new lover, a Rubenesque reflexologist, and with Frankie and Ben's six-year-old daughter, Delilah, the focus of a nasty custody battle. Among the supporting characters is a voluptuous Spanish hairdresser, who never goes much beyond petting because her mother will be waiting up for her. Then there's Cassandra's old friend Ana, who's decided she wants Cassandra to be the father—so to speak—of the child she intends to have.

Cassandra, who also is gay, is resourceful and witty, but even she is a bit overwhelmed by the complexities of human relations in this novel. There are enough changes of clothes and gender roles for several Shakespearean comedies, with Gaudí's Parc Güell serving as an inanimate Forest of Arden. No murders, but plenty of mystery. The sights are splendid, and the directions so specific that you may need no other map.

NOTED BUT NOT REVIEWED

CLIFFORD, Francis. *The Third Side of the Coin* (London, 1964; NY, 1965). An airport bank teller sees his chance, empties the till, and heads for the Costa del Sol, where an earthquake changes everything.

DUNNETT, Dorothy. *Ibiza Surprise* (1971, 1993). One of a series featuring artist-sleuth Johnson Johnson and his yacht.

MacINNES, Helen. *Message from Málaga* (1971, 1991). Spy stuff from a mistress of the genre.

SHELDON, Sidney. *The Sands of Time* (NY, 1988). The Basque ETA versus the sinister government cabal Sheldon calls "Opus Mundi." This bit of sleaze begins with a prison escape in Pamplona during the Running of the Bulls and chronicles the adventures of four nuns.

CLOSE-UP

Dining with Detectives

A N ARMY MARCHES on its stomach," Napoleon was supposed to have observed. So, too, many of the great fictional detectives. Among their eccentricities, dedicated eating and drinking figure largely. (Pun intended; there are any number of overweight detectives, the most celebrated being Nero Wolfe.)

Eating should also be one of the traveler's chief concerns—not just as fuel for the fray but as a way of getting to know a place and its people. Fiction's gourmandizing sleuths thus are excellent travel guides—especially those devoted to *la cuisine bourgeoise* or *paysanne* of their native turf. Superintendent Maigret once again is the model. Those who share his taste for good home cooking include Nicolas Freeling's Dutch Inspector Van der Valk and his French Commissaire Henri Castang, Roderic Jeffries's Inspector Alvarez of Majorca and Magdalen Nabb's Marshal Guarnaccia of Florence.

The aforementioned are consummate consumers, not cooks. Vázquez Montalbán's Pepe Carvalho, on the other hand, though he is usually fed by his sidekick, Biscuter, is quite capable of undertaking to roast a duck himself on a one A.M. whim. (See *The Angst-Ridden Executive* for a loving description of this early bird and its bacon, mushroom, truffle, and olive adornments.)

Carvalho's eating habits have inspired a hard-to-find cookbook, Vázquez Montalbán's *Las recetas de Carvalho* (Barcelona, 1989). Maigret's long-suffering wife also stars in a cookbook, *Madame Maigret's Recipes,* by Robert J. Courtine (NY, 1975). Nicolas Freeling's *The Cook Book* (London, 1972; Boston, 1991), however, is based more on the author's experience as a professional chef than it is on his detectives' eating habits.

In contrast to the reassuring image of Maigret trudging home to a plate of Mme. Maigret's coq au vin are the gourmet fantasies—all brand names and "stirred not shaken" fussiness—of James Bond and his imitators. There are also some self-conscious attempts to capitalize on the food/mystery affinity—Nan and Ivan Lyons's *Someone Is Killing the Great Chefs of Europe* (1976), for example, or Michael Bond's series of novels about restaurant reviewer Monsieur Pamplemousse. For consistently satisfying, hearty fare, the reader is advised to stick with Simenon, Freeling, and Vázquez Montalbán.

Here's a taste of each:

THE SOUPS OF FREELING: "Vera's potato soup was Slav, like her. One got a big bowl and three little bowls, with chopped chives, and little soldiers of fried bread, and rashers of bacon, grilled crisp and crumbled up. It put heart back into Castang." (*The Night Lords*)

Vera Castang's potato soup does not figure in Freeling's *Cook Book,* which preceded it by a number of years. But Arlette Van der Valk's pea soup from *Double-Barrel* is chronicled there; it is four pages and four days in the making.

CARVALHO ON COCIDO MADRILEÑO: "Carvalho spoke about the similar origin of pot au feu as an excellent cocido came into view. The chickpea, he said, marks the style of the Spanish pot au feu, and it is nearly always the dried vegetable that gives it its particular nuance. In Yucatán, for example, cocido is made with lentils, while in Brazil it is based on black beans. In the chickpea cocido of the peoples of Spain, the Madrid version is characterized by the use of chorizo sausage, while its Catalan counterpart relies on blood sausage and little meatballs." (*Murder in the Central Committee*)

MME. MAIGRET'S BOEUF BOURGUIGNON: "Make a marinade consisting of 2 small chopped leeks, 2 carrots cut in rounds, 2 large coarsely chopped onions, stalk of diced celery, 3 cloves of crushed garlic, a *bouquet garni,* salt and pepper, and a bottle of red Burgundy (or other sturdy red).

"Cut 1 3/4 lbs. stew beef into 2-inch pieces. Place in the marinade, covered, for 48 hours.

"Remove meat and drain it carefully. Strain the marinade.

"Melt 4 tablespoons of lard in dutch oven. Brown meat over high heat. Add the herbs from the marinade. Sprinkle 2 tb. of flour on the meat. Stir the meat with a wooden spatula so that the flour forms a crust on each piece.

"Heat the marinade and pour over the meat. Add 1–2 cups of hot water to cover meat well.

"Blanch 5–6 oz. of salt pork and add to the meat. Taste for seasoning. Cover and cook gently for 3 1/2 hours.

"Blanch 20 small white pearl onions and add to the meat. Take out the *bouquet garni.* Cook for 15 min.

"Remove from fire and add 1 tsp. of *marc de Bourgogne* (brandy). Before serving the meat, sprinkle with freshly cut parsley." (*Madame Maigret's Recipes,* presented by Robert J. Courtine [NY, 1975].)

III

ITALY

When one wanted to arrive overnight at the incomparable, the fabulous, the like-nothing-else-in-the-world, where was it one went? Why, obviously; he had intended to go there . . . to Venice. (Thomas Mann, "Death in Venice")

The trouble with this country is that it's a mass of anarchists and improvisors governed by bandits. (Magdalen Nabb, The Marshal and the Murderer)

Crime in Italy is a national industry. If an Italian isn't murdering someone in Calabria, it's only because he's too busy kidnapping someone else in Lombardy. Or embezzling public funds in Friuli. Or stealing little-known pictures from churches in Verona. Or burgling the Courthouse at Monza. That, at any rate, if The Times is to be relied on, is how they have spent the past week. . . . (Sarah Caudwell, Thus Was Adonis Murdered)

Both the Sicilian I am and the reasonable man I claim to be rebel against this injustice to Sicily, this insult to reason. . . . Is it really possible to conceive of the existence of a criminal association so vast, so well-organized, so secret and so powerful that it can dominate not only half Sicily but the entire United States of America? (Leonardo Sciascia, "The Day of the Owl")

Death in Venice (Of Course) and Elsewhere

MARSHAL SALVATORE GUARNACCIA of the Carabinieri (Florence). Vice-Questore Aurelio Zen of Criminapol (Rome). Commissario Guido Brunetti (Venice). Flavia di Stefano, assistant to the director of the National Art Theft Squad (Rome). Commissario Achille Peroni (Venice). Talented amateur Urbino Macintyre (Florence) . . . It would not be difficult to argue that this is the Golden Age of the Italian detective.

But where are the Italian writers?

With the exception of some works of Leonardo Sciascia, Carlo Emilio Gadda, and Umberto Eco, mainstream literary writers who have played on the borders of the genre, few Italian crime novels seem to find their way into English. The contemporary series characters listed above are all the creations of British or American novelists, and this in a country where the material is extraordinarily rich, where corruption is endemic on all levels of politics and society (and may be viewed as outrageous or hilarious depending on the quality and quantity of wine at luncheon). This is, after all, the country that gave American novelists and screenwriters the Mafia.

So where are the Italian writers?

It's a mystery.

Although most native contributions to the genre fail to find their way into English, many English and American writers of novels set in Italy write from an "Italian" point of view rather than a touristic one. Michael Dibdin is particularly successful in conveying the tragicomical cynicism about the police, the bureaucracy, and authority in general that informs Italian life and has reached a climax in recent years with the trials for corruption in the highest levels of government.

Not surprisingly, Italy's artistic wealth subsidizes any number of mystery plots—from Jonathan Gash's plot to steal all the antiques in Venice, to Timothy Holme's and Iain Pears's variations on the antiquarian romance, in which solution of a modern crime entails the solution of a centuries-old mystery.

There are good mysteries set all over Italy, but Venice exerts a special fascination for mystery writers. "Death and Venice go together," Jan Morris wrote in *The World of Venice*. Thomas Mann has something to do with that, of course. His extraordinary short story, with its vision of gondolas as coffins and its hallucinating scenes of pursuit through Venetian labyrinths, continues to haunt writers and readers about the city.

But Venice itself is a kind of *memento mori,* so filled with antique glories and so precariously perched, at the mercy of seasonal flood waters and unceasing industrial pollution from Mestre on the mainland. For writers who like a touch of the grotesque, it even offers an island of bones, Sant'Ariano (not to be confused with San Michele, the cemetery island).

Sant'Ariano doesn't make it into most guidebooks. It's the old Ossario (ossuary), where after twelve years in a conventional cemetery, impoverished Venetians of generations past were relocated to make room for others to rest (albeit briefly) in peace.

Michael Dibdin and Jonathan Gash make good use of the sensations engendered by the knowledge that the white objects crunching beneath one's feet are human bones. But, writes Dibdin in *Dead Lagoon,* "it was not only the thought of the unknown, uncountable dead whose remains had been tipped there like so much rubbish, thousands and thousands of bones and skulls, a whole hillock of them held in by a retaining wall. Almost as frightening as those reminders of mortality had been the evidence of life: a profusion of withered, gnarled, spiny plants and shrubs which sprouted from that sterile desert, and above all the host of rodents and reptiles which scuttled and slithered and nested amongst the bones."

READING LIST

CAUDWELL, Sarah. *Thus Was Adonis Murdered* (1981, 1982). Few mystery writers can rival Sarah Caudwell for sheer wit and style. Indeed her books, narrated by sexually enigmatic Hilary Tamar (is Hilary male or female?), evoke Evelyn Waugh or Nancy Mitford or P. G. Wodehouse more than they do Agatha Christie, but the plotting is fine too. Hilary is an Oxford professor of law; the other main characters are five young barristers—Bright Young Things of the eighties—whom Hilary insists on advising. They consume vast quantities of gin and cigarettes, make silly jokes about Cambridge, and cultivate a languid insouciance.

Though this is a quintessentially British series, the setting of this first volume shifts back and forth between London, where the young barristers—who have delicious names like Ragwort and Cantrip—seek to avoid as much work as possible, and Venice, where one of their number, Julia, has gone for a vacation and a bit of dalliance. Julia, who resembles "one of the more dishevelled heroines of Greek tragedy," is known for her incompetence in practical matters. Thus her friends, who gather every day to read her letters, are understandably distressed when a young man she takes to bed in Venice is promptly murdered and she is arrested. Led by Hilary, they puzzle out the solution from a distance.

DIBDIN, Michael. *Cabal* (NY, 1993, 1994). *Cabal* begins with a body falling from the balcony surrounding the dome of St. Peter's basilica, as the stunned congregation watches. It's worth watching.

The figure might have been falling through a medium infinitely more viscous than air, so slowly did it appear to descend, revolving languidly about its own axis, the long sustained keening wrapped around it like winding robes, the limbs and trunk executing a leisurely saraband that ended as the body smashed head first into the marble pavement at something approaching seventy miles an hour.

No one moved. The glistening heap of blood and tissue subsided gently into itself with a soft farting sound. Priest and congregation, tourists and attendants, stood as silent and still as figures in a plaster Nativity. In distant nooks and crannies of the vast enclosure, the final echoes of that long scream died away. Then, as strident as trumpets, first one, then many voices took up the strain, shrieking hysterically, howling, sobbing, and gasping.

It's hard to live up to a beginning like that, but Dibdin succeeds in a book that is fast-paced, original, and often hilarious.

The body so unceremoniously introduced into mass in the Holy City is that of a playboy aristocrat in serious need of money. He also is a member of a super-secret inner circle of the legendary Knights of Malta and privy to their plot to do something very dire. Needless to say, he did not jump of his own free will. It takes Aurelio Zen of Criminalpol, who is called in by the Vatican to serve as an independent investigator, about three minutes to figure that out. But, eager to get back to his girlfriend Tania's bed, he's quite willing to go along with any cover-up the Vatican has in mind.

Zen is a talented, imaginative, and efficient cop who seems always to be teetering on the edge of corruption. Certainly he's surrounded by it in the Italian government bureaucracy and, it seems, in the parallel Vatican bureaucracy. At the interface of the two, Zen feels himself "a speck of grit caught in the bearings of power." To make matters worse, he suspects Tania, his coworker and mistress, of having an affair. (What she's really up to is running a private business so financially successful that she fears it will undermine his manhood if he learns about it.)

This is a terrific book, which has great fun with many of the thriller conventions, with arcana both ancient (the Knights of Malta) and modern (a bizarre computer hacker), and with the clichés of Latin machismo. The settings—principally Rome and Milan—and the high-speed train, the *Pendolino,* that links them—are strongly drawn.

————. *Dead Lagoon* (London, 1994; NY, 1995). Another great beginning, this one on Venice's island of bones, where a drug trafficker has a gruesome encounter. Cut to Aurelio Zen, who has returned to his native Venice on a slightly illegal freelance assignment to investigate the mysterious disappearance of an American millionaire. Childhood memories, a new love interest, and an old neighbor who sees ghosts further complicate matters.

As usual Zen is trying, with little success, to be corrupt; he can't begin to compete with the cops and politicians he meets in this outing. In the background are the revelations of crime at the highest levels of the Italian government in the late eighties and early nineties—"a network of kickbacks, slush funds, golden handshakes, graft, incentives, backhanders and hush money"—and the subsequent indictments and trials. The foreground includes some very precise descriptions of Venetian street scenes, as well as some hallucinating images of corruption—for example, a cop literally drowning in shit. Even more horrific, ultimately, is the novel's vision of a New Europe on the splintered Balkan model. (See also Dibdin's other Zen novels: *Ratking* [1989], and *Vendetta* [1991], about a massacre at a billionaire's hideaway in Sardinia.)

DOWLING, Gregory. *See Naples and Kill* (NY and London, 1988). Both the beauty of Naples and the mess—its poverty, crime, corruption—are evoked in this lively novel by English writer Dowling. He's good on such details as the noise level in Naples; the importance of the word *casino* (which by complex derivation means "confusion, mess, cock-up"); the cultural clout of soccer hero Maradona; the benign nature of Italian Communists (they're "the cuddly variety, they don't bite"). And so dedicated is Dowling to scenic accuracy that he apologizes in an "afterword" for taking "liberties . . . with the geography of the south side of Ischia."

Dowling's protagonist is half-English, half-Italian January Esposito. Jan, who lives in London, is mourning the loss of his girl and his translating job when his half-brother Luigi, a would-be big-time criminal, turns up. Soon there are dead bodies to be dealt with, and Jan follows his brother to Naples, where some fairly entertaining bad guys are planning the assassination of a VIP amid the ruins of Pompeii.

Though given to silly disguises and snappy retorts, and always on the verge of taking a pratfall, Jan nevertheless is an effective and resourceful detective. If you think Chevy Chase as Fletch is funny, and if you're also amused by an English village named "Thrubton Nempwell" and the many ways Italian speakers can mangle its pronunciation, you'll enjoy this book. I did.

GADDA, Carlo Emilio. *That Awful Mess on Via Merulana* [Milan, 1957], translated by William Weaver (NY, 1965, 1984). The work of one of the greatest Italian writers of this century, *That Awful Mess* is much more likely to evoke comparisons with James Joyce than with Agatha Christie. True, it begins with two crimes—a burglary and a murder—but the mechanics of whodunit interest Gadda much less than philosophical questions of cause and effect, experiments with language, and his multileveled portrayal of Rome. Rome, writes Italo Calvino in an introduction to the 1984 edition, is "the true protagonist of the book, with its social classes ranging from the middle bourgeoisie to the underworld, the voices of its various dialects surfacing in the melting pot, its extroversion and its murkiest unconscious."

GASH, Jonathan. *The Gondola Scam* (NY, 1984, 1985). Resourceful rogue Lovejoy is in good form in this outing. His blathering about his success with "birds" gets tiresome, but the scam of the title is worthy of his talents—as quick-change artist, amateur puzzle-solver, "divvie" (diviner), and faker of antiques. The plan put to him by a millionaire collector: to steal all the antiques in Venice before it sinks into the sea. Except, of course, it's more complicated than that. There's not much plausible about this adventure, but it's fun and the scenery's great. (See also Gash's *The Vatican Rip* [1981], in which Lovejoy is challenged to extract a Chippendale table from the Vatican.)

GILMAN, Dorothy. *Mrs. Pollifax and the Second Thief* (NY, 1993, 1995). The CIA's old lady agent, as adept at karate as she is at gardening, is sent to Sicily to help an old friend. One hour after completing this entry in a very popular series, I had forgotten almost everything about it—except that it involved a lot of car chases and some conscientiously described scenery.

HIGHSMITH, Patricia. *The Talented Mr. Ripley* (NY, 1955, 1992). Tom Ripley is an otherwise undistinguished young American gifted with good taste in clothes and art and considerable acting ability. He also is a psychopath. In an updated version of Henry James's *The Ambassadors*, Ripley is dispatched to Europe by a wealthy man who wants Ripley to find his son, an acquaintance of Ripley's named Dickie Greenleaf, and to persuade him to give up painting and return to the family business. Ripley finds Dickie living in "Mongibello," a little town on the Amalfi coast probably modeled on Positano. Though he doesn't think much of Dickie's paintings or his bumptious, overeager girlfriend, Marge, Tom greatly admires his personal style and his tasteful possessions. He abandons his mission and moves in with Dickie. When Dickie tires of him, Ripley simply kills him and takes over his identity—his passport, his clothes, his accent, and his income. The mystery here is if—and how—Ripley/Dickie will avoid exposure.

This classic of psychological suspense also offers splendid glimpses of the expatriate *dolce vita* in postwar Italy—on the Amalfi coast, in Naples, Rome, Venice, and Sicily. (For the later adventures of Ripley, see Chapter I, "France.")

HOLME, Timothy. *The Assisi Murders* (London, 1985, 1988). Commissario Achille Peroni of Venice, "the Rudolph Valentino of the Italian police," accompanies his sister, Assunta, on a sightseeing "pilgrimage" to Assisi. Peroni's lust for a fellow pilgrim leads him into involvement in a contemporary murder case; meanwhile, his vulnerability to semimystical "plunges into the past" draws him into the mysteries surrounding a thirteenth-century woman follower of Assisi's St. Francis and a great art treasure. His housewife sister, Assunta, is busy rekindling a romance with the great love of her youth. Plenty of touristic local color, but the plot is overly complicated and fantastic. What puzzles most is the tone of the telling, which shifts from lightly ironic to darkly portentous from page to page. Peroni's other cases include *A Funeral of Gondolas* (Venice), *The Neapolitan Streak* (Naples), and *The Devil and the Dolce Vita* (Venice).

LANGTON, Jane. *The Dante Game* (NY, 1991). Langton's Homer Kelly, retired detective turned Harvard professor, usually sticks close to home—Boston and Concord, Massachusetts—and to the literary lights associated with the region (for example, *Emily Dickinson Is Dead*, 1984). In this outing, however, he grabs at a chance to teach for a year in Florence, and his creator grabs at every chance to weave quotes from, and parallels to, *The Divine Comedy* throughout. Though the novel involves drug-dealing, murder, a dissident priest turned hit-man, and a plot to kill the Pope, the tone is relentlessly lighthearted. The author's sketches of Florence are charming.

LEON, Donna. *Death at La Fenice* (NY, 1992, 1995). In the first of Donna Leon's series featuring Commissario Guido Brunetti of the Venice police, a famous conductor dies from a dose of cyanide during an intermission of *La Traviata* at the beloved opera house of the title (which in real life was recently devastated by fire). The conductor reputedly is both a former Nazi and a serious homophobe. He has other nasty secrets. Among the suspects: the prima donna, whom the conductor is blackmailing, and her lesbian lover.

Brunetti's "clothing marked him as Italian. The cadence of his speech announced that he was Venetian. His eyes were all policeman." He is a clever, compassionate, somewhat melancholy type, with a loving aristocratic wife. His home makes him happy. What makes him melancholy is his view of Venice as a city on the skids, threatened by age and corruption, oil spills and other forms of pollution.

————. *Death in a Strange Country* (NY, 1993, 1995) is about the murder of a young American soldier from the nearby base at Vicenza, whose body is found floating in the canal in front of Santi Giovanni e Paolo (otherwise, the Zanipolo). Dealing with corruption in high places, pollution, and other problems not confined to but well expressed in Italy these days, it maintains the high standard of the debut. It is a book one may enjoy without knowing Venice, since it is subtly instructive throughout, but to read it while seated on a canal step in front of the Zanipolo—now that is a special pleasure.

MARSH, Ngaio. *When in Rome* (NY, 1971). One of the grande dames of the British mystery (a Dame Commander of the British Empire in fact) sends her long-running series character, Inspector Roderick Alleyn, to Rome to look into an international drug operation. In order to get close to a suspect, Alleyn joins a small and very expensive tour group. Naturally there's a murder and naturally the tour group members, wittily sketched stereotypes all, are the likely suspects. There are some wonderful sights, especially a slightly fictionalized version of the Basilica di San Clemente (here called San Tomasso), a three-level place of worship of which the lowest level is a third-century Mithraic temple. Much less successful are Marsh's stabs at depicting *la dolce vita*. And her attempts at druggy hipness are merely embarrassing.

MURPHY, Haughton [pseudonym of James Duffy]. *A Very Venetian Murder* (NY, 1992). On their twenty-second annual vacation in Venice, retired Wall Street lawyer Reuben Frost and wife Cynthia, a former ballerina, attend the Party of the Year, held in the Palazzo Labia surrounded by Tiepolo's frescoes of the life of Cleopatra. Subsequently Reuben solves the murder of the host of the party, a famous dress designer (and a nasty piece of work). There's a lot of chitchat about the merits of the Hotel Cipriani versus the Gritti Palace, and every mouthful of every meal—at Da Arturo, Antica Besseta, Caffè Orientale, etc.—is lovingly described. This is also the only mystery I know to include a bibliography (of books about Venice). In short, this is the almost perfect mystery for our purposes. There are only two problems: 1) Reuben and Cynthia's self-satisfaction with their very comfortable and oh-so-tasteful life is hard to take; 2) the book is dull.

NABB, Magdalen. *Death in Springtime: A Florentine Mystery* (GB, 1983, 1989). The third in the Marshal Guarnaccia series begins charmingly with a freak March snowstorm: "the entire population of Florence [wakes up] blinking in amazement and consternation." But the main setting is the little village of Pontino (which is not on my map) in the Tuscan foothills. Since it's not his territory, Guarnaccia plays only a peripheral role in solving the mystery of a wealthy young American's kidnapping. He's not greatly missed. The Pontino brigadier, who knows "every blade of grass" in his territory; a lovestruck young lieutenant; and an amused and amusing "substitute prosecutor" are all sharply drawn, as is the very serious and competent Captain Maestrangelo.

Nabb's focus in this novel is on the Sardinian immigrants who herd sheep and make admirable ricotta in the hills outside Florence. Scorned by many Florentines, some of the Sardinians have developed profitable sidelines: kidnapping and drug-dealing. Though the mystery plot suffers in the process, Nabb sketches a vivid picture of the shepherds' rugged, archaic way of life.

————. *The Marshal and the Murderer* (GB, 1987, 1988). At his station house in a wing of the Pitti Palace, Guarnaccia is approached by a young Swiss woman whose roommate has disappeared. The marshal makes some routine inquiries in the potteries outside Florence where she had been working. Soon thereafter, her body is found in a waste heap of ceramic shards, and Guarnaccia is assigned to collaborate on the case with the jolly local marshal, Niccolino.

Here again the focus is on an isolated and inbred community, an unnamed town on the road to Pisa whose chief support is its small ceramic factories. (Nabb, who was once a potter and ceramics teacher in Florence, appears to know the environment well.) The murder and its investigation bring to the surface tensions and prejudices dating from the last years of World War II, a time of terrible deprivation and great brutality, in particular by the Germans against the Tuscan partisans. "Racial hatred [in this case, anti-German] is like a volcano," says one wise old character. "The flames of the great eruption of the last war may have died down but the volcano goes on smoldering. Nothing has changed. It only needs an excuse, economic depression, threatened vested interest, whatever you will, and it's ready to erupt all over again."

Salvatore Guarnaccia is a very low-key type and owes a lot to Maigret. His chief characteristics seem to be his small-town Sicilian origins (Syracuse), his bulging eyes and sleepy manner, and his inarticulate love for his young sons. He is modest about his detective skills, insisting he has no brains and no ideas, only a "mind full of images" derived from "simple observation." He is "one of those people who notice things," and that's usually enough. (See also the other Guarnaccia titles: *Death of an Englishman* [1981]; *Death of a Dutchman* [1982]; *Death in Autumn* [1985]—a body clad in fur coat, jewelry, and nothing else is fished out of the Arno; *The Marshal and the Madwoman* [1988]—a local crazy is found with her head in her oven; *The Marshal's Own Case* [1990]; *The Marshal Makes His Report* [1992]—death of a Florentine nobleman.)

PEARS, Iain. *The Titian Committee* (GB, 1991; NY, 1993). The Titian Committee is an international group of experts charged with seeking out, authenticating, and cataloging every known work of the Venetian master. A cantankerous clan, they have gathered for their annual meeting at the deluxe Fondazione Giorgio Cini (real) on the Venetian island of San Giorgio Maggiore. One of their number is found stabbed to death in the greenhouse of the Giardinetti Reali. Because of the art angle, gorgeous but volatile Flavia di Stefano of the Rome-based art theft squad is sent to write a quick, politically correct report. Of course things don't work out that easily. Flavia and her faithful admirer, bumbling English art dealer Jonathan Argyll (predictably, he falls into a fetid canal), are soon up to their ears in a case that comes to hinge on the identity of the model for the central figure in a Titian triptych in Padua. This is a lively, agreeable art puzzle in which the solution of the old mystery of the painting sheds light on the new.

SCERBANENCO, Giorgio. *Duca and the Milan Murders* [1966], translated by Eileen Ellenbogen (NY, 1970). Scerbanenco is considered one of the first important Italian crime novelists. His protagonist, Duca Lamberti, is a physician who has lost his license and served time for euthanasia. Approached by a sleazy type to perform an illegal operation to restore a lost virginity, Duca goes to the police and becomes an undercover operative in a case involving several murders and World War II betrayals. The setting is Milan, particularly the outer suburbs.

SCIASCIA, Leonardo. "The Day of the Owl" [Italy, 1961], in *The Day of the Owl; Equal Danger* (Boston, 1984). (Also published as "Mafia Vendetta," NY, 1964). From a modern master, a novella, set in Sicily, about the murder of a local businessman. For Sciascia and his detective, the mystery of the death is less important than its political ramifications, which lead to meditations on fascism, corruption, and the Mafia and their intertwined and all-pervasive roles in Sicily.

SICILIANO, Enzo. *Diamante* [Milan, 1984], translated by Patrick Diehl (San Francisco, 1987). Set in the province of Calabria in the toe of the Italian boot, this peculiar novel begins like a gothic romance, with a young innocent responding to an ad for a live-in librarian at a remote Calabrian villa. The residents of the house behave oddly; there are locked rooms, an unseen piano player, a missing will. Unlike the conventional gothic protagonist, however, this one is male. The other characters include an exceedingly raunchy village priest. There is a lot of unattractive sex and some carrying on about Calabrian codes of revenge, honor, justice, etc. The mafia works its way into the plot toward the end. Best left to languish in obscurity.

SKLEPOWICH, Edward. *Death in a Serene City* (NY, 1990, 1992). The passions that lead to murder are as nothing compared to writer Urbino Macintyre's passion for his adopted city of Venice, where this American *venezianizzato* has settled into a reclusive and exquisitely tasteful bachelorhood—modeled on that of Huysmans's Des Esseintes, but "purged of its many decadent excesses." But the murder of his faithful laundress and the disappearance of a mummified saint from one of Venice's more obscure churches get Urbino's inquisitive juices flowing. By novel's end, he and his sidekick, the Contessa da Capo-Zendrini, the elegant and devout English widow of a Venetian nobleman, are ready to move on to their next case.

This is a very literary book, with lots of allusions to the famous sensibilities that have resonated to the Serenissima in the past. Sklepowich pays erudite tribute to a number of Venice's most famous vistas. He also offers glimpses into many odd or obscure corners of Venice's present and past—the island of bones in the lagoon, for example, and the ballet slippers that mysteriously appear on Diaghilev's grave. The plot is less successful. At the end of this rather long book, I didn't totally grasp the mystery's solution—nor did I much care. I was, however, ready to book the next flight on Alitalia. (See also Sklepowich's *Farewell to the Flesh* [1991], in which Urbino investigates the murder of an English photographer during Carnival, and *Liquid Desires* [1993], in which murder strikes close to home for the contessa.)

VERALDI, Attilio. *The Payoff* [Milan, 1976], translated by Isabel Quigly (NY, 1978). According to the jacket copy, Veraldi has translated more than one hundred mystery novels from English into Italian, including most of Raymond Chandler. The latter influence is evident. What we have here is an attempt at Neapolitan hard-boiled, with mixed results.

The protagonist, Sasà Iovine, does little jobs for Michele Miletti, "possibly the richest man in Naples." Now, however, Sasà is being cut in by Don Michele on a corrupt municipal deal that will be his first chance at big money. Under the circumstances, he can't afford to turn down the old man's request that he go find his runaway eighteen-year-old daughter. What he finds instead are the murdered bodies of Don Michele's young wife and her lover.

The corpses proliferate in this very violent book; so do the crooks, all of whom outclass Sasà in nastiness—especially the sinister twin brothers who beat him within an inch of his life, and a disgusting fat mobster who tortures him by forcing him to ingest spaghetti (not as far-fetched as it sounds). There is a great deal of frenetic action in this book, which moves around Italy. Yet the novel as a whole is oddly slow-moving—like a movie in which a self-indulgent director holds each shot a few seconds too long. It could have been better.

NOTED BUT NOT REVIEWED

CORNELISEN, Ann. *Any Four Women Could Rob the Bank of Italy* (NY, 1984). But in this book, set in Tuscany, it's six women and an Italian mail train carrying a million dollars.

CRESPI, Camilla. *The Trouble with Going Home* (NY, 1995). Simona Griffo, sleuth in a series set in New York, goes home to Rome and immediately witnesses a murder outside her mother's house.

DAVIS, Lindsey. *Silver Pigs* (NY, 1989). First of a series, set in Rome in the first century A.D., and starring Marcus Didius Falco, investigator for the Emperor Vespasian.

FRIEDMAN, Mickey. *Venetian Mask* (NY, 1987). A group of friends come to Venice for Carnival . . . and find death.

GILBERT, Michael. *The Family Tomb* ([NY and GB, 1969]; NY, 1986). An English bookstore manager in Florence is drawn into an elaborate plot involving Etruscan tomb robbery. (Also published as *The Etruscan Net.*)

LLEWELLYN, Caroline. *The Masks of Rome* (NY, 1988, 1989). The heroine is an art conservator in Rome, who stumbles into art fraud and becomes a murderer's target.

MacINNES, Helen. *The Venetian Affair* (NY, 1963, 1969). An American journalist is caught up in Cold War intrigue, which takes him from Paris to Switzerland and Venice.

MURRAY, William. *A Fine Italian Hand* (NY, 1996). A magicians' convention brings Shifty Lou Anderson, Murray's racetrack series character, to Milan. Murder follows.

PETERS, Elizabeth. *The Seventh Sinner* (NY, 1972, 1986). Someone is stalking Jean Suttman, a young American studying art in Rome.

ROTSSTEIN, Aaron Nathan. *Judgment in St. Peter's* (NY, 1980, 1981). An American lawyer seeks revenge for his family's slaughter in the Holocaust.

SAYLOR, Steven. *Roman Blood* (NY, 1991). First of a series set in the first century B.C. The detective is Gordianus the Finder, protégé of young Cicero. Four sequels followed, of which the most recent at this writing is *A Murder on the Appian Way* (NY, 1996).

WHITTEN, Les. *A Killing Pace* (NY, 1983). An international arms salesman is overcome by "late-blooming morality" when guns he has sold are used by the Italian Red Brigade in a terrorist attack. His reform takes him to Italy and up against the Mafia.

CLOSE-UP

If You Read Italian

By Carmen Iarrera

HERE'S A SHORT list of some of the best Italian mystery writers who have described our cities with great attention. Look for them in Italian bookstores; at this writing, none of them has been translated into English.

ON MILAN

The most famous novels of **Renato Olivieri** are *Maladetto ferragosto* ("Damned August Holiday"), *L'indagine interrotta* ("The Interrupted Investigation"), and *Villa Liberty.* His protagonist is Giulio Ambrosio, who is a police commissioner in a foggy Milan as full of atmosphere as Simenon's Paris.

Milan is hard, dark, bloody, and dangerous in the novels of **Andrea Pinketts,** who looks to the hard-boiled American writers as his masters. His novels are *Lazzarro vieni fuori* ("Come Out, Lazarus"), *Il vizio dell'agnello* ("The Vice of the Lamb"), and *Il senso della frase* ("The Meaning of the Sentence").

Laura Grimaldi, formerly the director of *Il Giallo Mondadori* and *Segretissimo,* the most important Italian mystery and spy story publications, now devotes full time to her own writing. Her latest crime novels are *Il sospetto* ("The Suspicion"), *La colpa* ("The Fault"), and *La Paura* ("The Fear"), which make up a trilogy in which both the innocent and the guilty are described with great understanding and humanity.

ON TURIN

A journalist for one of Italy's most important newspapers, *La Stampa,* **Bruno Ventavoli** is the author of *Assassino sull'Olimpo* ("Murder on Olympus") and *Pornokiller,* in which he depicts perfectly not only the world of porn-movie production, but also a suburban Turin populated by East European immigrants drawn to Italy by delusions of a better life and easy money.

ON GENOVA

Carlo Alberto Rizzi is a former company manager from Genova. His first novel, *I Cioccolatini di Soziglia,* is set at the beginning of the century in Genova and a little village on the seaside. As the murder investigation involves more and more people, the novel slowly becomes a choral portrait of a rich family and a village.

ON SICILY

Silvana la Spina's *Morte a Palermo* ("Death in Palermo") and *L'ultimo treno da Catania* ("Last Train from Catania") describe obscure, subtle, and twisted characters in decaying and fascinating cities.

ON BOLOGNA

Loriano Macchiavelli: In his first novel, *Fiori alla memoria* ("Flowers in Memory"), he gave birth to Antonio Sarti, who is the protagonist of most of his other novels and especially of *Passato, presente e chissà* ("Past, Present and Goodness Knows"), from which a TV serial has been made. All his work is strongly linked to the life of his city, Bologna.

ON ROME

Corrado Augias, journalist and essayist, has written many crime novels: *Quel treno de Vienna* ("That Train from Vienna), *Il fazzoletto azzurro* ("The Blue Handkerchief"), *L'ultima primavera* ("The Last Spring"), and *Una ragazza por la notte* ("A Girl for the Night"). His preferred setting is Rome, from the beginning of the century to the present. He writes with irony about politicians, journalists, shady operators, and ambitious nice girls.

IV

EASTERN EUROPE AND THE BALKANS

CZECHOSLOVAKIA 1960: Prague . . . is still the most Ruritanian of the capitals of Europe . . . an aura of romance lingers over the city. At sunset lamps are lit in the linden trees on the embankment. A hundred points of saffron reflect the last light of day from the pinnacled Hradcany on the Heights. As the neon slogans begin to flash in the Vaclavske Namesti [Wenceslas Square], so the turreted grey buildings and the cobbled courtyards of the old town come into their own. One feels the presence of Black Michael and enigmatic young countesses; one is no more than a stone's throw from Zenda. (Lionel Davidson, The Night of Wenceslas)

YUGOSLAVIA 1966: The nation was like a carefully assembled jigsaw puzzle. From a distance one saw only the picture which had been created, one of progress and peace and harmony, independence from Russia, industrial progress, increasing westernization, a burgeoning tourist trade, and so on. But closer up the cracks appeared. Closer up one saw that the whole was composed of an infinity of little oddly shaped pieces held precariously together. Croatians, Serbs, Slovenes, Dalmatians, Montenegrins, Bosnians, Hercegovinians, Macedonians, all carefully if tenuously interlocked in a pattern called Yugoslavia. (Lawrence Block, The Canceled Czech)

TRANSYLVANIA 1993: We had traveled through a valley of forests and small farms, of villages of blue- and green-painted houses very neatly kept. Some of the houses had elaborately carved wooden gates in front, wide as the length of the house. Words we couldn't read formed patterns with vines and flowers on the gates, sometimes freshly painted, sometimes splintered and worn. Most of the gates had long birdhouses like dormitories built along the top.

57

> *Large, ungainly stork nests balanced on roofs and on electrical*
> *poles. . . . Occasionally a long-beaked head peeked out to look at us. We*
> *passed farmers in the fields ploughing furrows for planting; sometimes*
> *they worked the land with horses, more often by hand. The men wore*
> *fedoras and the women kerchiefs, and there were Gypsy families too, in*
> *brighter colors, hoeing poorer land.* (Barbara Wilson, *Trouble in Tran-*
> *sylvania*)

A History of Death

IN LIONEL DAVIDSON'S *The Night of Wenceslas* (1960), the narrator describes the evening crowds in Prague's Wenceslas Square: "noisier,
more vivacious than London crowds. Open necks, open faces, a new
breed. They seemed to be streaming down the road together, millions
of them. At the end of the street the monstrous picture of Lenin looked
down . . . [with the inscription] 'Every hand, every brain for the building of socialism.' . . . The town of my childhood had been taken over. It
lay asleep beneath their vigorous sandals."

Thirty-five years later that town, one of Europe's most beautiful and
unspoiled, is wide awake, and Wenceslas Square is jammed with tourists
of all types, especially the backpacked youth of North America. The
Czechs seem an adaptable people; they speak of "the old days" with such
detachment that it is hard to recall that Czechoslovakia's Velvet Revolution only took place in 1989. It is also easy to forget that in 1989, Czech
"political correctness" was redefined for the fifth time in this century.

There are still some rough edges to the Velvet Revolution. Two friends
report separate nasty encounters with traffic police, and everyone warns
of the chicanery of cab drivers. The minister of the interior, however, tells
an international gathering of crime writers that the nation is fortunate in
having a seasoned professional police force untainted by the politics of
the past. The crime writers look skeptical, but Josef Skvorecky's Lieutenant Boruvka certainly was a credit to his force. Of course he fled the
country in 1968.

So where are the commies of yesteryear? Specifically, where are the
estimated 120,000 Czech secret police of the Communist era? Larry
Beinhart (the immediate source of that estimate) has one fictionalized sug-

gestion: many of them, adapting readily to capitalism, are putting their training to use in the lucrative field of industrial espionage.

Meanwhile in the Balkans, war rages. It's hard to imagine a time when people might be traveling to the former Yugoslavia for pleasure—or for any but the grimmest sort of business. But who would have imagined ten years ago that Prague would almost overnight become one of the top tourist destinations in Europe? Even as I write this, busloads of American pilgrims are arriving in the Croatian town of Medjugorje, hoping the Virgin Mary will make one of her scheduled appearances.

Furthermore, the Balkans provide the only opportunity in this book to praise the work of one of the best American mystery writers, Rex Stout, whose detective, Nero Wolfe, was a native of Montenegro.

The reading list that follows, however, is heavily weighted toward the Czech Republic, currently the most popular of the former Iron Curtain countries with travelers and arguably that with the richest literary tradition.

READING LIST

AMBLER, Eric. *A Coffin for Dimitrios* [in England, *The Mask of Dimitrios*] (London and NY, 1939; NY, 1990). Charles Latimer, a British detective novelist visiting Istanbul, becomes obsessed with the real-life mysteries surrounding Dimitrios Makropoulos, whose dead body he views in a Turkish morgue. With some clues from a police dossier, Latimer sets off to follow Dimitrios's trail from his humble beginnings in Izmir, through his multiple careers as murderer, paid assassin, spy, drug smuggler. The trail leads Latimer to Sofia, Belgrade, Athens, Switzerland, and Paris. Along the way we are given vivid, edgy pictures of a part of the world where, in the 1920s and '30s, "the war to end all wars" has done nothing of the sort: Turkey, Greece, the Balkans, Central Europe. Now, seventy-five years later, the ancient enmities of this part of the world are again news. And *A Coffin for Dimitrios*—with its hair-raising description of the all-but-forgotten 1922 massacres in Izmir, for example—still has much to show us. "Hope had come and gone, a fugitive in the scented bosom of illusion. Men had learned to sniff the heady dreamstuff of the soul and wait impassively while the lathes turned the guns of their destruction."

———. *Judgment on Deltchev* (GB, 1951, 1989). In an unnamed

Balkan city based on Sofia, Bulgaria (according to Ambler's autobiography), a nationalist hero named Deltchev is being tried for treason by the Soviet puppet government. The narrator, Foster, a famous English playwright, has been dispatched by a clever editor to cover the trial. As one cynic observes, "the trial of a political leader on ideological grounds is most theatrical to Western ways of thinking." Other Western reporters also are on hand for what is expected to be a tragic farce: Deltchev is clearly doomed—and clearly innocent.

Or is he?

Foster is soon up to his ears in ambivalence and ambiguity, as Ambler demonstrates his mastery of psychology and atmosphere. There is little local color, and what there is tends to be totalitarian black and gray. But read *Judgment* for its evocation of a time and place and for Ambler's taut, clean style that occasionally flares into aphorism—as in his glance at "the terrible anxiety of men who, having sacrificed their principles, fear that the sacrifice may after all go unrewarded."

BEINHART, Larry. *Foreign Exchange* (NY, 1991, 1992). In trouble with the IRS, New York City PI Tony Cassella has gone to ground in the Austrian ski resort of St. Anton. There, using the name Rick Cochrane, he has opened the region's first Laundromat and settled down with his French girlfriend and their new baby, Anna Genevieve, who reduces this tough guy to some seriously sentimental blather. When a young American skier and her rich Japanese lover are killed in an avalanche, new parent Rick/Tony is vulnerable to a mother's plea for information about her daughter's last days. But it is soon evident that there are a number of suspicious types interested in the dead skiers and that this may be a rare case of murder-by-avalanche! (The how-to of this remains vague.)

In any case Tony's investigation becomes an excuse for travels (accompanied by girlfriend, baby, mother, and mother-in-law) in the new Mittel-Europa of 1990. There are set pieces of booming capitalist Vienna, "the Mall Without Walls"; of shopping-impaired Budapest, where "the Big News in town was the opening of the Nike shop—the first twenty-four-hour-a-day store in Europe"; of freedom-drunk Prague, "where the pubs rang with capital letters. Freedom. God. Revolution. Atheism. Capitalism. Free Markets. Humanism. The Values of Socialism. The Triumph of Art."

Informative, well-written, and entertaining, despite an implausible plot and an embarrassment of baby talk.

BLOCK, Lawrence. *The Canceled Czech* (NY, 1966, 1994). Evan Tanner hasn't slept a wink in the sixteen years since a piece of Korean shrapnel destroyed the "sleep center" in his brain. He earns a living writing term papers and working as a freelance secret agent. His hobbies include languages and Lost Causes; he belongs to the Flat Earth Society, the Jacobite League, the Stern Gang, the Slovak Popular Party, and the Council for a Greater Serbia, among others.

In this sequel to *The Thief Who Couldn't Sleep* (also 1966), Tanner's assignment is to rescue from a Prague jail an odious old Nazi who is about to be tried by the Czechs for his war crimes. The purpose is to safeguard for the United States the Nazi's papers, which include invaluable information about a global neo-Nazi network.

The Canceled Czech's virtues include its quirky and resourceful hero; terse, workmanlike prose; and good pacing. What it lacks is a sense of place. Tanner covers a lot of territory (Bohemia, Moravia, Slovakia, Hungary, Yugoslavia, Greece) with almost no attempt at description. Moreover, it is a mistake to invent a castle for a city dominated by two of the world's most famous: both the very real Hradcany, which looms on the heights above Prague's Vltava River, and Franz Kafka's fictional masterpiece.

On the other hand, Tanner is a prescient map reader. See the quotation at the head of this chapter.

ČAPEK, Karel. *Tales from Two Pockets* [1929], translated by Norma Conrada (NY, 1994). These tales from a great Czech playwright and novelist (*The War of the Newts, R.U.R.*), are mysteries only in a very broad sense—mysteries of human nature and human justice, say—though some do involve detectives and ratiocination. Written for a newspaper audience, they are clever, colloquial, and wise—and seem to reflect the hopeful period in Czech history during which they were written.

DAVIDSON, Lionel. *The Night of Wenceslas* (GB, 1960, 1994). Davidson's acclaimed thriller is a bit reminiscent of *Our Man in Havana* in that the protagonist's weaknesses conspire to turn him all unwitting into not just an amateur spy but a very effective one. Nicolas Whistler, a feckless young Londoner whose family were war refugees from Czechoslovakia, is trapped by his own greed into undertaking a dubious mission to Prague. He *thinks* he'll be bringing *out* the secret formula for a new technique in Bohemian glass-making; in reality he will be bringing *in* a British atomic secret.

The early scenes in Prague are colored by Nicolas's feeling of enchantment in rediscovering as an adult the city he left at age six. But once he has twigged to his real mission, the novel becomes a classic pursuit story as Nicolas flees the secret police through half-remembered streets, now swollen by thousands of country people brought in to take part in some gigantic socialist parade. It's a John Buchan-esque chase in an urban setting, and Nicolas proves equal to the challenge.

DURRELL, Lawrence. *White Eagles over Serbia* ([1957]; NY, 1995). "Something very big is happening in the mountains of South Serbia" in this twice-surprising tale from the author of the *Alexandria Quartet*. The first surprise is that Durrell ever wrote a spy thriller; the second is that it is such an anachronistic one, owing much more to *The Thirty-Nine Steps* (1915) than to *From Russia, with Love* (1957). According to one Durrell biographer, the original publisher insisted the book be marketed as a juvenile. The book offers lots of mountainous Serbian scenery and detailed descriptions of the burbling Ibar and Studenitsa rivers where the hero, a British agent and passionate fisherman named Methuen, casts for trout. What Methuen is really supposed to be doing is finding out what's going on among Black Peter and the White Eagles—not a rock group but an army of royalist guerrillas dedicated to Tito's overthrow and led by a charismatic ruffian known as "Black Peter." Methuen does his job and the Cold War continues.

FREELING, Nicolas. *The Seacoast of Bohemia* (GB, 1994; NY, 1995). Like Larry Beinhart, Nicolas Freeling seems to have been traveling in the new Eastern Europe. His longtime character, French policeman Henri Castang, now an adviser to the European Community based in Brussels, is lured into doing some investigating by a mother whose child disappeared a number of years earlier. Proceeding by intuitive leaps, Castang soon finds himself on the road east; also like Beinhart's hero, Castang brings along his own family problems (in this case his Czech wife, Vera).

The plot—involving the Nazi past as well as contemporary traffic in prostitution—is thin. The scenery—Bohemia, Prague, Berlin, Copenhagen—is better. But both are really just pretexts for Freeling/Castang's cranky, conservative reflections on the EC, *Peer Gynt*, the Nazi and Communist legacies, national differences, Pilsner Urquell, good and bad taste, the superiority of German bread, the music of Smetana and Janáček, etc., etc. The urge to pontificate, always lurking in Freeling's books, is unresisted in this one. The style is extremely mannered—rife with capital letters and literary allusions. If you're not already a Freeling fan, this is not a good place to begin. (For other Castang titles, see Chapter I.)

As for the title, it's an allusion to Shakespeare's famous little error in *The Winter's Tale:* Bohemia has no seacoast. Unless, like the Castangs, you choose to count the shores of the Bohemian lake known as the Lipno See.

SJOWALL, Maj, and Per Wahloo. *The Man Who Went Up in Smoke* (see Chapter VIII). Swedish police inspector Martin Beck goes to Budapest on business and is enchanted.

SKVORECKY, Josef. *The Mournful Demeanour of Lieutenant Boruvka* [1966], translated from the Czech by Rosemary Kavan, Kaca Polackova, and George Theiner (NY, 1987). This is the first of four collections of linked tales written by one of Eastern Europe's most admired writers. Among the murder victims: a dancer, a mountain climber, a spry old Italian mobster, a sad old Czech lady. Each case calls for the logical or the intuitive powers of Lieutenant Boruvka of the Prague police. The homicide detective is a clever and good man, whose conscience sometimes gets him in trouble. He is also a slightly comic figure—round of face and body, henpecked by his wife, manipulated by his beloved teenage daughter, and hopelessly in love with a woman known as Eve Adam. All this is reflected in Boruvka's characteristic "mournful" (or "melancholy" or "gloomy" or "sadeyed" or "mute, despairing") expression, to which the pathetic awfulness of murderous human nature also contributes.

————. *Sins for Father Knox* [1973], translated by Kaca Polackova Henley (NY, 1989, 1991). Ten witty stories in the classic puzzle mode, with parodic touches. In each case, the reader is invited not only to solve a crime, but to identify which of Ronald Knox's "Ten Commandments" for detective story writers Skvorecky has violated. The "detective" in most of these cases is Boruvka's beloved Eve Adam, but the lieutenant and his daughter also turn up. The settings range from Prague to San Francisco and are not central to most of the tales. (A good thing, too, since Skvorecky seems to think that a practical route from Manhattan's Fifth Avenue to the West Side docks goes through the Bronx and Queens.)

————. *The End of Lieutenant Boruvka* [1975], translated by Paul Wilson (NY, 1990). In the two earlier volumes, political references are few and oblique. But in 1968 Skvorecky emigrated to Canada. In this volume, set during the 1968 "Prague Spring"—the eight months of liberalization under Alexander Dubček—and the Russian invasion and harsh "normalization" that followed, politics is inescapable, like the distant rumble of the Soviet tanks.

A sense of tragic history informs this book, which also seems to benefit from an excellent translation, the perspective of distance, and—need I add?—the freedoms of Skvorecky's new homeland. The five closely linked tales focus on the effects on Boruvka of the painful compromises he must make with his conscience to keep his job and his home and his self-respect in a land where political *incorrectness* can be a capital offense. In the end the pain of compromise is too much. An act of conscience frees him, and Boruvka finds peace in prison and "the deep, dreamless sleep of people who, though they may be misguided, are kind and honorable."

It's not really the end, though. In *The Return of Lieutenant Boruvka: A Reactionary Tale of Crime and Detection,* translated and adapted by Paul Wilson (1991), Boruvka has escaped from his Czech prison and is working as a parking lot attendant in Toronto, where he is able to give the feminist detective agency where his daughter works some useful tips.

STOUT, Rex. *The Black Mountain* (NY, 1954, 1993). If you've never read a Nero Wolfe novel, you really should take a break and read one or two others before traveling to *The Black Mountain* (English for "Montenegro"). Though as always the writing—in the voice of Wolfe's legman and amanuensis Archie Goodwin—is fine, the plot is atypical. The arrogant, reclusive Wolfe, who rarely leaves his Manhattan brownstone except to dine at Rusterman's Restaurant, in this case travels all the way to Montenegro in what was then Tito's Yugoslavia. The reason is in character, however: to bring to justice the murderer of his lifelong friend Marko Vukcic, proprietor of that same Rusterman's Restaurant and supporter of a group of Montenegrin freedom fighters known as "the Spirit of Black Mountain" (fictional as far as I have been able to determine).

In the rough terrain of his native land, the sedentary Wolfe suffers all sorts of physical and mental indignities among bloody-minded Titoist bureaucrats, Montenegrin guerrillas, and Albanian Stalinists. The usually irreverent Archie also suffers, forced to keep quiet because he (unlike Wolfe) doesn't speak Montenegrin, Serbian, Albanian, and Italian.

According to his biographer, the closest Stout himself ever got to Montenegro was passing through Dubrovnik in 1928. But the book offers a lot of secondhand information about Yugoslavia in the years after the 1948 break with Stalin but before the more tolerant and open form of communism known as "Titoism" was fully established. And though the setting and physical activity are unusual, Wolfe remains his cranky self. Invited near novel's end to meet the U.S. ambassador to Rome, Wolfe frowns. "She's a woman," he says, declining.

So much for Clare Boothe Luce.

WILSON, Barbara. *Trouble in Transylvania* (Seattle, 1993). This is the second adventure of Cassandra Reilly, translator, indefatigable traveler, amateur detective. (See Chapter II, "Spain," for her *Gaudí Afternoon*.) In this outing, Reilly—a lesbian, of a certain age and not too happy about it—is visiting a friend in Budapest before boarding the Trans-Mongolian Express for China, when she gets drawn into the titular trouble. A woman she met on the train to Budapest is accused of the murder of a nasty spa owner (and snake-oil salesman) in the region of Romania long (but not too accurately) associated with the misdeeds of Dracula (a.k.a. Vlad the Impaler).

Cassandra and two friends head for the spa town of Arcata (not on my map) in Transylvania. They find the countryside beautiful and benign but the political history worthy of Vlad. The legacy of the late dictator Ceauşescu is poverty and suspicion. Tensions between the Romanians and the minority Magyars of formerly Hungarian Transylvania are frighteningly high. The subplots include the poignant story of a tiny Romanian orphan adopted by Americans. The only vampires are metaphorical, but there are a number of those.

After a long lament for her people's plight, one Romanian optimist finds the silver lining: "Thank you, God, at least we are not Yugoslavia."

Glum though this may sound, Cassandra Reilly is a cheeky, resilient soul, with an acute sense of the ridiculous; there is plenty of that in the spa world of mudpacks and galvanic baths and aging flesh.

NOTED BUT NOT REVIEWED

DAVIS, J. Madison. *Bloody Marko* (NY, 1991). Marko Renovich is brought back to his native Yugoslavia to stand trial for fifty-year-old war crimes. The novel traces his story back to the beginning.

GRANGER. Bill. *The Infant of Prague* (NY, 1987). A leading Czech cultural figure wants to defect, and a Chicago church's statue of the "Infant of Prague" has begun to weep. So begins another adventure for the superspy called The November Man.

HAGGARD, William. *The Notch on the Knife* (NY, 1973). Haggard's series character, Col. Charles Russell of the "Security Executive," is called to a country that sounds a lot like Yugoslavia to help an old comrade-in-arms who is now the nation's dictator.

LITTELL, Robert. *The Amateur* (NY and London, 1981). After PLO terrorists kill his fiancée, CIA cryptologist Charlie Heller blackmails the agency into training him to take revenge. Set mainly in Langley and Prague.

————. *The October Circle* (Boston, 1976). A group of idealistic Bulgarians in 1948—and twenty years later, when the Soviet intervention in Czechoslovakia has shaken the Communist world.

MacINNES, Helen. *The Snare of the Hunter* (NY, 1974). An American journalist is dispatched to help his lost love—daughter of a great Czech writer and ex-wife of a high-placed member of the secret police—to escape from Czechoslovakia in 1972.

MacLEAN, Alistair. *Force 10 from Navarone* (London, 1968). The heroes of MacLean's famous war novel, *The Guns of Navarone,* are parachuted into Bosnia-Herzegovina to find out why communication with the pro-Allied Partisans has broken down. See also MacLean's *Partisans* (1983).

SEYMOUR, Gerald. *The Heart of Danger* (NY, 1995). The Balkans now: a mass grave in Croatia, a mad Serbian "warlord," and the mysterious death of an English woman.

CLOSE-UP: VIENNA

I never knew Vienna between the wars, and I am too young to remember the old Vienna with its Strauss music and its bogus easy charm; to me it is simply a city of undignified ruins which turned that February into great glaciers of snow and ice. The Danube was a gray flat muddy river a long way off across the Second Bezirk, the Russian zone where the Prater lay smashed and desolate and full of weeds, only the Great Wheel revolving slowly over the foundations of merry-go-rounds like abandoned millstones, the rusting iron of smashed tanks which nobody had cleared away, the frostnipped weeds where the snow was thin. I haven't enough imagination to picture it as it had once been, any more than I can picture Sacher's Hotel as other than a transit hotel for English officers or see the Kärntnerstrasse as a fashionable shopping street instead of a street which exists, most of it, only at eye level, repaired up to the first story. A Russian soldier in a fur cap goes by with a rifle over his shoulder, a few tarts cluster round the American Information Office, and men in overcoats sip ersatz coffee in the windows of the Old Vienna. At night it is just as well to stick to the Inner City or the zones of three of the Powers, though even there the kidnappings occur—such senseless kidnappings they sometimes seemed to us—a Ukrainian girl without a passport, an old man beyond the age of usefulness, sometimes, of course, the technician or the traitor. (Graham Greene, The Third Man [1950])

WHEN IN VIENNA: Catch a guided tour following in the tracks of Joseph Cotten and Orson Welles in *The Third Man*. It will take you to all the important locations in the 1949 film classic—from the top of the Riesenrad, the great Ferris wheel in the park known as the Prater, down to the sewers where Harry Lime makes his last stand. To get the foul smell out of your nostrils, you might as well have one of the delicious pastries for which Vienna is so well known and a *Mélange* (coffee with hot milk) at the Sacher Café or the Mozart Café. (Located behind the Opera, both figure in the movie.) For information on *Third Man* tours, consult the concierge of your hotel or stop by the tourist information office, Vienna 1, Kärtnerstrasse 38 (open daily nine A.M.–seven P.M.).

A City in Greeneland

By Helga Anderle

NO DOUBT GRAHAM Greene's *The Third Man* is, internationally, the most famous crime story set in Vienna. It was not written to be read, however, but to be seen—intended as nothing more than raw material for the film that Greene had agreed to make with director Carol Reed. Greene readily admitted that the film was better than the story. He came to bombed-out, occupied Vienna in February 1948 to do some research for the movie treatment, and the plot quickly evolved after he was introduced to Vienna's underground: a labyrinth of thousands of kilometers of water channels and sewers underneath the city.

The city was still divided into four zones, each controlled by one of the Allied powers—the United States, France, Great Britain, and the Soviet Union. The sewers were a perfect traffic system, allowing criminals, spies, and racketeers, such as Greene's Harry Lime, to pursue their business, crossing from one military zone to the other without danger of being caught. Access was through one of the many advertising kiosks scattered everywhere around town. Once you found a door, an iron staircase led you down into the sewers and you could conveniently vanish from sight.

Although Greene is usually thought of as a spy novelist, Harry Lime is not a spy but a racketeer, dealing in a new American miracle drug, penicillin. Not legally available to Austrian doctors and hospitals, it brought enormous profit on the black market. Watering down the penicillin increased the profits but led to the deaths of a number of children. When the police got on to him, Lime staged his accidental death. Nobody would have questioned it except his devoted friend Holly Martins, who arrives for a visit just in time for the funeral.

After the Allies pulled out (the Russians were the last to leave, in 1955), Vienna—an outpost of the West easily accessible from the East—remained a boomtown of espionage and other illegal commerce. It figures as such in a variety of novels.

While Graham Greene got quite an authentic impression of postwar Vienna during his fortnight stay, British author Philip Kerr (who was born in 1956) apparently relied heavily on *The Third Man* movie for his 1991 novel, *A German Requiem*. Despite its title, this last book of Kerr's trilogy *Berlin Noir* (published in one volume in 1993) is set almost entirely in Vienna during 1947 and '48. Many sequences of Kerr's story are directly inspired by the movie. When Berlin-based PI Bernie Gunther is hired to prove an alleged murderer innocent and save him from being hanged, his first steps in Vienna lead him to the Central Cemetery. Inevitably he takes a ride on the Riesenrad and frequents the same cafés and nightclubs as the characters in *The Third Man*. Quite originally, however, he meets a "chocolady" who aspires to a role in "a British movie starring Orson Welles."

Though his descriptions of his roamings through Vienna ring true ("compared with Berlin, Vienna looked tidier than an undertaker's shop window"), nothing else is what it seems to be. Most of the spies he meets turn out to be counteragents, and from the kind chocoladies, Bernie gets not only love but gonorrhea. And when he dives deeper and deeper into the Nazi subcultures, he discovers that some SS men believed to be dead are quite alive and enjoying opulent lives on the payrolls of the U.S. or Russian secret services.

No wonder that in this grisly novel, the Viennese take their share of abuse. For Kerr they are as phony as their bombastic Ring buildings: "They are all front. Everything that's interesting about them seems to be on the surface. Inside they're very different . . . All Viennese were born to be spies." But some could also make a living as pastry cooks. "To come to Vienna without a sweet tooth? Why that's like a blind man taking a trip on the Big Wheel in the Prater. You don't know what you're missing. Why don't you try a little?"

In Larry Beinhart's *Foreign Exchange* (NY, 1991, 1992), there are many allusions to *The Third Man*, even a character who calls himself Harry Lime. Some forty years later the ruins are gone, however, and Beinhart's protagonist Tony Casella finds Vienna "perfect": "The boulevards are wide. The sidewalks are immaculate. Traffic flows. Nothing is in disrepair. The lawns, the shrubs, the trees are groomed . . . Pedestrians never cross on a red light. There is a great deal of that which means capital Culture— public sculpture on imposing architecture, famous paintings, museums and live music from dead civilizations."

Erotomaniac Casella especially notices the many naked female statues ("who with their stocky bodies and their hard and pointed tits look as if Viennese sculptors had fallen in love with hordes of German masseuses").

Unlike the usual lone-wolf PI, Tony Casella is a family man who pursues his case with wife, mother, and baby daughter in tow, so that his work is frequently interrupted by shopping sprees. Traveling through Austria, Casella's mother, who grew up believing America to be the richest nation of the world and Europe a place to send CARE parcels, is shocked to see "how rich, new and clean everything looks." And of course she can't help noticing "how expensive everything is."

In Robert Andrews's *Death in a Promised Land* (NY, 1993, 1994), the discovery of a murderous conspiracy reaching from the inner circles of the White House to Russia sends CIA agent Bradford Sims to Vienna. After having slept off the jet lag at the Ambassador Hotel, agent Sims quite fittingly has a rendezvous with a colleague near the famous Ferris wheel. "It was one of Vienna's famous landmarks and figured in an agency cult classic, 'The Third Man,' a motion picture of intrigue and espionage in which Orson Welles met Joseph Cotten in one of the cabins. 'Der [sic] Riesenrad,' Sims remembered it in German. 'All we need is Harry Lime and a little zither music,' Houghton mused."

A widely traveled author, Helen MacInnes favors European settings for her novels. In *Prelude to Terror* (NY, 1978), she sends New York art expert Colin Grant to Vienna on a secret mission for a rich and mysterious art collector to acquire a famous painting that is being smuggled out of Hungary. A walk on the Ring, the elegant boulevard surrounding the old city, gives Grant a chance to philosophize about the Viennese taking life easy despite the Iron Curtain. "Sunshine and flowers and trees, bustling traffic, well-dressed people, a general feeling of optimism—it seemed as though the nightmare of 1945 was buried with the discarded rubble. Perhaps they were putting a good face on it all, like the modern buildings that obliterated the war damage. If I were a Viennese, thought Grant as he crossed the wide square before the Opera House, once gutted by flames and now duplicated in splendor, I'd always be conscious that Czechoslovakia's barbed wire and Hungary's armed watchtowers were less than thirty miles away. So what would I do? Enjoy today, and concentrate on tomorrow's neutrality, that comforting if fragile word. Eat, drink—appropriately, he was approaching the Kärntnerstrasse, heading for one of its restaurants—and give a damned good imitation of being merry."

Today, despite its being one of the safest cities of Europe and the world (street muggings are rare, the homemade crime rate low), the downfall of communism in the surrounding countries has attracted all kinds of post–Cold War criminals to Vienna. Russian mafiosi, frequently former KGB agents, control prostitution, narcotics, and arms traffic; occasionally hired killers are flown in from Moscow to get rid of rivals; former Yugoslavs and Poles specialize in car theft; Romanian gangs in safe-cracking; instead of penicillin the hot black-market commodity is plutonium; there is money-laundering and illegal immigration. Luckily, neither the middle-class Austrian nor the tourist is likely to run into these gruesome individuals, except that they might unsuspectingly sit next to one in a café. Austria, however, is no longer "an island of the blessed," as Pope Paul VI once called it. And *The Third Man* of our day remains to be written.

V

——————=«(●)»=——————

GERMANY

BERLIN/THE WALL: *Leamas went to the window and waited, in front of him the road and to either side the Wall, a dirty, ugly thing of breeze blocks and strands of barbed wire, lit with cheap yellow light, like the backdrop for a concentration camp. East and west of the Wall lay the unrestored part of Berlin, a half-world of ruin, drawn in two dimensions, crags of war. . . .*

. . . suddenly he felt the coarse, sharp contact of the cinder brick. Now he could discern the wall and, looking upwards, the triple strand of wire and the cruel hooks which held it. Metal wedges, like climbers' pitons, had been driven into the brick. Seizing the highest one, Leamas pulled himself quickly upwards until he had reached the top of the wall. (John le Carré, *The Spy Who Came in from the Cold*)

BONN/BAD GODESBERG: *At twenty-five minutes past eight, the Drosselstrasse in Bad Godesberg had been just another leafy diplomatic backwater, about as far from the political turmoils of Bonn as you could reasonably get while staying within fifteen minutes' drive of them. It was a new street but mature, with lush, secretive gardens, and maids' quarters over the garages, and Gothic security grilles over the bottle-glass windows. The Rhineland weather for most of the year has the warm wet drip of the jungle; its vegetation, like its diplomatic community, grows almost as fast as the Germans build the roads, and slightly faster than they make their maps. Thus the fronts of some of the houses were already half obscured by dense plantations of conifers, which, if they ever grow to proper size, will presumably one day plunge the whole area into a Grimm's fairy-tale blackout. . . . A kilometre southward, unseen Rhine barges provided a throbbing, stately hum, but the residents grow deaf to it unless it stops. In short, it was a morning to assure you that whatever calamities you might be reading about in West Germany's earnest, rather panicky newspapers . . . Bad Godesberg was a settled, decent place to be alive in, and Bonn was not half so bad as it is painted.* (le Carré, *The Little Drummer Girl*)

71

WHEN IN BERLIN: Visit the Café Kranzler. "Just a little way down the street beyond the shell of the Gedächtniskirche with its slick modern tower—like a tricky sort of hi-fi speaker cabinet—aping the old broken one is Kranzler's, a café that spreads itself across the Kurfürstendamm pavement," notes Len Deighton in *Funeral in Berlin.* Deighton's agent meets his informant Johnny Vulkan one Sunday in the Kranzler, where in fine weather they set out tables and chairs on the pavement. The meeting is not unique. In other novels, too, the Kranzler is the setting for conspiratorial contacts between agents. The café has been a Berlin landmark since its opening in 1932. At first it was a writers' and artists' rendezvous; then, after the war, the spot where Allied officers got together; later, the place where over coffee and cakes West Germans showed off their first modest postwar prosperity to anyone strolling past.

Tales of Two Capitals

By Thomas Przybilka and Reinhard Jahn

B ONN WAS A Balkan city," writes John le Carré in *A Small Town in Germany,* "stained and secret, drawn over with tramwire. Bonn was a dark house where someone had died, a house draped in Catholic black and guarded by policemen." No question, le Carré disliked Bonn right from the start. In the more than forty years during which the little town on the Rhine near Cologne was the capital of the Federal Republic, many Germans also had an ambivalent attitude toward the sleepy "Federal Village." In 1949, four years after the end of the Second World War, Bonn was chosen by the government of Chancellor Konrad Adenauer to be the temporary capital of the Federal Republic of Germany (BRD), newly formed from the American, British, and French occupation zones. The old "imperial capital" of Berlin, meanwhile, was isolated in the Soviet occupation zone, which in 1949 became the German Democratic Republic. That second German state (DDR), sheltered under Moscow's umbrella, in 1961 sealed itself hermetically against West Germany with its "Zone Border."

Berlin—or, to be precise, the eastern part of the city—was named as the DDR's capital by the East German government. The temporary two-state Germany lasted for forty years. West Berlin, controlled by the Allies, was totally cut off from the surrounding area of East Germany by warlike border installations and the Berlin Wall, until a new Germany was created in 1990 through reunification. In 1991 its parliament decided that the capital would no longer be peaceful Bonn on the Rhine, but once again Berlin.

For forty years, from 1949 to 1989, the Cold War, the power struggle between the political systems of the USSR and the USA, was conducted with every means at their disposal by the secret services of East and West, particularly along the dividing seam in Germany. No wonder, then, that the spy story and the political thriller flourished against the backdrop of the old and new German capital. Meanwhile, the fact that peaceful Bonn was in reality less often the setting for international intrigue does not mean that the "Small Town in Germany"—as John le Carré dubbed it—offered no material for first-class spy stories.

Bonn's famous (or notorious) "Diplomats' Racetrack," the multilane highway running from central Bonn to the diplomats' suburb of Bad Godesberg, leads, in Ross Thomas's 1966 first novel, *The Cold War Swap,* to "Mac's Place." The bar run by ex-CIA man McCorkle and his partner Padillo becomes the pivotal point of a coldly calculated CIA operation. The American government wants to exchange a written-off special agent for two scientists who have defected to the East and whom the United States would like to have back. McCorkle realizes that the operation is no routine transaction when the barkeeper at Mac's Place is shot dead before his eyes, just as he confides to him his secret recipe for mixing a Seven-Layer Mint Frappé. The operation takes McCorkle and Padillo out of cosy Bad Godesberg and behind the Iron Curtain, straight into a KGB trap, from which they manage to extricate themselves, albeit not unscathed.

The German version of Mac's Place has long since ceased to exist. McCorkle and his partner, along with their German staff, left Bonn for Washington, D.C., where they reopened the bar for later novels.

Yet even though Bonn, as a former police chief put it, has "never, thank God, reached world ranking in terms of crime," it has been, like any other capital city with its government departments, ministries, and embassies, a hotbed of spies from every sovereign country, but most of all from the DDR. During the 1980s, Markus Wolf, the legendary spymaster of the

DDR's Ministry of State Security ("Stasi"), concentrated on variations on the "Romeo agent" theme—using seduction as a way to gather information from lonely, vulnerable women in key government jobs.

One fictional variation on this theme is Martin Walser's *No Man's Land* (a translation of his 1987 *Dorle und Wolf*). The protagonist, Wolf Zieger, who grew up in the DDR and later moved to the Federal Republic, feels loyalty to his native country and offers his services as a spy in order to reduce the DDR's deficit in high technology. To gain access to key information, he becomes one of Markus Wolf's "Romeo agents." He marries Dorle, secretary in the Defense Ministry in Bonn, and he has an affair with her colleague Sylvia, who supplies him with the secret material that his case officers need. When after nine years he grows weary of espionage, his East German case officers show little understanding of his desire for a quiet family life, and pile on the pressure.

Like Wolf Zieger, Otto "the Raven" Reimann, in Brian Freemantle's *Little Grey Mice,* is a Romeo agent whose target is a woman bureaucrat in Bonn. Freemantle tells his tale in the same cool, professional way as Reimann does his job for his KGB supervisors, seducing Elke Meyer, who has an important job in the chancellor's office, in order to find out what the new Germany's political position on NATO will be after reunification. Bonn is the pivot and the crux of Otto Reimann's operation, and it is where, despite his espionage successes, he comes unstuck. He cannot easily escape the demons that he conjures up through his love entanglement with the "little grey mouse" from the chancellor's office. Tough luck for the Raven; fortune in misfortune for the "grey mouse."

In Robert Ludlum's action thriller *The Aquitaine Progression,* the plot is less gray and shadowy than is Freemantle's. In his hunt for the men behind one of Ludlum's usual world-encompassing conspiracies, the hero, John Converse, also ends up in sleepy Bonn. Converse meets an important informant at the Alter Zoll, the old, chestnut-ringed bastion on the southeast rim of Bonn's Old Town. Soon afterward he is unable to prevent the murder of the American ambassador in the Hofgarten, a park in front of Bonn University. However, the little town on the Rhine is no more than an atmospheric backdrop in Converse's hunt for the power-hungry generals who aim to establish a new world dominion embracing the whole of Europe.

It is mostly the small, easily comprehensible spying operations that take place in Bonn: stories of petit-bourgeois entanglement in betrayal and treachery. In that respect, those writers who dismiss Bonn as an unimposing town, which was never able to develop the flair of a true capital city (and never wanted to), are absolutely right.

The really big spies, the really big secret service operations of Cold War fiction, are in Berlin. There, John le Carré's Alec Leamas waits at the Wall for *The Spy Who Came in from the Cold;* there Adam Hall's agent, Quiller, takes on a neo-Nazi conspiracy in *The Quiller Memorandum;* there, in the mid-sixties, the *Funeral in Berlin* is staged for Len Deighton's nameless agent as he seeks to bring a top East German scientist across the border for the British secret service.

Likewise, Deighton's Berlin-born Bernard Samson, British spy and tragic hero of the 1980s trilogy *Berlin Game, Mexico Set,* and *London Match,* is always lurking around the Wall, which was erected in August 1961 by the National People's Army and the People's Police to stop the ever-growing tide of refugees from the DDR flowing into the western sector of the city. Over the years, the East German state perfected its 155-kilometer "anti-imperialist defensive barricade" around West Berlin, turning it into a lethal border where guards were under orders to shoot to prevent any attempt at escape. By the end, the barrier consisted of a 4.1-meter-high, 16-centimeter-thick wall of concrete slabs, reinforced along the top with a thick concrete tube or a metal mesh fence. Running up to it on the eastern side was a 10-meter "Death Strip" with watch towers and bunkers, dog runs, patrol paths, and a contact fence that, at a touch, set off visual and acoustic alarms.

On November 9, 1989, following political upheavals and popular protests in the DDR, all the hitherto strictly controlled border crossings were finally opened, leading to the reunification of Germany.

Shortly before those days in 1989, Adam Hall's Quiller returns to the divided city in a strange collaboration with the KGB to thwart an attempt on the life of Mikhail Gorbachev: "The East Germans are fervently hoping for some kind of reunification," Hall writes in *Quiller-KGB,* "because so many of them have got relatives in the West and they've been cut off from them all this time by the Wall. On the other hand, some people are scared to death, because if Europe becomes denuclearized—which is the way things are heading—the US is going to withdraw most of its forces and that'll leave West Germany without a security umbrella. . . ."

While the city was divided, Checkpoint Charlie, the foreigners' border crossing at the corner of Kochstrasse and Friedrichstrasse, was the focus—the eye of the needle—for numerous risky spy operations by the British SIS and American CIA, not only literary ones. "You are leaving the American Sector," reads Alec Leamas on the famous placard in le Carré's classic *The Spy Who Came in from the Cold* (1963), as he waits for a defector from the DDR, as yet unaware that he himself is a mere pawn in the game played by "Control," his chief, who is using Leamas in order to discredit Mundt, the East German spymaster, in the eyes of his own people. Like Leamas, Len Deighton's Bernard Samson waits at the Wall in *Berlin Game* (1983) for a top East German spy, "Brahms IV," who is to deliver important material about a mole in the British secret service.

In the succeeding books of the Samson Trilogy, long after Bernard has discovered that Fiona, his beautiful wife, has not only been unfaithful to him with his colleague Bret Rensselaer but is also the mole they are hunting, he returns again and again to the haunted streets of Berlin: "Berlin is a sort of history book of twentieth-century violence," Deighton writes in *London Match*, "and every street corner brought a recollection of something I'd heard, seen or read. We followed the road alongside the Landwehr Canal, which twists and turns through the heart of the city. Its oily water holds many dark secrets. Back in 1919, when the Spartakists attempted to seize the city by an armed uprising, two officers of the Horse Guards took the badly beaten Rosa Luxemburg—a Communist leader—from their headquarters at the Eden Hotel, next to the Zoo, shot her dead and threw her into the canal" *(London Match)*.

In *Winter: A Berlin Family* (1987), Deighton, the "poet of the spy story," leads us back into the period before the Nazis seized power in Germany and then, on a broad canvas, up to the Allies' victory over Nazi Germany.

The era of Hitler's dictatorship and the Second World War has been used by many thriller writers as background for conventional crime stories, but the British writer Philip Kerr, in his 1989–91 "Berlin Noir" trilogy, was the first to hit on the idea of putting a hard-boiled private eye to work in the historical Berlin of 1936 to 1947. Bernhard "Bernie" Gunther has resigned from his post as police detective at headquarters in Alexanderplatz, and, after working for a while as a hotel detective in the Adlon, has set up his own small detective agency. *March Violets,* the first novel in the trilogy, is set against a backdrop of the preparations for the 1936 Olympic Games; Gunther, searching for an industrialist's daughter's jewelry, which is supposed to have vanished after a fire, becomes acquainted not only with the cells at Gestapo headquarters in Prinz-Albrecht-Strasse but also with the Nazis' reign of terror in Dachau concentration camp, into which he smuggles himself on the trail of the vanished gems.

With his indifferent attitude toward the Nazi regime and his capacity to come to terms again and again with inhuman circumstances, Bernhard Gunther behaves as many Germans did during those years. "Survival, especially in these difficult times," he says in *The Pale Criminal*, "has to count as some sort of an achievement." And he allows himself to be roped into a power play between Reinhard Heydrich and Heinrich Himmler. *A German Requiem* is set in 1947, in the ruins of occupied Berlin and Vienna.

Another British writer, Robert Harris, in the scenario for his political fiction *Fatherland* (1992), has gone even further, tackling the question of what the face of Germany might have been had Adolf Hitler's aggressive power politics met with success. In his widely successful and—especially in Germany—hotly debated thriller, the year is 1964, and the German nation is preparing for the Führer's seventy-fifth birthday. The long campaign against Russia is on the verge of a victorious conclusion; and in the United States, with which Germany made peace in 1946, John F. Kennedy is president.

The Berlin in which Kriminalkommissar Xaver März is investigating the death of a top-ranking Nazi Party member is a gigantic metropolis. Yet untouched by the pompous grandeur with which the Nazi rulers surround themselves, there is a dark, deadly side to the state. During his investigation, März, along with American journalist Jane MacGuire, finds traces of the buried past. He learns that the Jewish population of Germany has been brutally expelled or murdered so that the rulers could enrich themselves from the fortunes of the dead. Harris's knowledgeably written novel shows us how Berlin might have looked, with Albert Speer's gigantic edifices, triumphal arches, magnificent avenues and conference halls, had history taken a different turn.

The real Berlin of today, in reunited Germany, has a quite different appearance, as Russian detective Kommissar Arkadi Renko gets to see during his inquiries in Martin Cruz Smith's *Red Square* (1992). On the trail of valuable Russian Modernist paintings, Renko, who made his first appearance in Smith's 1981 novel, *Gorky Park*, ends up in reunited Berlin. He finds a city full of contrasts: dilapidation alongside luxury; the knitting together of the once-divided city is highlighted with painful clarity.

"The Wall is gone and Berlin is finally free to bloom," says a new-style entrepreneur. "Think of it: over two hundred kilometers of Wall erased, an extra thousand square kilometers in the center of Berlin to be developed. It's the greatest real estate opportunity in the second half of the twentieth century."

READING LIST

Books discussed in the preceding essay are indicated by an asterisk at the end of the reading list.

ARJOUNI, Jakob. *Happy Birthday, Turk!* [Zürich, 1987], translated by Anselm Hollo (NY, 1993). Kemal Kayankaya is a private detective of the really tough variety in Frankfurt am Main, one of Germany's toughest cities. He has to find the murderer of a Turkish guest worker who was killed in the red-light district near the main railway station. The trail leads through the brothels and the drug scene of Germany's banking and financial capital. At the end, the sleuth establishes that although he was on the right track, he hasn't found the right murderer. Arjouni, a young shooting star on the German crime writing scene, has read lots of Chandler and even more Hammett. In *Happy Birthday, Turk!*, he has written Germany's first genuine hard-boiled whodunit.

BAXT, George. *The Alfred Hitchcock Murder Case* (NY, 1986). A good, inventive story of how film director Alfred Hitchcock gets involved in a murder case in the twenties, during a spell in Munich, and how the details of that case later inspire his films. A special delight for all Hitchcock fans and for all cinema lovers (who if they come to Munich should not miss a visit to the Bavaria-Filmstudios on Geiselgasteig).

BIERMANN, Pieke. *Violetta* [Berlin, 1990], translated by Ines Rieder and Jill Hannum (London and NY, 1996). *Violetta* is the second in a series of seven crime novels (but the first to be translated) that Biermann, a Berlin journalist, translator, and two-time winner of the German Crime Award, plans to write about her formerly divided city, its neighborhoods and its people. The first book, *Potsdamer Ableben* ("Death in Potsdam," 1987), was set among journalists, artists, and the more unsavory types— junkies and prostitutes—who frequent the area between Europa Center and Tiergartenstrasse. Her protagonist is Detective Chief Inspector Karin Lietze. In *Violetta*, Lietze and her assistants pursue a strange serial killer who stamps the foreheads of his foreign victims with letters indicating their origins—*T* for Turk, *P* for Pole, *C* for Chilean. Biermann writes in a sometimes dry and sardonic but also sometimes very witty style. She's a master of Berlin slang, known in Germany for its cynical world view. *Violetta* captures the atmosphere in Berlin just before the Wall came down in 1989; it's a very exact but very personal portrait of the town.

BÖLL, Heinrich. *The Lost Honor of Katharina Blum* [Germany, 1974], translated by Leila Vennewitz (NY, 1975). With this brilliant and aggressively written thriller about mass media methods and the police hunt for the political terrorists of the Red Army Faction (RAF), Heinrich Böll, the 1972 Nobel literature laureate, prompted intense political discussions in the Federal Republic. The background to this explosive story is Böll's home city of Cologne and the annual carnival with its great processions. During carnival time, a special police unit storms the apartment of Katharina Blum, a lawyer's secretary, who is alleged to have helped Goetten, a terrorist, to escape. They fail to find the wanted man, but continue to investigate the young woman. The sensationalist press portrays Katharina as a super-terrorist and in so doing sets off a chain of violence.

CHILDERS, Erskine. *The Riddle of the Sands* (London, 1903; NY, 1915, 1976). Davies and Carruthers, two young British patriots, set out from Flensburg on an autumn sailing trip along the German coast. The year is 1902, Germany is ruled by Kaiser Wilhelm II and is engaged in a dangerous rivalry with Great Britain. No wonder, then, that yacht owner Davies suspects the mysterious mariner Dollmann, whose daughter Davies has fallen in love with, of being a German spy. Thus the sailing adventure between Frisia and the East Frisian Islands becomes a brilliant spy novel, which ranks as not only the first in its genre but also one of the best.

The author's own fate was the stuff of fiction. Childers (1870–1922), a clerk in the British House of Commons and participant in the Boer War, frequently sailed his yacht amid the sandbanks of the Frisian coast. In 1914 he smuggled 1,500 Mauser rifles by yacht into Dublin to arm the Irish republicans, whose cause he had adopted. In 1922 he was convicted of treason by a British military court and executed by firing squad.

CLIFFORD, Francis [Arthur Bell Thompson]. *The Naked Runner* (London and NY, 1966). The story takes us back to the divided Germany of the Cold War years. Sam Laker was not always an unprepossessing representative for office furniture, so the favor an old friend from the secret service asks is no ordinary matter. While visiting the Leipzig Trade Fair in the DDR, Laker is to make contact with a woman agent. In the process, he is arrested by East German Stasi Captain Hartmann. Yet instead of charging Laker with espionage, Hartmann demands that Laker should shoot a renegade East German official in Copenhagen. Although Francis Clifford worked in the offices of the British Special Operations Executive during the war, his spy story does not sound particularly credible. However, the oppressive atmosphere in the former DDR, marked by ever-present fear of the informers of state security (Stasi), is well captured.

KIRST, Hans Hellmut. *A Time for Scandal* (London, 1973, also published as *Damned to Success*); *A Time for Truth* (London, 1974); *A Time for Payment* (London, 1976). In these three novels, published in Germany 1971–73, Kirst has written "a Munich Trilogy" of police procedurals. In Kirst's Munich, illegal business operations and political intrigues lie barely hidden under the façade of high society, providing plenty of material for the former journalist. His novels, though a bit given to moralizing, are definitely worth reading. Whether the case involves the death of a high-class prostitute, the muzzling of a critical journalist, or a sexual killer whose actions threaten Oktoberfest, the inquiries of Kirst's eager inspectors always lead into high places and uncover dirty political intrigues. Kirst is not the German Ed McBain, but his novels are full of action and suspense.

LE CARRÉ, John. *A Small Town in Germany* (NY, 1968). Much sensation and controversy greeted le Carré's novel about the takeover of power by an anti-West, clearly Fascist-oriented "Movement" in West Germany. In 1980, according to le Carré's story, West Germany is destabilized through strikes and the uprising of the discontented middle classes, workers, and students. In the midst of this situation, a British Embassy employee in Bonn vanishes with secret papers about Anglo-German relations, and the British secret service sends Alan Turner to the Rhine to find him.

———. *The Little Drummer Girl* (NY and London, 1983). The novel begins in Bonn, then moves to the Mideast. See discussion in Chapter X.

MARTIN, Hansjörg. *Sleeping Girls Don't Lie* [Reinbek, 1966], translated by Joachim Neugroschel (NY, 1976). The story begins with a dead girl in a train compartment, into which advertising copywriter Hans Obuch innocently stumbles. Was it suicide or murder? Hans is not satisfied with the police investigations. The story of his own inquiries in a small northern German town is told with a quiet and amiable humor which has made Hansjörg Martin one of the most popular crime writers in Germany.

Sleeping Girls Don't Lie is a leisurely, conventional whodunit with the atmosphere of a small town in the 1950s, when Germany was experiencing a general rise in prosperity, the result of the *Wirtschaftswunder* (economic miracle).

MIEHE, Ulf. *A Dead One in Berlin* ([Munich, 1973]; NY, 1976). Film producer and script writer Ulf Miehe tells the story of a young film team in Berlin that contacts a big gangster for research purposes. He inspires them with an idea for a Big Deal—but only for a movie, of course. When they begin to work on their plan, however, the reader begins to wonder. Do they really just want to make a movie? The clever confusion of reality and fiction in this novel creates an ironical gangster ballad.

PIRINCCI, Akif. *Felidae* (Munich and NY, 1989). The author, who says "I love cats even more than my wife," has created a cat detective named Francis who tells of his adventures in the backyards of nineteenth-century mansions, a paradise for cats in a prosperous part of Bonn, where the Turkish-born Pirincci himself lives. Francis tries to solve a series of mysterious murder cases among his own species. In his inquiries he encounters a religious sect and its fascist leader who suffers from delusions of his own omnipotence.

*DEIGHTON, Len. *Funeral in Berlin* (London, 1964).

*————. *Berlin Game* (London, 1983; NY, 1984); *Mexico Set* (London and NY, 1985); *London Match* (London, 1985; NY, 1986).

*————. *Winter: A Berlin Family* (London, 1987; NY, 1988).

*FREEMANTLE, Brian. *Little Grey Mice* (NY, 1992).

*HALL, Adam [Elleston Trevor]. *The Quiller Memorandum,* also known as *The Berlin Memorandum* (London and NY, 1965).

*————. *Quiller KGB* (London, 1989).

*HARRIS, Robert. *Fatherland* (NY and London, 1992).

*KERR, Philip. *March Violets* (London and NY, 1989); *The Pale Criminal* (London and NY, 1990); *A German Requiem* (London and NY, 1991). Also published in one volume as *Berlin Noir* (London and NY, 1993).

*LE CARRÉ, John. *The Spy Who Came in from the Cold* (NY, 1964; London, 1963, 1994).

*LUDLUM, Robert. *The Aquitaine Progression* (NY, 1984).

*SMITH, Martin Cruz. *Red Square* (NY, 1992, 1993 pb). See also chapter IX, "Russia."

*THOMAS, Ross. *The Cold War Swap* (NY, 1966). For the post-Bonn adventures of McCorkle and Padillo, see *Cast a Yellow Shadow* (NY, 1967);

The Backup Men (NY, 1971); and *Twilight at Mac's Place* (NY, 1990, 1991).

*WALSER, Martin. *No Man's Land* [Germany, 1987], translated by Leila Vennewitz (NY, 1989).

NOTED BUT NOT REVIEWED

ALBRAND, Martha. *Endure No Longer* (Boston, 1944; London, 1945). This novel describes life in prewar Germany. Not much suspense, but a lot of background about the Third Reich.

ALLBEURY, Ted. *The Only Good German* (London, 1976), also published as *Mission Berlin* (NY, 1986). In Berlin and Hamburg a British agent hunts a neo-Nazi terrorist organization.

————. *The Seeds of Treason* (London, 1986; NY, 1987). Another Allbeury novel about the British secret service in divided Berlin—including a romantic but unconvincing love story that breaches the Iron Curtain.

————. *The Special Collection* (London, 1975). While West German politicians try to start a peaceful East-West dialogue, KGB hardliners prepare a violent coup d'état.

ANDERSCH, Alfred. *The Redhead* [Germany, 1960], translated by Michael Bullock (London, 1961). A young woman who wants to escape her married life is used by an Englishman in a revenge plot against a former Nazi. A panorama of the Germany of the sixties wrapped into crime fiction.

BEHN, Noel. *The Shadowboxer* (NY, 1969; London, 1970). In Germany in 1944, an American agent finds a way into a concentration camp. Ultimately he must face the fact that he is being used by his American masters to promote a provisional German government. A strange and disturbing plot.

BUCKLEY, William F., Jr. *The Story of Henri Todd* (NY and London, 1984). The Berlin Wall is just about to be erected when Blackford Oakes, CIA super-agent, is sent to Berlin to find out about a secret plan of the DDR leadership to stop emigration into the "Golden West."

DAVIS, J. Madison. *The Murder of Frau Schuetz* (NY, 1988). A hero of the Afrika Korps is ordered to investigate the murder of the commandant's wife in a concentration camp on the Eastern front near the Carpathians. An early chapter takes place in a Berlin severely damaged by bombing. The prologue and epilogue take place in Vienna.

FOLSOM, Alan. *The Day After Tomorrow* (NY, 1994). At an international congress in Geneva, an American surgeon meets the man who killed his father twenty years earlier. The hunt for the killer leads him to Berlin, where he gets caught in the trap of a mysterious organization. A political and psychological thriller.

FORSYTH, Frederick. *The Odessa File* (London and NY, 1972). In this well-researched thriller, a journalist infiltrates an organization of old and young Nazis.

ISAACS, Susan. *Shining Through* (NY and London, 1988). A nice Jewish girl from Queens is sent on a secret mission to wartime Berlin.

KAYE, M. M. *Death Walked in Berlin* (London and NY, 1955). Also published as *Death in Berlin* (NY, 1983). The young niece of a British occupation officer becomes involved in a murder case.

MacLEAN, Alistair. *Where Eagles Dare* (London and NY, 1967). British command forces must rescue an Allied officer held in a Nazi fort in Bavaria.

ROSS, Angus. *The Hamburg Switch* (London and NY, 1980). Former Secret Service agent Marc Farrow tries to get an East German scientist out of the DDR, covering a lot of ground in the process.

SHERMAN, Dan. *The Prince of Berlin* (London, 1985). A story about CIA secret missions in Berlin from 1945 to 1985. Written in the style of John le Carré, with a cynical attitude toward American politics.

CLOSE-UP

If You Read German

By Regula Venske

HERE ARE FIVE talented German novelists with three things in common: none has been translated into English, each has a strong sense of place, and all are highly recommended.

ON BERLIN

Dagmar Scharsich's *Die Gefrorene Charlotte* ("Frozen Charlotte") recreates the atmosphere of East Berlin as it was just shortly before the fall of the Wall; former East Germans still hate her naive and gullible, though charming, first-person narrator, believing that she represents the West German stereotype of East Germans as slow-moving and backward.

ON DORTMUND

Sabine Deitmer's crime novels—*Kalte Küsse* ("Cold Kisses," 1993); *Dominante Damen* ("Dominant Ladies," 1994, winner of the second-place German Crime Award in 1995), and *Neon Nächte* ("Neon Nights," 1995)—could be situated in any big, anonymous industrial city like Dortmund in the Ruhrgebiet, an industrial area in northwest Germany. Deitmer's police investigator, Beate Stein—tough, green-eyed, heterosexual, feminist—solves cases dealing with sexual abuse of children within the family, prostitution, and women's fear of going out in the dark. She has a wonderfully biting humor, but she is also sensitive enough to accept help from a blind girlfriend. The publication of Deitmer's short story collection *Bye bye Bruno* in 1988, followed by *Auch Brave Mädchen Tun's* ("Good Girls Do It, Too") in 1990, made her one of the most "dominant" (and best-selling) contemporary German crime writers.

ON COLOGNE

If you like unconventional and courageous women, state attorney **Gabriele Wolff** is the right author to take you to Cologne cathedral or to events of the carnival season. She sends her alter ego off into dangerous places and situations, and casually tells you a lot about the German legal system along the way. Three Wolff titles are *Kolscher Kaviar* ("Cologne Caviar," 1990); *Himmel und Erde* ("Heaven and Earth," 1993); and *Armer Ritter* ("Poor Chap," 1993).

ON BREMEN

Bremen is Anywhere—a provincial town with Big City pretensions. In his series of ten Bremen police novels, **Jürgen Alberts** depicts the provincialism of German politics between 1975 and the reunification. His books are satirical, mean, and witty. The latest, about corruption at the local TV station, is called *Medien Siff* ("Media Scum").

ON HAMBURG

The standard question I'm asked by newspaper interviewers is: "Why are there so many excellent crime writers living in Hamburg?" I don't know, and I also don't know why the male among them still cling to the myths of the Reeperbahn (Hamburg's notorious street of sex) and the clichés of the red-light district with desperately stubborn nostalgia. Anyway, I like **Doris Gercke** and her lady investigator, Bella Block, best, as in *Auf Leben und Tod* ("Mortal Business"), her latest, which is written in a clear and poetical language.

VI

THE NETHERLANDS

THE SMELLS OF HOLLAND: *There was a smell of rotted dead leaves from last autumn, of rain-slimed and exhaust-blackened tree trunks, of sodden muddy grass alongside the pavements. The street lamps had a depressed droop like undernourished tulips: the shimmering halo of light, reflected off raindrops, hung around them like bad breath. But this is part of it, thought Van der Valk, not discontented, without this there would be no spring, no hairy pussy willows reminding him of the scent of mimosa far down in the South. He had bought some mimosa that morning for his wife . . . His wife's smile and the scent of mimosa, vividly pictured and for one instant recaptured, would be almost the last things in his life. That and the moisture on his loden coat, and the dead leaves, and a wet leather glove: the smells of Holland.* (Nicolas Freeling, *Aupres de ma Blonde*)

THE CAPITAL: *Amsterdam, by its tolerance for unconventional behavior, attracts crazy people. Holland is a conventional country; crazy people have to go somewhere. They go to the capital, where the lovely canals, thousands and thousands of gable houses, hundreds of bridges of every shape and form, lines of old trees, clusters of offbeat bars and cafes, dozens of small cinemas and theaters encourage and protect the odd. Crazy people are special people. They carry the country's genius, its urge to create, to find new ways. The State smiles and is proud of its crazy people. But the State does not approve of anarchism. It limits the odd.* (Janwillem van de Wetering, *Death of a Hawker*)

THE COUNTRYSIDE: *One of the charms of Holland is that it is so completely itself—unique, unmistakable, changeless in spite of change, familiar when seen for the first time. The scenes that the Breughels and Potter and Vermeer and Ruisdael painted are still there, and over great stretches of countryside only the functional electric watermills alongside the ancient windmills indicate the change of century. In any Dutch*

landscape four-fifths of the canvas is filled with the wide, windy sky; the
remaining fifth will show either red-brick, steeply gabled houses or fresh
green fields, flat as paper, sprinkled with sleek, black-and-white cows.
There is certain to be water about, and very probably a boat or two. . . .
(Patricia Moyes, *Death and the Dutch Uncle*)

WHEN IN AMSTERDAM: Go book-shopping. Amsterdam is a city of
bookstores and Holland a land of readers—among them van de
Wetering's Commissaris, who buys second-hand travel books at the
stalls on the Oudemanhuispoort ("The Old Man House Gate,"
after a home for the elderly). Don't worry about a language problem: most stores stock some books in English, and a number specialize in them. Pick up used Freelings and van de Weterings at
The Book Exchange (Kloveniersburgwal 58) or De Siegte (Kalverstraat 48–52). For new English books, try The English Bookshop
(Lauriergracht 71) or W. H. Smith (Kalverstraat 152).

Dutch Interiors

A MSTERDAMMERS DON'T LIKE police; maybe it goes back to the Nazis,
the Occupation," says a character in Carolyn Hougan's thriller *Shooting in the Dark*. Or maybe it's just because legal parking spaces are in such
short supply. Nonetheless, that lovely, overcrowded city—with its unsettling mixture of prurience and primness, its prostitutes whose show-
windows gleam from daily washing—has produced two of the best
modern series of police novels: the Van der Valk stories of Nicholas Freeling and the Grijpstra/de Gier tales of Janwillem van de Wetering. Both
series are written in English. (A third police series, the Dutch-language
DeKok novels by "Baantjer," is popular in the Netherlands but seems to
be losing something in translation.)

Freeling and van de Wetering are superb travel writers, and their novels abound in precise descriptions of Dutch places and insights into
Dutch minds. Neither author seems much concerned with police procedure, and their detectives are more intuitive than rational in their crime-
solving. Both authors tend to break the classic puzzle rules—introducing
the murderer late in the game, for example.

In most ways, however, the two series are very different. And otherwise congenial people may differ passionately about which is better. Freeling's books are longer, slow-moving, more ambitious both stylistically and intellectually. Piet van der Valk is part highbrow, part cunning peasant. Though his detecting style is "friendly, very talkative, with a lazy, joking manner, good at creating confidences," he also is given to bouts of rather pompous moralizing about the ills of society and to attacks of misogyny. (He describes one annoying person in *Because of the Cats* as "a restless, unsatisfied woman who really needed to be raped by three drunken sailors.")

Freeling's Van der Valk has a French wife named Arlette, but on the job he's a loner. Van de Wetering offers a team: Sergeant de Gier is a handsome bachelor who cultivates geraniums, has an occasional love affair, but lives alone with a demanding cat. Adjutant Grijpstra, the senior partner, is an artist *manqué,* with a fat wife he detests and a couple of children. They are longtime partners and friends who needle each other, talk tough, drink quantities of coffee and *jenever.* Both have sweetness in their souls, which surfaces when de Gier plays flute to Grijpstra's drums.

Also very much part of the team is their boss, the Commissaris, an old and wise man who suffers dreadfully from rheumatism and cultivates a Zen-like detachment, but who is spry enough to play a central role in most of the books. There is also a brash young constable named Cardozo.

There is a warmth and humor in the van de Wetering novels that is lacking in Freeling's. On the other hand, van de Wetering's books are more formulaic, without Freeling's experiments in point of view and his complex character development. In truth, Grijpstra and de Gier are engaging collections of traits rather than fully developed characters. They undergo some changes during the course of the series but nothing to compare with the complicated stages of Van der Valk's career and personal life, culminating in his murder in the splendid 1972 volume, *Aupres de ma blonde.* (Freeling subsequently revived him in *Sand Castles.*)

Several good books by other writers are described below. But in the policing of the Low Countries, van de Wetering and Freeling are without peer.

READING LIST

BAANTJER [Albert Cornelis]. *DeKok and the Disillusioned Corpse* [1977], translated by H. G. Smittenaar (1993). A corpse is found in Amsterdam's "Brewers Canal." Inspector DeKok quickly detects that the deceased was an apprentice to a cat burglar known as Slippery Eel, but the inspector has his work cut out for him learning anything more. (Also available in English: *DeKok and the Sorrowing Tomcat, DeKok and the Romantic Murder, DeKok and the Dying Stroller,* and a growing list of other jaunty titles.)

DeKok—a.k.a. "the gray sleuth"—is allegedly brilliant, has an admiring young sidekick named Vledder, and hates bureaucracy. He also has startling eyebrows, an irresistible grin, and resembles a "good-natured boxer." These formulae are repeated in book after book—as are several longer set pieces, such as a description of the red-light district. Especially annoying is a characterization of the Warmoesstraat police station as "the Dutch Hill Street," which even occurs in the translation of a novel published in Dutch in 1974 (*The Sorrowing Tomcat*). The TV series first aired in 1981.

It's hard to imagine what these books are like in the original Dutch because they have so obviously been revised for an American audience, explaining things every Dutch person would know. In *The Disillusioned Corpse,* for example, we get a quick rundown on the amazing damming of the saltwater Zuiderzee to create farmland and a freshwater lake. The translation is clumsy, rendering place-names into literal English, thereby sacrificing both flavor and usefulness. (You won't find Brewers Canal on any map of Amsterdam; Brouwersgracht is another matter.) But if you run out of Freelings and van de Weterings, a Baantjer may serve to while away a rainy Dutch afternoon.

FREELING, Nicolas. *Love in Amsterdam* (London, 1962, 1985) [also published as *Death in Amsterdam*]. "Here in Amsterdam love causes the police no end of trouble," muses Inspector Van der Valk. In his first outing, Van der Valk shares the spotlight with the chief murder suspect, Martin, whom he befriends in an unorthodox fashion. The murder victim is Martin's former girlfriend, Elsa, a woman of dubious virtue but enduring allure. The novel is divided into three parts, each named for a place: "The House in the Josef Israelskade" is the site of the murder; "Matthew Marisstraat 87" flashes back to the confused and sinister years just after World War II, when Martin first met Elsa, who was living at that address near the Museumplein; "The House of Keeping" is the jail where Martin awaits the outcome of Van der Valk's investigation.

———. *Because of the Cats* (London, 1963, 1965). Now a chief inspector in the juvenile division, Van der Valk becomes fascinated with the criminal activities (burglary and rape) of a gang of teenagers from the fictional North Sea "new town" of Bloemendaal aan Zee. These feckless rebels come from well-off families and homes filled with "glossy toys— the flowers of the Euromarket"; they also are into sex, drugs, and a cult. The book's most sympathetic character is a traditional whore-with-a-heart-of-gold and a fondness for classical music.

————. *The King of the Rainy Country* (NY, 1965, 1985). Van der Valk is ordered to find a millionaire who has disappeared with a young girl. The trail takes him to Cologne, Innsbruck, Chamonix, and Strasbourg— and into digressions on the art of the slalom, the difference between Northern European passion and that of the South, the romance of Mayerling, precious stones, Baudelaire's *Spleen* (the source of the title), and much more. He also gets shot.

————. *Strike Out Where Not Applicable* (London, 1967, 1969). Slowed down by his injury, Van der Valk becomes commissaire of the criminal brigade in the attractive old town of Lisse, center of the Dutch tulip fields. His pleasant new life is disrupted by the murder of a piggish local restaurateur. This novel is especially good on landscape and on the details of Dutch provincial life—food, for example.

*Auprès de ma Blonde (in Britain, *A Long Silence;* NY, 1972). Van der Valk is promoted to principal commissaire ("an animal high in police hierarchies") and sent to the Hague to take part in a blue-ribbon commission on reforming the penal code. In his free time, Van der Valk is drawn into what he comes to think of as his "private case," a little mystery involving an Amsterdam jewelry store and an almost Dickensian set of characters. On page 87, he is shot dead. Freeling abruptly introduces himself into the story as a friend of Van der Valk's as well as his chronicler, apologizes for having underestimated Van der Valk's wife Arlette in a dozen books, and (as author) sends her back to Amsterdam to find out who killed her husband. It's a daring gambit, but the book works. And Arlette, "a wife-slave, and happy about it," turns into a formidable heroine. (Freeling subsequently gave her a new husband and her own detective business in *The Widow.*)

Others books in the series, and their principal settings other than Amsterdam, are: *Question of Loyalty* (a.k.a. *Guns Before Butter,* 1963); *Double-Barrel* (1964)—the northeastern Dutch province of Drente; *Criminal*

---

*vaut le voyage (see page 4).

Conversation (1965); *Tsing-Boom* (1969); *The Lovely Ladies* (a.k.a. *Over the High Side*, 1971)—Dublin; *The Widow* (1979)—Strasbourg; *Sand Castles* (1989)—the province of Groningen in northern Holland.

HOUGAN, Carolyn. *Shooting in the Dark* (NY, 1984). This first novel plays variations on the conventions of the romantic suspense genre with wit and intelligence. Unceremoniously dumped by her husband of seven years, New Yorker Claire Brooks impulsively flees to Amsterdam. It is 1980; Queen Juliana is abdicating in favor of her daughter Beatrix, and Claire is just in time for the ceremonies and the riots that followed. Also gathering in Amsterdam are the members of a very powerful and very secret international cabal known as the Circle Group. There are dire games afoot and Claire quickly finds herself in the middle of them—and in bed with an attractive American reporter. The action is skillfully integrated with sightseeing—an assassination outside the Rijksmuseum, a chase through the Keukenhof Bulb Gardens—in this superior tourist's tale.

MacLEAN, Alistair. *Puppet on a Chain* (NY, 1969). A monumentally silly thriller in which British Interpol cop Paul Sherman tells about his trip to Amsterdam to break up an international drug ring. He is assisted in this project by two beautiful, "highly trained," and extremely dopey female agents. Judging from the number of near-fatal mistakes he makes, Paul's not very good at his job. What he *is* good at is surviving violent and ingenious attempts on his life—including one in a rural setting that suggests the author's been reading Shirley Jackson's "The Lottery."

MOYES, Patricia. *Death and the Dutch Uncle* (NY, 1968). Moyes's series character, Superintendent Henry Tibbett of the CID, and his plucky but dull wife, Emmy, fly to Holland in hopes of preventing the assassination of a member of an important international commission. Their mission takes them to Friesland in the north. There they rent a boat and tool around, getting into trouble (Emmy almost suffers death-by-windmill) before Henry solves his case, which has its roots in the Dutch underground during the Nazi occupation. The plot is unmemorable, but there are good descriptions of Amsterdam and—more unusual—of the little towns and watery byways of rural Friesland. Moyes tips her hat to Nicolas Freeling by having Tibbett call on Van der Valk for assistance, though their meeting takes place off-page. Other Moyes novels are discussed in Chapter XX, "The Caribbean."

SIMENON, Georges. *Maigret in Holland* [1940], translated by Geoffrey Sainsbury (NY, 1993). When a French citizen, a professor on a lecture tour, is suspected of murder in the pristine little Dutch town of Delfzijl on the North Sea, Inspector Maigret—for semiofficial reasons that are never quite clear—is sent to investigate. He is hampered by his inability to speak the language. But human nature transcends language, and the Divine M. M., en route to a solution, ponders the passions and resentments simmering beneath the surface of bourgeois respectability—"the stale perfume of a provincial town. Sewing meetings . . . Whispered gossip. Heart-to-heart talks with an undercurrent of cattiness."

VAN DE WETERING, Janwillem. *Outsider in Amsterdam* (NY, 1975, 1986). Adjutant Grijpstra and Sergeant de Gier get right to work in this first novel of the series, whose plot involves both Amsterdam's colonialist past and its hippie/druggy 1970s. The leader of the "Hindist Society," a quasi-religious group with an unsavory commercial sideline, is found hanged in a ramshackle gable house in the Haarlemmer Houttuinen, a busy main thoroughfare. The house's residents—and the main suspects—include the sympathetic outsider of the title, a native of the former Dutch colony of Papua New Guinea, whose passion is his restored 1943 Harley-Davidson motorcycle.

————. *Tumbleweed* (NY, 1976, 1978). A Curaçao-born and very upscale call girl, who dabbles in magic, is found fatally stabbed in her expensive houseboat on the river Schinkel. The murder weapon is a British commando knife, apparently thrown by an expert. At least two of the suspects qualify. One is a rich businessman with a second home on the little island of Schiermonnikoog in the North Sea, where de Gier and Grijpstra, in a very funny scene, are forced to indulge in some strenuous bird-watching. The Commissaris, meanwhile, is following other leads in Curaçao, where the Caribbean sun does wonders for his rheumatism and a meeting with a kind of shaman restores his soul. One of the best of the Grijpstra/de Gier/Commissaris outings.

————. *The Corpse on the Dike* (NY, 1976, 1987). The murder of a reclusive rich man living in a dilapidated house on a dike in Amsterdam North is made even more mysterious by the murder weapon, a handgun (outlawed and hard to come by in Holland). Some evocative sketches of Amsterdam neighborhoods both obscure (Bickers Island) and notorious (hippie-haunted Dam square).

————. *Death of a Hawker* (NY, 1977, 1978). A rich street vendor is killed in his home, while outside rioters protest the spread of the subway into the Niewmarket area. De Gier falls in love. Grijpstra steps in dog shit in a rare literary treatment of the omnipresent challenge to the Dutch reputation for cleanliness: unregulated canine defecation.

————. *The Blond Baboon* (NY, 1978, 1987). In which Grijpstra finds the perfect café and de Gier falls into the Amstel River. Both events occur as they and the Commissaris seek the murderer of a Belgian nightclub singer turned successful furniture importer, who lives in a handsome turn-of-the-century house on the Mierisstraat. Perhaps because it begins with a ferocious gale that threatens the country's man-made defenses, the novel is suffused with affection for Amsterdam's architectural variety, its odd people, its watery byways.

Others in the series: *The Japanese Corpse* (1977)—de Gier and the Commissaris follow a case to Japan (see Chapter XIII); *The Maine Massacre* (1979)—ditto Maine; *The Mind Murders* (1981); *Hard Rain* (1986); *The Hollow-Eyed Angel* (1996).

VERONESE, David. *Jana (A Tale of Decadence)* (London and NY, 1993). This self-conscious exercise in decadence, set mostly in Amsterdam in the mid-eighties, features sex, drugs, violence, and great paintings. The narrator, Eddie Verlaine, is an expatriate American who deals in secondhand furs and the like. He falls under the spell of the mysterious Jana—all black leather clothing, platinum hair, and chic nihilism—and into the hands of her sinister confederates. When he returns to his flat in London, he finds he's transported not just furs but a fortune in heroin. There are excellent evocations of the sights and sounds of the red-light district, the Waterlooplein flea market, and other seedy haunts. Eddie is also a bit of an aesthete who pays ritual visits to Vermeer's *Kitchen Maid* in the Rijksmuseum, and the author writes well about it. But the nightmarish quality of Eddie's adventures will be off-putting to many.

VII

━━━━━◦((◉))◦━━━━━

IRELAND

Murderer's ground. It passed darkly. Shuttered, tenantless, unweeded garden, whole place gone to hell. Wrongfully condemned. Murder. The murderer's image in the eye of the murdered. They love reading about it. Man's head found in a garden. Her clothing consisted of. How she met her death . . . The weapon used . . . The body to be exhumed. Murder will out. (James Joyce, *Ulysses*)

The west coast of Ireland, he thought, was a landscape of harshness and exiguity, a million miles from the green and pleasant land of England. It was a landscape carved by a warped history, eaten to rock bottom by the forces of erosion, now almost irreducible in its barrenness. It was a landscape of green patches precariously struggling against the wildness of encroaching heather; drystone walls instead of hedges; stunted trees bending before wet winds; futile roads winding towards long-abandoned homes and bare hilltops; and lonely beaches among black rocks and the tormenting crash of the sea. (Patrick McGinley, *Bogmail*)

WHEN IN DUBLIN: Have coffee or lunch at Bewley's Oriental Café on Grafton Street, a Dublin institution for generations, refurbished in recent years. Here John Brady's Matt Minogue regularly stops by to eat sticky buns, and Peter McGarr stages a particularly bloody battle in *The Death of a Joyce Scholar*.

Murderer's Ground

PERHAPS BECAUSE POLITICAL murder is an all too familiar part of Irish reality, the conventional murder mystery has not flourished there. Even in Irish police procedurals, the culprit is likely to be the IRA—or its British or Protestant enemies. Solving the mystery is sometimes just a matter of figuring out who belongs to which Provo faction.

The best-known contemporary detective novels set in Ireland, Bartholomew Gill's Inspector McGarr tales, are second-rate as mysteries, only a bit better as local color. Fortunately, a newer series, John Brady's novels featuring Inspector Matt Minogue, is more promising. Both Brady and Gill are Americans, however. The author of still another new series, Eugene McEldowney, is a Dublin journalist. His two novels are set north of the border and feature Cecil Megarry, a Belfast police detective.

When I met Dublin novelist and journalist Vincent Banville a few years ago, we talked about the lack of homegrown Irish detectives—particularly private eyes. Banville remarked that he was working on this and, sure enough, his first John Blaine adventure, *Death by Design,* was published in Dublin in 1993.

The IRA terrorist thriller (as opposed to the mystery with a political villain) has become a distinctive subgenre in recent years. A few of the best are included below, but the settings they portray—especially the gritty, edgy, deadly streets of Belfast and Derry—will not be attractive to most travelers.

Sui generis, but wonderful, are the novels of Patrick McGinley and, of course, Flann O'Brien's *The Third Policeman.*

READING LIST

BANVILLE, Vincent. *Death by Design* (Dublin, 1993). Vincent Banville has so deeply absorbed the lessons of Hammett and Chandler and Ross MacDonald that this novel at times verges on parody. The protagonist, John Blaine, is an American-style tough guy with a stage Irishman's accent and a hefty dose of Irish sentimentality. He is a classically seedy PI in a country without much use for his profession; "it was the Irish way to keep such things within the family circle or to send for the priest." A former hurling champ whose beloved wife, Annie, has left him, Blaine drinks too much, smokes too much, and lets the dirty dishes pile up in the sink. He has the Irish way with words—particularly dirty ones; he is a master of scatological invective.

Hired by a rich woman to find her long-lost son, Blaine follows the case into a Dublin netherworld, where somebody is slitting the throats of down-and-outs.

Underneath Blaine's tough guy façade is a squishy, sensitive New Man who listens to Janis Ian records and calls for "a quick Bushmills to deaden the taste of unrequited love." What is genuinely tough is Banville's portrayal of Dublin—corrupt, filthy, menacing, heartless, and architecturally ruined by its would-be conservators. "Dear old dirty Dublin," Blaine muses, "what a pass you've come to: riddled and moth-eaten and down on your knees."

BENNETT, Ronan. *The Second Prison* (London, 1991). Kane is a former IRA terrorist who has spent twelve of his thirty-three years in Long Kesh and other prisons. At once a "hard man" and an idealist, he has been sustained by belief in his cause and by loyalty to his mates. Emerging from jail, he must come to terms with the venality and betrayals of his former comrades, and with the shattered illusion that he is in control of his own life. Part IRA thriller, part psychological study, this first novel by an Irish writer was short-listed for an *Irish Times*/Aer Lingus award.

BLAKE, Nicholas [C. Day-Lewis]. *The Private Wound* (London and NY, 1968). A young Anglo-Irish writer returns to the West of Ireland where he was born, seeking peace and solitude to write. It is the summer of 1939, war looms (with Ireland defiantly neutral), and the atmosphere in rural "Charlottestown" in County Clare is vaguely sinister. The narrator plunges into a torrid affair with a local landowner's wife. Halfway though the novel she is murdered. Not much of a mystery, this is an elegant evocation of a bitter time, a beautiful place.

BRADY, John. *Kaddish in Dublin* (London, 1990; NY, 1992). The third in Brady's Inspector Matt Minogue series begins with the murder of a member of Dublin's small Jewish community. A self-styled PLO group claims credit, but Minogue turns up another suspect, the conservative Catholic brotherhood known as Opus Dei. This is Dublin for Advanced Tourists, a city of bus strikes and urban blight, permeated by "the sulphurous stink of the Liffey, long an open sewer, and the tangy hop smell of the Guinness brewery." (See also Brady's *A Stone of the Heart* [1988], set at Trinity College; *Unholy Ground* [1989], in which a murder threatens Anglo-Irish border talks; and *All Souls* [1993], in which a burned-out Minogue returns to his native County Clare.)

CROFTS, Freeman Wills. *Fatal Venture* (London, 1939; N. Ireland, 1987). Although Crofts, a master of the classic British puzzle novel, lived most of his life in Belfast, only a few of his books have Irish settings. In this charmer, a young London travel agent, Harry Morrison, gets caught up in an ambitious scheme to make a fortune by turning an over-the-hill ocean liner into a floating casino that will cruise the British "home waters," visiting the Orkneys, Shetlands, Hebrides, and the coasts of Ireland.

The murder of Morrison's business partner takes place at White Rocks, near the Giant's Causeway on the spectacular Antrim Coast in Ulster. Fortunately, Crofts's series detective, Inspector French, is available to solve it. Crofts is not much for elaborate descriptions; he prefers lists of names and railway timetables. But this tale enchantingly evokes a more leisurely era of travel. (See also Crofts's *Sir John Magill's Last Journey* [1930].)

DILLON, Eilís. *Death at Crane's Court* (London, 1953; NY, 1988). The murder victim is the obnoxious new owner of a deluxe retirement hotel on Galway Bay. The suspects comprise most of the hotel's elderly, eccentric residents, including one lady who fertilizes her fabulous garden plot with cats she raises for that purpose. The original of the hotel is probably long extinct, but when I bought a copy of this book in Kenny's great bookstore in Galway City, Mrs. Kenny remarked that the unnamed bookstore in Chapter 10 was an earlier incarnation of Kenny's.

Dillon's *Death in the Quadrangle* (London, 1956; NY, 1968) is an amiable academic mystery set in a university called King's, whose fictional campus adjoins Dublin's very real Phoenix Park. The amateur detective is a retired teacher of English literature, Professor Daly, who played a less central role in *Death at Crane's Court*. The other academic types are relentlessly odd. (A third Daly adventure is *Sent to His Account* [1954].)

FALLON, Ann C. *Hour of Our Death* (NY, 1995). The fifth novel featuring Dublin solicitor James Fleming, who dabbles in sleuthing as a hobby. In this one, the Virgin makes an appearance to three villagers of "Buncloda," near Enniscorthy (County Wexford). The chief "visionary," young Mary Dowd, is encouraged by an ambitious young priest, hordes of pilgrims descend on the village, and two of the visionaries are murdered. The details of village life seem authentic, but the prose is flat, and the sleuth, though described as "charming," quite without any discernible personality. (See also Fallon's *Dead Ends* [NY, 1992]—murder on Halloween in a fancy country inn—and three other titles.)

GILL, Bartholomew. *McGarr on the Cliffs of Moher* (NY, 1978). The body of a beautiful New York *Daily News* reporter is found near the tourist attraction of the title. She's carrying $27,000 of her paper's money to pay for an IRA story, the first of many unlikely details. Most preposterous is Chief Inspector Peter McGarr himself, who, despite his lofty position in the Garda Soichana (Ireland's national police), spends most of his time getting in fistfights, drinking all night, and cutting legal corners. But Gill does write with precision of the scenery of the Clare peninsula from Lahinch to Kilbaha and drops in some useful history. Fun for the first-time tourist to Ireland's West.

————. *The Death of a Joyce Scholar* (NY, 1989). The eponymous murder occurs during Bloomsday celebrations in Dublin; the site is the "murderer's ground" in *Ulysses*. A promising beginning, but McGarr is as ridiculous as ever, and author Gill can't decide whether he wants to explain Joycean aesthetics or to get it on vicariously with a group of sexually depraved academics. Even worse is *The Death of an Ardent Bibliophile* (1995), in which the keeper of Marsh's Library in Dublin is a coprophile as well as a bibliophile and models his sex life on Jonathan Swift's nastier impulses. (See also *Death on a Cold, Wild River* [1993] and at least seven more McGarr tales.)

HYNES, James. *The Wild Colonial Boy* (NY, 1990). Clare Delaney of Philadelphia and Brian Donovan of Detroit meet on a bus headed south across the border from Derry to Donegal Town. They are classic innocents abroad—except Brian is carrying ten pounds of Semtex plastique for a renegade IRA Provo. The explosive is intended to blow sky high a conciliatory political move on the part of the Provo leadership. This is a first-rate thriller, which uses setting exceptionally well. A crucial meeting takes place on the Devil's Causeway, Ulster's most dramatic landscape. A glorious Donegal sunset is observed through the scope of an assassin's rifle. But check the terrorist climate before reading this one on a trip to Ireland (or England). It's scary.

McELDOWNEY, Eugene. *A Stone of the Heart* (London and NY, 1995). In his second outing, Cecil Megarry of the antiterrorist Special Branch of the Royal Ulster Constabulary has returned to the force after a three-month suspension (see the first Megarry novel, *A Kind of Homecoming* [1994]). He's assigned to a bank robbery in which the robbers ignored thousands of pounds in favor of some papers in a safe-deposit box. The paper trail leads to a political kidnap scheme, a figure high up in British intelligence, and a killing deep in Megarry's past. This is a solid police procedural set against the grimy, bitterly sad background of this divided city and its ancient quarrels.

McGINLEY, Patrick. *Bogmail* (1978). There's no question *who* the murderer will be. Spoiled priest turned Donegal pub-owner Roarty intends to do in his bartender, Eamonn Eales, who has already been partly successful in his designs on Roarty's daughter. The question is *how*. Poisonous mushrooms fail, but volume 25 of the 11th edition of the *Ency-*

clopaedia Britannica does the trick and the body is buried in a bog. Then the mystery becomes: Who is the self-styled "bogmailer" taunting Roarty with witty extortion letters? One of the rural intellectuals and eccentrics who booze and talk through the evening in Roarty's pub? Or perhaps it's the Englishman Potter, whose conversational talents have won him a place at the bar. We couldn't find the parish of Glenkeel on the map of Donegal, but many other places named in this magic landscape of bog, glen, lough, and mountain are quite real. "A word of advice then. Surrender to the genius of the country." (See also McGinley's *Goosefoot* [1982] and *The Trick of the Ga Bolga* [1985].)

O'BRIEN, Flann [Brian O'Nolan]. *The Third Policeman* (London, 1967, 1988). Written in 1940 but not published until after O'Brien's 1966 death, this minor classic stands the conventions of the detective novel on their heads for darkly comic purposes. The narrator kills a man with a bicycle pump to get money to publish a scholarly treatise. But when he goes to collect the loot from his victim's house, he finds the corpse quite talkative. What follows bears comparison with *Through the Looking-Glass* in its absurd, dreamlike logic. (Indeed there's a hint that even time and eternity are done with mirrors.) The best moments involve two village policemen—paragons of "constabulary virtuosity"—who excel at finding missing bicycles they themselves have stolen. Their motive is noble: to keep riders who overuse their bikes from merging with them according to "the Atomic Theory." O'Brien's language is superb and unique.

SEYMOUR, Gerald. *Harry's Game* [in Great Britain, *The Killing of Henry Denby*] (NY, 1975). A former British official in Ulster is assassinated by an IRA type known for most of the book only as "The Man." British soldier Harry is sent undercover into a Catholic neighborhood of Belfast to take out "The Man." "Three hundred years Post-Cromwell, and nothing changed. Blood of martyrs on the streets again." This is Seymour's first and best-known IRA thriller. He returns to the theme in *Field of Blood* (1985) and *The Journeyman Tailor* (London, 1992; NY, 1993).

SIMPSON, Howard R. *Cogan's Case* (Dublin, 1992). One of the paperback "Glendale Crime Series" of Irish mysteries, published by Glendale Press. This one is set in Cork, in the fictional fishing village of West Portal. A brutal murder on a French trawler moored there leads to the temporary partnership of Finbarr Cogan of the Garda and Roger Bastide of Marseilles Homicide; behind the murder is a Marseilles/Dublin drug ring. There's lots of action—and plenty of West Cork scenery. Much is made of the stereotypical contrasts between the gourmandizing, womanizing Bastide (who appears in other Simpson books) and Cogan, a stolid, dumpy family man from Kinsale. Also contrasted are the trigger-happy Marseilles *flics* and the underequipped, underarmed, often blundering Garda. "This is West Cork not Miami," after all. Vulgar fun.

NOTED BUT NOT REVIEWED

ADCOCK, Thomas. *Drown All the Dogs* (NY, 1994). New York police detective Neil Hockaday, protagonist of two previous Adcock novels, ventures across the sea to solve the mystery of his father's disappearance during World War II.

FREELING, Nicolas. *You Who Know* (NY and London, 1994). When an Irish friend and colleague is killed in Brussels, Henri Castang, Freeling's series character, travels to Ireland and elsewhere looking for answers.

GASH, Jonathan. *The Sleepers of Erin* (NY and London, 1983). Lovejoy, antiques (Celtic), and fraud—the mix as usual, only this one's set in Ireland.

INNES, Michael [J. I. M. Stewart]. *The Case of the Journeying Boy* (NY and London, 1949; NY, 1983). A classic spy adventure of "pursuit and flight," set in the Irish countryside and involving a bumptious lad and his stodgy tutor.

WHITE, Terence de Vere. *The Distance and the Dark* (London, 1973, 1978). Fallout from the Troubles up North brings tragedy to the Anglo-Irish gentry and Irish country folk alike.

VIII

SCANDINAVIA

In November the frost set in. I have respect for the Danish winter. The cold—not what is measured on a thermometer, but what you can actually feel—depends more on the strength of the wind and the relative humidity than on the actual temperature. I have been colder in Denmark than I ever was in Thule in Greenland. When the first clammy rain showers of November slap me in the face with a wet towel, I meet them with fur-lined "capucines," black alpaca leggings, a long Scottish skirt, a sweater, and a cape of black Gore-Tex.

Then the temperature starts to drop. At a certain point the surface of the seas reaches 29F, and the first ice crystals form, a temporary membrane that the wind and waves break up into frazil ice. This is kneaded together into a soapy mash called grease ice and gradually forms free-floating plates, pancake ice, which, on a cold day at noon, on a Sunday, freezes into one solid sheet.

And it gets colder, and I'm happy because I know that now the frost has gained momentum; now the ice will stay, now the crystals have formed bridges and enclosed the salt water in pockets that have a structure like the veins of a tree through which the liquid slowly seeps . . . it's one reason for believing that ice and life are related in many ways. (Peter Hoeg, *Smilla's Sense of Snow*)

Of Ice and Ideology

THE CRIME NOVEL has thrived in Scandinavia at least since the twenties, when the Swedish writer Martin Gunnar Serner, under the name Frank Heller, wrote a series of stylish thrillers—some set in Sweden, but most on the Continent—featuring as detective an exiled Swedish bon vivant and gentleman-crook named Filip Collin. For most contemporary American and British readers of mysteries, however, *the* Scandinavian detective is gloomy, dyspeptic Detective Chief Inspector Martin Beck, head of Sweden's National Homicide Squad and protagonist of ten novels, published in the 1960s and '70s by the husband-and-wife team of Per Wahloo and Maj Sjowall.

The Beck novels are unusual for several reasons, not the least of which is that they began to be translated into English early on and quickly gained an enthusiastic American audience. By the sixth volume each addition to the series was routinely appearing in the United States within a year of its publication in Sweden. American enthusiasm for Sjowall and Wahloo probably helped a number of other Scandinavian mystery writers in the realistic mode, such as K. Arne Blom and Poul Orum, who also found English-language publishers in the sixties and seventies.

Some of the qualities that made the Beck series popular in the United States—as well as in Europe and the USSR—are obvious: they are well written, intelligently plotted, and sometimes very funny police procedurals, modeled in part on those of Ed McBain, and featuring several interesting continuing characters in addition to Beck. What makes their popularity in the United States a little surprising is their overt political content. Sjowall and Wahloo were Communists who, according to Wahloo, set out "to use the crime novel as a scalpel cutting open the belly of an ideologically pauperized and morally debatable so-called welfare state of the bourgeois type. . . ." In the Beck series, according to one critical study, the mystery genre is used "to indict the conspiracy between a supposedly socialist government and the capitalists in whose interests they govern." Sjowall and Wahloo maintained that "the so-called Welfare State abounds with sick, poor, and lonely people, living at best on dog food, who are left uncared for until they waste away and die in their rathole apartments." The authors also target the growth of crime and violence in Swedish society and the growing paramilitary power of the newly nationalized police. One member of Beck's team hears "the rats of fascism pattering about behind the wainscoting."

Though contemporary Sweden certainly looks prosperous to American eyes, the authors' gibes at the sky-high taxes that fuel the social welfare system will not seem dated to anyone who has recently dined out in Stockholm. As Martin Beck pays his bill after a snack at the famous Golden Peace (Den Gyldene Fredan), "he had reason to note that this was his first restaurant meal for some time. During his period of abstinence the prices, already exorbitant, had gotten ridiculous."

Sjowell and Wahloo deliberately set out to write ten Beck books as a way of examining the condition of Sweden during the decade they encompass. The series grows more political as it progresses—moving from questions of individual guilt and innocence to generalized indictments of Swedish capitalism and American imperialism. The novels are firmly grounded in real time and the characters' movements can be precisely tracked on a street map. But as travel literature they leave something to be desired. There are few descriptive passages, except in *The Man Who Went Up in Smoke*, when Beck goes to Budapest. Only the most dedicated fan will be tempted to seek out the landmarks of Martin Beck's Stockholm: his postdivorce apartment at Kopmangatan 8 in Gamla Stan (Stockholm's Old Town); South Police Headquarters on Vastberga Avenue, where he has his office; Stadsgarden Quay, the wharf area that was his favorite part of Stockholm as a child.

The Beck novels rank with the best European mysteries ever written. Among Scandinavian crime novels in translation they have only one rival, the fascinating and unique 1993 best-seller, *Smilla's Sense of Snow* by Peter Hoeg.

READING LIST

BARNARD, Robert. *The Cherry Blossom Corpse* [in England, *Death in Purple Prose*] (NY and London, 1987; NY, 1988). Barnard's Perry Trethowan of Scotland Yard reluctantly accompanies his sister to a romance writers' conference in Bergen, Norway. The scenery is gorgeous, the plot satiric. Clues to the inevitable murder are provided by the setting and by local drinking habits.

————. *Death in a Cold Climate* (NY, 1981). Set in Tromsø, Norway, three degrees north of the Arctic Circle: "The day, such as it was, would last no more than an hour or so, and then everything would be wrapped up in fitting, natural darkness." On such a December day, a young foreigner disappears in Tromsø; his naked body is found in the snow when the spring thaw finally begins. The possible motives include sex and North Sea oil; the suspects are a randy "perfect Norwegian housewife" who has been abandoned by her husband, and various unattractive members of Tromsø's English-speaking community who hang out in a pub called The Cardinal's Hat. As always Barnard is witty and observant. His minor characters have an almost Dickensian vitality.

BLOM, K. Arne. *The Moment of Truth*, translated by Erik J. Friis (NY, 1977). Set in Lund, a university town in southern Sweden, in 1973, this tale by a well-known and prolific Swedish writer, the current president of The International Association of Crime Writers, begins with a peaceful demonstration against "a foreign guest" from a politically unpopular country (the United States?). The demonstration escalates and the police respond violently. This incident is followed, without obvious connection, by a foray into the mind of a serial killer whose specialty is policemen's wives. The rest of the book moves back and forth between the killer and the police team assigned to the case. The Lund setting is perfunctorily described, including the cathedral ("a tourist attraction"), where the novel reaches a climax. See also Blom's *The Limits of Pain* (translated 1979), also set in southern Sweden.

FRANCIS, Dick. *Slayride* (NY, 1973). David Cleveland, investigator for the British Jockey Club, is called in to consult when a British jockey disappears along with the day's take from Oslo's Øvrevoll racetrack. Shortly after his arrival, Cleveland finds himself swimming for his life in the freezing waters of Oslo Fjord. Soon a dead body is found, and it's business as usual for a Dick Francis hero: plenty of physical and mental stress, a bit of sex, some smart detecting. Less horse lore than usual and only a few Norwegian touches—some dramatic scenery, and cloudberries for dessert. Not his best work.

HOEG, Peter. *Smilla's Sense of Snow* [Denmark, 1992], translated by Tina Nunnally (NY, 1993, 1995). When a small boy named Isaiah, an immigrant from Greenland living in a Copenhagen housing project, plunges to his death from the roof of a warehouse, his friend Smilla Qaavigaaq Jaspersen knows it can't be an accident. Isaiah had an intense phobia about heights and would never have been on the roof of his own free will. Smilla sets out to find what really happened in a richly patterned plot that makes vivid use of its Danish and Greenland settings.

Published in the United States to critical acclaim, this unusual thriller went on to hit the best-seller lists. At the heart of its appeal is its narrator and heroine, Smilla Jaspersen, the misfit daughter of an Inuit hunter from West Greenland and a wealthy Danish doctor. Smilla dresses like her father's daughter (cashmere and elegant boots) but knows snow and ice like her mother's. By instinct as well as training, she is a mathematician and glaciologist who has outfitted and served as navigator on expeditions to Greenland, tagged polar bears, and done research in "glacial morphology." During the course of this novel her multiple skills are put to use in unraveling a complicated and action-filled plot that links Isaiah's death to two mysterious expeditions to Greenland, an Allied code-breaking operation in 1946, a tropical drug-smuggling ring, an astounding scientific discovery, and a number of unnatural deaths. The landscape and world views of Greenland and Denmark are contrasted to good effect.

SJOWALL, Maj, and Per Wahloo. The ten Martin Beck novels, in order of Swedish publication, are:

Roseanna [Sweden, 1965], translated by Lois Rotà (NY, 1968; 1993). Melancholy, wife-harried Martin Beck is called in when a young woman—an American tourist—is raped and murdered near Motala on Lake Vattern in this somewhat routine police procedural.

The Man Who Went Up in Smoke [Sweden, 1966], translated by Joan Tate (NY, 1969; 1993). Beck's family holiday on an island in the Stockholm archipelago is interrupted when he is sent to Budapest to investigate the disappearance of a Swedish journalist. Beck "could not remember ever being given such a hopeless, meaningless assignment." But he gets along well with his counterpart in the Hungarian police, and the authors wax uncharacteristically eloquent on the beauties of Budapest.

The Man on the Balcony [Sweden, 1967], translated by Alan Blair (NY, 1968; 1993). A series of brutal muggings in Stockholm parks, followed by the rape/murder of an eight-year-old girl, keep Beck and his colleagues busy and depressed.

The Laughing Policeman [Sweden, 1968], translated by Alan Blair (NY, 1970; 1992). The homicide squad must solve the mass murder of nine bus-riders, who include a blackmailer, the policeman trailing him, and seven innocent bystanders. The murderer is a prosperous businessman.

The Fire Engine That Disappeared [Sweden, 1969], translated by Joan Tate (NY, 1971).

Murder at the Savoy [Sweden, 1970], translated by Amy and Ken Knoespel (NY, 1971). An unscrupulous and exploitative businessman, shot at the Savoy Hotel in Malmö, proves to be more villain than victim.

The Abominable Man [Sweden, 1971], translated by Thomas Teal (NY, 1972). Again the villain is the victim—in this case, a corrupt cop.

The Locked Room [Sweden, 1972], translated by Paul Britten Austin (NY, 1973, 1992). Three cases for Beck and his boys: the murder of a wretched old man behind locked doors; a young woman who becomes a sort of ideological bank robber; the antics of some engaging professional crooks and some ludicrously incompetent cops.

Cop Killer [Sweden, 1974], translated by Thomas Teal (NY, 1975).

The Terrorists [Sweden, 1975], translated by Joan Tate (NY, 1976; 1978 pb). Beck and his team succeed in protecting an unpopular U.S. senator visiting Stockholm from would-be assassins. But in the eerily prophetic climax of the novel (written ten years before the killing of Olaf Palme), a Swedish prime minister is shot down.

NOTED BUT NOT REVIEWED

ALBRAND, Martha. *Nightmare in Copenhagen* (NY, 1954). A young American scientist, summoned to Denmark by an old friend, finds himself caught up in international intrigue over a new explosive.

BODELSEN, Anders. *Think of a Number* [Denmark, 1968], translated by David Hohnen (NY, 1969). A young Danish bank clerk is lured into bank robbery and other crimes.

EKMAN, Kerstin. *Blackwater* (London, 1995; NY, 1996). A literary thriller set in northern Sweden.

JOENSUU, Matti. *The Stone Murders* [Finland, 1983], translated by Raili Taylor (NY, 1986). Vicious teenagers and frightened cops in Helsinki. Written by a sergeant in the Helsinki police.

NIELSEN, Torben. *An Unsuccessful Man* [Denmark, 1973], translated by Marianne Helwig (NY, 1976). Set in Copenhagen, where police superintendent Ancher ("the very image of a Danish Maigret") investigates a purported suicide and the murders of two little girls.

ORUM, Poul. *Nothing But the Truth* [Denmark, 1974], translated by Kenneth Barclay (NY, 1976). Set in a port town in West Jutland, this police novel begins with the discovery of a floating corpse with a bullet hole in its head.

CHECKLIST

Other European Destinations

Austria

ALBRAND, Martha. *A Call from Austria* (NY, 1963).

AMBLER, Eric. *Uncommon Danger* [*Background to Danger*] (NY and London, 1937).

MacINNES, Helen. *Above Suspicion* (London and NY, 1941)—spy thriller.

————. *Horizon* (London, 1945; NY, 1946).

————. *Prelude to Terror* (NY and London, 1978).

STEWART, Mary. *Airs Above the Ground* (NY and London, 1965).

Cyprus

HAGGARD, William. *The Expatriots* (London, 1989; NY, 1990).

KAYE, M. M. *Death Walked in Cyprus* (1956); as *Death in Cyprus* (NY, 1984; London, 1985).

Greece

AIKEN, Joan. *The Butterfly Picnic* (London, 1972).

CAUDWELL, Sarah. *The Shortest Way to Hades* (NY, 1985)—the wittiest of current mystery writers.

COLE, G. D. H. *Greek Tragedy* (London, 1939)—murder on a Mediterranean cruise.

DICKINSON, Peter. *The Lizard in the Cup* (NY and London, 1972)—Greek millionaires and the Mafia.

GODDARD, Robert. *Into the Blue* (London, 1990; NY, 1991).

HIGHSMITH, Phyllis. *Two Faces of January* (London and NY, 1964).

INNES, Hammond. *Levkas Man* (London and NY, 1971).

MacINNES, Helen. *Decision at Delphi* (NY, 1960; London, 1961).

MICHAELS, Barbara. *The Sea King's Daughter* (NY, 1975).

STEWART, Mary. *This Rough Magic* (NY and London, 1964)—classy romantic suspense.

————. *My Brother Michael* (NY and London, 1960).

WHITNEY, Phyllis. *Seven Tears for Apollo* (NY, 1963)

Portugal

PATTERSON, Harry. *To Catch a King* (NY and London, 1979).

Switzerland

DÜRRENMATT, Friedrich. *A Dangerous Game* [1956] (London and NY, 1960; U.S. title: *Traps*)—an important Swiss playwright and novelist who used the conventions of the detective novel for serious moral and literary ends.

————. *The Judge and His Hangman* [1952] (London, 1954; NY, 1955).

————. *The Pledge* [1958] (NY and London, 1959).

————. *The Quarry* [1959] (NY and London, 1962).

EDWARDS, Anne. *Haunted Summer* (NY and London, 1972).

FLEMING, Ian. *On Her Majesty's Secret Service* (NY and London, 1963)—in which Bond gets briefly married.

MOYES, Patricia. *Season of Snows and Sins* (NY and London, 1971).

TREVANIAN. *The Eiger Sanction* (NY, 1972; London, 1973)—espionage and mountain-climbing.

IX

RUSSIA

It was very cold, with the special dreary cold that always settled over Moscow after the holidays. It was the heavy sort of cold that made all men appear identical as they drew their jaws deep into their scarves and stooped against the wind. Women who had reached a smileless age hobbled along under great mountains of clothing, trailing bags stuffed with whatever the day had offered. (Ralph Peters, *Flames of Heaven*)

Moscow was a thieves market for foreign sharks and hustlers, from multinational conglomerates to desperate insurance brokers from Sioux Falls . . . Moscow was a salesman's paradise; its citizens' pent-up urge to consume made them ripe for the plucking. (David Madsen, *USSA*)

"I think people get the kind of government they deserve. In this case, probably better."

"That's not true, Sam. The Russians may not understand democracy, but in some curious way they are passionately devoted to svoboda—freedom."

Hollis [of the CIA] shrugged.

[Lisa Avery said] "I always thought that communism is an historical fluke here. It won't make it to its hundredth birthday."

Hollis replied dryly, "I'd hate to think what these people will come up with next." (Nelson DeMille, *The Charm School*)

Good-Bye to All That

By Anthony Olcott

FOR MOST OF this century, Russia—or at least Moscow—has been a godsend for the practitioners of the mystery and, even more so, the thriller genres, because the props of Russian "local color" have been so easy to haul onstage. Apart from the journalists, junior diplomats, and occasional graduate students who wrote most of these books, until just a few years ago almost no one was able to visit Russia, and even if they were, they were confined to the same three square miles around Red Square as were the diplomats and journalists. Thus the novelists' descriptions of the Ukraine Hotel, Arbat Street, and the Red Arrow overnight train to Leningrad squared perfectly with the experiences of those few travelers able to check up on these authors' authenticity.

Surprisingly few of these journalists- and diplomats-turned-authors could speak Russian, but even in their ignorance they knew more of the language and local customs than did most tourists, who were unlikely even to be able to decipher the mysteries of Russia's distinctive alphabet. Thus, as long as a book offered up the handful of facts that everybody "knows" about Russia—that it is cold, the people drink vodka, and the politics are both byzantine and brutal—all an author had to do to make his scenery look authentic was throw in a few phrases that purported to be Russian, add a few names that sounded like someone gargling a handful of Scrabble tiles, and then send his hero across Red Square in a blizzard. As he trudged he might ponder a quote from Pushkin, Pasternak, or—if the book came from near the "Evil Empire" end of the literary spectrum—from Sun-tzu's *The Art of War.*

Of course, Russia's isolation began to end, slowly, in the 1970s and 1980s, and then with a rush, as Gorbachev's *glasnost* and *perestroika* hurtled the USSR toward collapse. For mystery and thriller writers, Gorbachev's "openness" was literal—for the first time, John le Carré could travel to Moscow and Leningrad, Martin Cruz Smith could visit the Russian Far East, David Ignatius could go to Tashkent, and Lionel Davidson could (apparently) visit deepest Siberia. The result was a breathtaking leap forward in authenticity, as these highly talented writers (and others) were now able to bring us their crisp, vivid observations of the decaying, half-unbuilt, half-destroyed splendors of the late Soviet Empire.

However, that "openness" worked both ways. For the first time Russians began to be able to read the mysteries and thrillers we had written about them, and we began to be able to read theirs. Although there was much mutual politeness in them, such cross-cultural encounters usually left both parties puzzled, because—as we began to discover—there was very little overlap between what *we* consider to be a crime and what *they* consider to be a crime.

To be sure, in both Russia and America such social infelicities as murder, theft, and drug trafficking are formally crimes, and the novels about them treated them as such. However, the causes of these crimes, and the way that a detective might go about solving them, proved to be quite different in the two systems.

American detective stories tend toward a cowboy's view of the universe. The world is an evil place, the wickedness of which can be kept at temporary bay only by the courage, intelligence, and moral conviction of the lone misfit, who is willing to buck the system, even if it means his death.

Transposed to Russia, this type of hero works quite well in espionage and thriller plots, where he (almost never she, for some reason) can be a Westerner. Lionel Davidson's *Kolymsky Heights* (1991) is a prime example; the hero, Johnny Porter, manages to insert himself surreptitiously into farthest Siberia and then, at the price of enormous physical suffering, to get himself out again. James Burch's *Lyubyanka* (1983), Andrew Garve's *Two if by Sea* (1949) and *The Ashes of Loda* (1964), John Kruse's *Red Omega* (1981), Anthony Hyde's *Red Fox* (1985), and both of John le Carré's "real" Russian books, *Russia House* (1989) and *Our Game* (1995), all work thoroughly convincing and satisfying variations on the non-Russian hero. The details of the scenery in these books are usually right, but what is more important, so too is the sensibility of the hero reacting to the scenery, trying to absorb the cold and sinister brutality of that vast, tormented land.

The problems of differences in mentality show up much more vividly in those books by foreigners which attempt to use Russians as their heroes. To Bolsheviks crimes by and against individuals were of little significance. In a socialist system, the desire to rob or to murder was a holdover from the capitalist past, but so too was the petit-bourgeois mentality that would be concerned about *being* robbed, or even, in many circumstances, murdered. After all, in the Communist system, the only person who could accumulate goods enough to make it worth someone's while to steal them was almost certainly a criminal himself.

This did not mean, however, that there was no such thing as crime. To the Russian cast of thought, there was enormous scope for misdeed, but this was of a political nature, the crimes of one class against another, or of a small group of traitors against the people as a whole. As village detective Aniskin explains to a miscreant he has just arrested, a man who had always voted against the Party's candidates so that the village votes would be 99.99 percent, rather than unanimous:

> "I could have arrested you a million times before and you would have ended your life in a camp, but I believe in Soviet power and I put my faith in it completely. There was no prison that is worse than your life . . . Nothing could be more terrible than being one hundredth of one percent, while the people are the rest. You died thirty years ago!" (Vil Lipatov, "The Elk Bone," Moscow, 1970)

What was important in the Soviet system was not the individual—either as criminal or as victim—but rather the social phenomena that either had failed to make crime unnecessary or continued to regard individual possessions as something about which the state should bother itself. As the NKVD man points out, politely but definitively, to Investigator Nikulin in Ivy Litvinov's *His Master's Voice* (1930):

> "It's an open question, however, who is more dangerous to society . . . a man who deprives it of a not particularly valuable life, or one who continues for years systematically undermining trade and the development of industry, thus affecting the lives of countless hundreds. If I could rid society of the speculators I would leave it to deal with the murderers itself."

It should also be remembered that the NKVD's indifference to murder was not just to solving it, but also to committing it. Real murder was so rare in England that it is little wonder that fiction about murder became a genre of endless fascination, but in Russia, where the state itself murdered millions of its own citizens for "crimes" as insignificant as having been born Ukrainian, Tatar, or the child of a writer, what interest might the circumstances of a single death hold?

As a consequence, for all their authenticity of setting, nearly all of the American books that attempt to give us not only Russian scenery but also Russian psychology invariably strike Russians as odd and exotic, if not outright deranged, while American readers find mysteries translated from the Russian to be, at best, incomprehensible, and at worst, inconsequential. Russians tend to conclude that, for all the shrewd brilliance of what Martin Cruz Smith notices about Russia in *Gorky Park, Polar Star,* and *Red Square,* and for all the gripping excitements of his plots, the turns of Arkady Renko's mind tell them a great deal about how Americans think and behave, but very little about themselves (the same criticism is made of my own Ivan Duvakin, whom Russians also regard as pretty much an American in a fur hat).

For our part, Americans have understandable difficulty in getting excited about, for example, Vil Lipatov's story "A Village Detective" (Moscow, 1970), which revolves about the theft of an accordion: This, village detective Aniskin informs us with complete seriousness, is "equivalent to [the theft] of a good cow, and ranks very little lower than that of a motorcycle. If my memory does not deceive me, we have not had such a serious case in this village since 1948. That was when Valka Suchkov pinched two lengths of German woolen cloth from a wounded soldier back from the front." Nor do we fare much better with Mikhail Chernyonok's *Losing Bet* (1984), in which the primary villain buys books in places of low demand and resells them in cities of high demand. To us this is entrepreneurial, and a virtue; to the Russians this is speculation, and a crime.

Might we then conclude that all such differences have been swept away by the coming of capitalism and democracy, or will be shortly? The Russians can now drive Cadillacs and Rolls-Royces, so surely they must object when these are stolen? And murder, in a society that now values its individual citizens enough to permit them to vote, must surely be a crime that needs to be solved?

Perhaps . . . but the available literature so far suggests that there continues to be very little confluence between our notion of crime and theirs. Most Russians see privatization as "piratization," the same theft of public resources that once was conducted on a small scale by blue-collar drunks hustling kopeks to buy cheap vodka, and now is conducted on a nationwide scale by the factory managers, and their bosses, who are hustling dollars by the million, even billion, in order to buy private jets and beach-side villas.

In a land where a handful of public officials have essentially stolen an entire country—talk about "heists of the century"!—it is difficult to ignite public imagination with the theft of anything smaller, just as it remains difficult to get readers to care about individual deaths in a land where the old and infirm die of hunger and cold in the train stations, and where the healthy and well-placed "clarify their relations" with small private armies, or in the case of Chechnya, with a large public one.

For the time being at least, the vicarious traveler should continue to regard Russia as a place where the scene and the crime are best and most authentically rendered separately. To convey the shock of Russia's sensual distinctiveness, we do best with a hero who is a foreigner, and so can notice the millions of strange sights, odd smells, and weird juxtapositions to which a Russian born and bred would never react.

If what we wish to see, though, is the psychology of real Russian crime, we will do best to rely upon the Russians. Some of them, it is true, may continue to bother us about missing accordions and black-market books. However, most of the best Russian writers of this century have in one way or another been doggedly pursuing answers to that quintessential Russian question: *"kto vinovat?"*, or Who is guilty?—guilty of creating the Soviet Union, and then of killing it; of nationalizing all the property, and then of privatizing it; of turning entrepreneurs into criminals, and now criminals into entrepreneurs.

READING LIST

ALEKSANDROV, Nikolai. *Two Leaps Across a Chasm* (NY, 1992). Truth in advertising—I translated this book. I did so, however, because I thought its portrait of the late Soviet era was marvelous. Based on an actual political and financial scandal, the novel tells of the efforts of Sergei Orlovsky, a *glasnost*-era reporter, to expose the interlocking protective mechanisms of corrupt government officials and their equally corrupt KGB friends. Unable to overcome the combined weight of these forces, Orlovsky succeeds in making an ally of Yosif Vashko, the lieutenant in the militia who had originally been sent to arrest him. The sort of honest cop who had thought that the loudly declaimed virtues of the system he was protecting were real, Vashko proves an industrious and imaginative enemy as he begins to understand how deep—and how high up—the country's corruptive rot has spread. For all of Vashko's efforts, however, the novel's ending proves as Russian as a bowl of cold borscht.

CHERNYONOK, Mikhail. *Losing Bet* [Moscow, 1979], translated by Antonio Bouis (NY, 1984). Smoothly and colloquially translated, this is part of a series about Anton Birukov, a militia detective in Novosibirsk. The novel opens with a young woman being flung from the balcony of an apartment, but since she doesn't die until nearly the book's end, it's long unclear whether or not this is a murder mystery. Birukov's investigation has more to do with the woman's past and her circle of acquaintances, neither of which is beyond reproach: this is the world of the black-market "fixers," who used their private initiative to smooth out the lumpy spots in socialist retailing. Like most Soviet mysteries, this is a procedural, but the differences between Russian and American procedures are eye-opening.

DAVIDSON, Lionel. *Kolymsky Heights* (NY, 1994). The long silence of Lionel Davidson might itself make a satisfying mystery: whatever made him write this book fourteen years after his previous one, however, this is vintage Davidson—masterfully told; exotic to the point of fantasy, but still somehow believable (well, almost); and unique. Spy satellites catch an explosion at an underground secret facility in deep Siberia; photos suggest that some of the survivors are chimpanzees, genetically engineered to be humanoid. The only spy who has a chance of bringing out the necessary "hum-int" is Johnny Porter, a Gitksan Indian of stamina and genius; among his other accomplishments, Porter speaks Japanese, Korean, Russian, English, and several of the languages of the northern peoples, all of them well enough to be taken as a native. This improbable hero is worth swallowing, though, for the beauty of Davidson's descriptions of northern Siberia—the rivers that become highways when they freeze; the fires that must be kindled under trucks before they will start; the alcoholism and disease that are ravaging Russia's Chukchis, Evenks, Nenets, and other northern peoples; and the sturdy individualism of the "Sibiriyaks," Russia's equivalent of our wild-westerners.

DINALLO, Greg. *Red Ink* (NY, 1995). One of the first of the post-Soviet mysteries, Dinallo's book is a sympathetic tale of infant democracy drowning in a tide of laundered party-mafia cash. Dinallo has clearly been to the new Russia, but he would have done better to center the novel on his secondary hero—Gabriella Scotto, tough gal agent from the U.S. Treasury—rather than on his Russian, Nikolai Katkov. Some of the touches with Katkov are marvelous, such as that he is a recovering alcoholic trying to fathom the imported mysteries of Alcoholics Anonymous, but there are enough of what the Russians call "cranberries" (factual errors in local color) to undermine the book's authenticity. A Russian would be unlikely to say a policeman was "as big as a refrigerator," for example, since Russian refrigerators are about four feet tall, nor would someone like Katkov ever accuse an ex-girlfriend of trying to pull "a guilt trip," describe a woman as having "*bronskys* out to here," or toast another drinker with the word "*Zadrovnye*" (which if it means anything would mean approximately, "I drink to your logging sled"). Still, stumble though he may on some of the little details, Dinallo gets the main outlines of the new Russia extremely well.

FLEMING, Ian, *From Russia with Love* (NY, 1957). Probably the archetype of the "Evil Empire" genre of thrillers. Most of Fleming's action takes place on the Orient Express, but the opening scenes in Moscow convey perfectly the lumpy somberness of Soviet offices, as well as the dark chill of the world around the Kremlin. Fleming shows a surprising flair for the Russian language—the head of his SMERSH, for example, is General Grubozaboyshchikov ("Coarse-slaughter"), while another character's mother-oath is delicately rendered as "Y*b**nna mat!" It is a bit puzzling, though, to wonder whose sensibilities those asterisks were meant to protect.

FRAYN, Michael. *The Russian Interpreter* (NY, 1966). Perhaps not strictly a thriller or a mystery, this novel reproduces better than any other I know the total paranoia which Soviet Russia was capable of inducing in visitors, even those who were fluent in the language and familiar with the mores. Paul Manning, the hero, is a Brit doing graduate research at Moscow State University. His path begins to be dogged by one Gordon Proctor-Gould, an "old friend" of whom Manning has never heard. Eventually Proctor-Gould meets Manning, and charms him into working as an interpreter for Proctor-Gould's sappy exercises in "international goodwill." The beautiful Raya appears, displacing Katya, Manning's gloomy and unromantic semi-girlfriend, before moving on to Proctor-Gould's bed. By degrees, everyone turns out to be someone else, and Manning ends up in Soviet prison. Frayn captures perfectly the baleful enigmas, the wilderness of mirrors, that was life in Moscow—at least for foreigners—for most of this century.

HYDE, Anthony. *The Red Fox* (NY, 1985). An unusually literate and high-minded thriller, written by a Canadian journalist who had been posted to Moscow. Hyde was one of the first to pick up on the bubbles of Russian nationalism beginning to make their way through the fetid politics of Brezhnev's stagnation period, which gives many of his observations real prescience:

> Was there really a *Russian* dissent within the "Soviet Union" [Hyde's hero wonders]—a dissent that might truly matter? In a way, I thought, this street proved [there might be]. The Bolsheviks had

tried to rename the Nevsky "Avenue of the 25th of October" but it just hadn't stuck. And a lot else hadn't stuck either. Since 1917 Russia had come a great distance, but so had the rest of the world; relatively little had changed. She was the *real* "sick man" of Europe, with a vast, rebellious empire, a desperately backward economy, and a cruelly repressive government.

However, Hyde sets that nationalism in pursuit of Anastasia, the Romanov daughter who was always rumored still to be alive, miraculously spared the bloody end that had caught her parents, sisters, and little brother in that basement in Yekaterinburg. The later course of history has dimmed somewhat the central point of Hyde's speculation—that finding a living thread back to the time before the Bolsheviks might cause the Russians to throw off their shackles—but the virtues of Hyde's lucid prose, and the well-observed authenticity of his Russian settings, place *Red Fox* among the best of the "Russian mysteries."

IGNATIUS, David. *SIRO* (NY, 1991). Ignatius works the Washington-insider's territory, telling stories about the CIA that claim solemnly to be fiction, but which simultaneously wink at us, suggesting that they might be true. Although not as strong as Ignatius's truly remarkable *Agents of Innocence,* which was set in the Middle East, *SIRO* is one of the few thrillers that realizes that there was more to the USSR than just Moscow. Anna Barnes and Alan Taylor, your typical multilingual, super-sexy, and highly proficient CIA agents, go about fomenting nationalist sentiments on the periphery of empire, in the hopes of weakening the USSR. Set in the 1970s, but published when it was clear that nationalist sentiments were indeed threatening the USSR, Ignatius's book manages to suggest that the clumsiness of the CIA as it let Iran slip from our grasp was somehow redeemed by the seeds of revolt it was simultaneously sowing in Uzbekistan, Armenia, and Azerbaijan. Most of the settings are in Europe or Turkey, but Ignatius also makes good use of street scenes in Tashkent, Erevan, and elsewhere:

> [Erevan] was a high, dusty city; most of the buildings had been constructed of the same pinkish stone. The city had a recurring architectural motif as well—a high, rounded arch with the graceful curves of the Armenian alphabet, which looked like it was all "U"s and "M"s.

KAMINSKY, Stuart M. *Death of a Dissident* (1981), *Cold Red Sunrise* (1988), *The Man Who Walked Like a Bear* (1990), *Death of a Russian Priest* (1992), and others. For us pedantic Sovietologists, Kaminsky's mysteries about Moscow cop Porfiry Rostnikov and his team are so full of "cranberries" that they could be used to garnish a darned big turkey, but Kaminsky writes with undoubtable verve. Read these as you might Edgar Rice Burroughs's Tarzan books, for the thrill of the plot and the grace of a story well told, rather than for solid information about what to expect when visiting Africa.

KERR, Philip. *Dead Meat* (London, 1993, NY, 1995). Although he presents this as a post-Soviet mystery, Kerr is really writing about the end of the Gorbachev era, when the stores were empty, the ruble uninflated, and the various mafias still only a dark cloud growling on the horizon. Kerr's first-person detective has been seconded from Moscow to St. Petersburg, to learn about the mafias; this is a neat solution to the problem of how a local detective supplies the kind of touristy "local color" descriptions that make this kind of book fascinating. Kerr's St. Petersburg is spot on—moldering buildings, dank canals, and neglected monuments to past glories. Perhaps surprisingly, Kerr's greatest strength is in the details of Soviet legal method, which are rarely elaborated in books (foreigners generally don't know about them, and Russians know them too well to bother explaining). He is also deeply sympathetic to the plight of good Soviet cops, who genuinely care about the crime that has all but devoured their country, but who have almost no resources with which to fight it.

There is, however, one very disconcerting quirk in Kerr's book—in order to gain authenticity, he gives some of his characters the names of real and well-known people—Sobchak, Kornilov, Voznesensky, Ordzhonikidze—and, what is even more alarming, he gives some of them names from the Russian classics—there is a Lebezyatnikov, a Stavrogin, a policeman named Svridigailov (sic), and even a Mr. Chichikov!

KOLBERGS, Andris. "The Shadow," in A. Kolbergs and V. Lagzdins, *The Shadow* (Moscow, 1991). Kolbergs is Latvia's most famous mystery writer, although this novella is more representative of the turn toward social commentary that mystery writers took in the early *glasnost* period. The story pursues what seem at first to be wholly unrelated threads—a successful but lonely woman senior executive; a struggling but gifted young glassblower; a wastrel son of a well-known professor, who despite having had every advantage of Soviet life is skidding toward a life of crime.

Commission of a petty swindle brings in the militia, who make a crucial error of identification, as a result of which it turns out that the three lives are in fact intimately related. Kolbergs's insistence that environment is the sole determinant of behavior is good Soviet criminology, but the needs of early *glasnost*, which was trying to point out how poisonous the Soviet social environment had become, allow the novella to wander through the lower depths of card sharps, prostitutes, black marketeers, recidivists, and misfits. The book also illustrates how closely the local militia were woven into the fabric of social life; the *chastkovoi*, or beat cop, knows every person in his district.

KRUSE, John. *Red Omega* (NY, 1981). This is a gem of a "what-if" adventure, about a CIA attempt to assassinate Stalin. Much of the book is set outside Russia, because the hero—"El Duro," youngest general in the Spanish Republican Army, and later a *zek* in the *gulag*—attempts so assiduously to avoid being recruited for this mission. Like *The Day of the Jackal,* the plot is basically absurd, but manages somehow to teeter so close to the possible that the novel is truly gripping. Kruse's details of Moscow during Stalin's last days appear thoroughly authentic, and the machinery of his plot inside the Kremlin also manages to seem authentic, if highly unlikely.

LAGZDINS, Viktor. In "A Night at Elk Farm," in A. Kolbergs's and V. Lagzdins's, *The Shadow* (Moscow, 1991). This may be the only Latvian locked-room mystery you will ever have occasion to read. It is the story of a birthday party at a cabin deep in the Latvian woods, attended by various forty-plus midlifers, including Girt Randier, a criminal investigator in the militia. Lucky thing, too, because midway through the party the birthday boy is discovered dead in the root cellar beneath the kitchen. The result is a classic British-style parlor mystery, complete with slowly revealed secrets, concealed adulterous affairs, financial misdealings, and minute but crucial time discrepancies in the tales these Latvian revelers tell. The translation makes the story murkier than it really is, and the conventions of the plot were outdated well before Latvia lost its independence the first time, but the novelty of the setting makes this tale of interest nonetheless. The text makes the obligatory Soviet noises, but the ennui and anomie of these Latvian intellectuals is very convincingly, and revealingly, drawn.

Le CARRÉ, John. *Our Game* (NY, 1995). Le Carré had the luck, or perhaps the prescience, to have this novel, which is set against a background of armed insurrection in the Caucasus, come out just as Moscow's armies began their real-life attempt to stomp Chechen independence into the mud. Having chosen the Ingush rather than the Chechens, le Carré was off by one people, but that did little to diminish the timeliness, or the importance, of what he was exploring. Since the bulk of the plot concerns the preoccupation of the narrator, Tim Crammer, intelligence officer in early retirement, with relations between Emma, his one-time girlfriend, and Larry Pettier, his former agent, who like all scholars of lesser North Caucasian languages is anarchic, charismatic, and sexy as the devil, the book has an oddly self-pitying quality. However, the scenes in "the new Russia" are as accurate—and as hair-raising—as anything that le Carré has written:

> I was facing a detachment of seven or eight armed men in flak jackets. Grenades hung from their belts . . . Two men marched me along a crimson corridor to a darkened observation balcony that looked down through smoked glass onto Moscow's rich, reclining in the plush alcoves of a nightclub. Slow waiters moved among them, a few couples danced. On foreshortened pillars, naked go-go girls rotated mindlessly to the rhythm of rock music. The atmosphere was about as erotic as an airport waiting room. The balcony turned a corner and became a projection room and office. A stack of Kalashnikovs stood against the wall . . . In a far corner a bald-headed man in underclothes was handcuffed to a chair. He was slumped forward, crouching in a mess of his own blood. At a desk not four feet from him sat a pudgy, industrious little man in a brown suit, passing hundred-dollar bills through an electronic money-detector and totting up his findings on a wooden abacus.

————. *The Russia House* (NY, 1989). In the first blossom of *glasnost*, le Carré was invited to Russia, to see the country about whose intelligence agencies he had written so many novels. This novel, the first result of those trips, has a thoroughly Cold War plot—someone is passing information; can we trust him?; better send some amateur enthusiast over to check—but the details of the setting and of the behavior of the Russian characters are given with clinical precision. Le Carré's major topic is the limitation of Cold War thought, and the impossibility of the Western intelligence services adjusting to the new realities of a crumbling Soviet Union, so there is a great deal of philosophizing, along the lines of this musing by Goethe, the informant: "How did our great vision [of the Russian Communists] crumble to this dreadful mess?" The real pleasure of the novel, though, is the density of le Carré's description, which is as good as going to Russia yourself:

> In a broad Moscow street not two hundred yards from the Leningrad station, on the upper floor of an ornate and hideous hotel built by Stalin in the style known to Muscovites as Empire During the Plague, the British Council's first ever audio fair for the teaching of the English language and the spread of British culture was grinding to its excruciating end.

LIPATOV, Vil. *A Village Detective* (Moscow, 1970). The fact that the author's first name is an acronym of "Vladimir Ilych Lenin" says all you need to know about the political orientation of the eight short stories and novellas in this collection, all of which have been translated by different people, none of whom speaks English as a native language. Still, for all the lumpiness of the prose, the doings of Fedor Aniskin, a village militiaman in a tiny remote village on the Ob River, have some genuine charms. Aniskin is a Siberian Nero Wolfe, indolent by nature and too plump to see his own feet, who prefers to solve the few crimes of which his fellow villagers are capable by deduction, based upon his knowledge of the locals. Only one story, "Three Winter Days," deals with a murder—which Aniskin nearly fails to solve because of the confusion wrought by the intrusion into the region of a logging crew. Aniskin triumphs in the end, but, interestingly enough, doesn't bother to chase the murderer, because the miscreant has run off into the taiga, where Aniskin is confident nature and the wilderness will mete out rough justice.

Not only are the details of a remote Siberian village totally convincing, but one of Lipatov's stories has what, for my money, is the *most* Russian "moment" anywhere in literature:

> In the little room which he called the office Aniskin opened both the small windows and got out a few sheets of paper, an untippable inkwell, and an old schoolboy's pen with a "rondo" nib. Having laid all this out on the table he sat down, put his arms on the table and said:
> "You'll have to excuse the cockroaches."

LITVINOV, Ivy. *His Master's Voice* (London, 1930; revised, 1973; re-published, 1989). An Englishwoman who married a Russian diplomat, Litvinov brings the sensibilities—and many of the tricks—of Agatha Christie to this book, but the precision of her Russian details is beyond reproach. The plot is set in 1926, when Russia's version of the Jazz Age was steaming its blissfully unaware way toward a collision with the iceberg of Stalinism. Arkady Pavlov, a successful businessman, has been found slumped dead over a recording by Chaliapin, stabbed in the back with a jeweled Caucasian dagger. The first—but far from the last!—suspect is Tamara Georgievna, a fiercely beautiful but reticent Georgian ballerina from the Bolshoi. Resolution of this mess requires rather more coincidences—misaddressed letters, overheard conversations, and chance acquaintances who just happen to remember the names and faces of the White Eagle underground anti-Bolshevik conspiracy of ten years before—than the genre really permits, but Litvinov's Procurator Nikulin is a likeable sort, who manages to explain a lot of Soviet police procedure.

LOURIE, Richard. *First Loyalty* (NY, 1985). Lourie is a translator and writer of such talent that his attempt at a thriller seems to highlight the mechanical obligations of the genre. The plot, which moves forward on several fronts at once, involves a think-tank in a closed Siberian city that has perfected a life-prolonging serum; a dissident Jew whose beautiful but disillusioned sister lives in Brooklyn; another dissident, this one a poet, who is really a creation of KGB disinformation; the master KGB disinformer himself; a New York literato-translator; and an NYPD cop named Solly who is suffering from a midlife crisis. The Russian settings are a bit generic, since they purport to show cities closed to outsiders, but Lourie's observations of Russian behavior—both émigré and Soviet—are murderously precise. The solemnity that the straight thriller requires rather dampens Lourie's wit, which shows off much better in another of his books, *Zero Gravity* (NY, 1987); neither a mystery nor a thriller, it is even more Russian, and highly recommended.

*MADSEN, David. *USSA* (NY, 1989). Madsen's is a bizarre and eerie book, because it gets nearly every broad outline of the future wrong—and yet manages in its details to be perhaps the best book yet written about the post-Soviet world. In Madsen's reckoning, the USSR does not collapse, but rather is defeated by the United States, in a nuclear exchange

vaut le voyage (see page 4).

that turns most of Siberia to glowing toast. Dean Joplin, Madsen's hero, a former CIA agent who was part of the American occupying administration, and who is now a Marlowe-like private detective, is blackmailed by a gung-ho U.S. government law enforcer into investigating the murder of a Russian businessman, representative of an American timbering firm, in the Kosmos Hotel.

Madsen's plot is fairly predictable (good guys turn out to be bad, and vice-versa), and in the end gets almost silly, but it is not the plot that makes Madsen's book remarkable. Rather it is Madsen's portrait of "commercial Russia" which is so uncannily prescient—the sleaziness, the collusion between the U.S. government, U.S. business interests, and "former commies," and the Third World juxtapositions of newly rich and newly poor in a post-Soviet commercial hell all seem drawn from life. To be sure, Madsen makes one or two wrong guesses about what post-Communist Moscow will be like: "The explosion of sex clubs, red-light districts, and all-night parties that often followed a dictator's dismissal (Franco's Spain for example) had never happened in Moscow. Night life was safe—and earnest."

PETERS, Ralph. *Flames of Heaven* (NY, 1994). A richly detailed, apocalyptic book from the genre of the encyclopedia-thriller. Set in Moscow, Tashkent, Samarkand, and other points of the former USSR, Peters's novel tells the story of the USSR's collapse through the interwoven lives of good soldier Misha Samsonov, poor-little-rich Uzbek girl Shirin Talala, quasi-dissident painter Sasha Leskov, and his even more dissident brother Pavel, who also is a KGB colonel. Peters knows Russian and Russia intimately, although he sometimes demonstrates this mastery by having his characters drop remarks to one another like "Of course you know the Registan [Hotel] in Samarkand?"

Peters also shows his Russianness in his antipathy toward the Uzbeks, who are the bad guys of this book. His view of Central Asia and the yellow-peril threat its "cold-hearted, slant-eyed, inscrutable" people are supposed to present for Russia and its infant democracy springs directly from sodden late-night conversations around ash-strewn kitchen tables in Moscow and Leningrad.

SEMYONOV, Julian. *Petrovka 38* (NY, 1965). Semyonov was probably Russia's most popular and most successful writer, producing both mysteries and thrillers. When his serial, *Seventeen Moments of Spring*, was broadcast, detailing the doings of Sterlitz, a Soviet agent who was supposed to have penetrated the Nazi High Command, all of Russia literally came to a halt; it is rumored that Brezhnev even had Politburo meetings rescheduled so as not to miss Semyonov.

Perhaps not so gripping, this novel nevertheless has many virtues, particularly because of the detailed portrait it gives of the doings of ordinary Soviet policemen; "Petrovka 38" is the address of Moscow's criminal investigation headquarters. Semyonov's novel was the first intimation we had that, in addition to the grand political crimes like Left-Deviationism, Toadying to Revanchists, and Harboring Bukharinite Inclinations, Soviet Russia also suffered from lesser crimes, like murder, armed robbery, breaking-and-entering, and drug addiction. Fortunately, Semyonov's cops Kostyenko, Roslyakov, and Sadchikov (to whom Semyonov gives a stutter, annoyingly reproduced in the text) are able to catch the one sicko who has caused all these crimes, and Moscow is able at novel's end to return serenely to the tasks of building communism.

SMITH, Martin Cruz. *Gorky Park* (NY, 1981). A blockbuster when it came out, Smith's first novel about misfit and loner Arkady Renko continues to find readers fifteen years later. Smith was the first foreigner to get beyond the stage-scenery of touristy Moscow, conveying the claustrophobic, insecure lives of ordinary Russian citizens in a state that valued them at nothing. Smith has a sure eye for authentic details, conjuring up Moscow in all its sullen vastness, crouched beneath a leaden sky. In its day, this book's ending strained credulity, since it was at that time so difficult for most Russians to leave the USSR. That "poetic license" has grown less glaring with time, leaving the virtues of Smith's strong characterization and swift plotting more burnished than ever.

————. *Polar Star* (NY, 1989). It is difficult to imagine the reader who would wish to check on the authenticity of details in Smith's second Arkady Renko mystery. Set on a Soviet fishing trawler in the Bering Sea, the book is a veritable thesaurus of synonyms for "freezing," "slimy," and "dark." However, Smith's portraits of Soviets have grown richer, clearly a product of his own increased knowledge about the USSR. The victim is a Georgian girl, and the suspects include Estonians, Russians, Ukrainians, and even an Uzbek girl (though it is hard to imagine what father in that fiercely patriarchal people might have let his daughter travel alone so far from home; equally difficult to picture on board a trawler is a fisherman named Izrail Izrailovich). Renko's political disgrace, which has sent him to the *Polar Star,* is vividly rendered, and the villain's demise, when it comes, is luridly and imaginatively Russian.

Smith's efforts at authenticity include his characters' names, which are usually a weakness in Russian books by foreigners; however, his solution of using a lot of real names is a little disconcerting, since names like Patiashvili, Chaikovskaya, and Marchuk all belong to real and well-known people, none of whom is easy to picture on this ice-covered fishing boat.

————. *Red Square* (NY, 1992). By the time he was composing his third Renko book, Smith had become a best-seller in Russia, and so an honored and frequent guest. The increase in his familiarity with Moscow shows in this book, which is set on the eve of the 1991 attempted coup (although Smith uses his poet's license to compress some of the events leading up to the coup, leaving only a few months for events that really took about two years). Smith renders beautifully the scruffy flea markets, the moneychangers-in-Mercedes, the various mafias (from Chechnya, Kazan, Almaty), and, best of all, the "political shape-changers" who were beginning so fluidly to transform themselves from Communists into democrats. Renko grows more cynical with every book: "Arkady knew from experience that there were two types of investigations: one that uncovered information, and the more traditional type that covered it up. The second was more difficult since it demanded someone to cover the crime scene and someone to control information in the office." This hardened disaffection makes the ending, a damp-eyed victory for apparent democracy on the barricades of Yeltsin's White House, ring a little hollow, but in no way mars the book. Smith's habit of giving secondary characters the names of real people—Minin, Gubenko, Platonov, Federov—remains disconcerting, but this is without question the best of his three excellent books about Russia.

TARASOV-RODIONOV, Alexander. *Chocolate* (NY, 1932). No Western reader would recognize this as a genre book, but it is perhaps the most perfectly and profoundly Russian of all mysteries. Comrade Zudin is a Chekist, one of the iron Bolsheviks who dispenses life and death as the god of Revolution requires. After more than a decade of service, however, Zudin's revolutionary acuity has grown dim; in a momentary blink of his political consciousness Zudin permits himself to accept the gift of a pair of silk stockings (for his wife) and chocolate (for his children) from a ballerina under interrogation. The error is a fatal one, for Zudin finds himself arrested and, eventually, shot.

As in Arthur Koestler's *Darkness at Noon* (another good political thriller), the mystery *Chocolate* explores—and solves, at least on its own terms—is that of why a man would come not only to confess to crimes he has not committed, but even further to understand that his refusal to accept that false blame is itself a crime, for which he deserves punishment anyway. In Tarasov-Rodionov's words:

> And perhaps, to stigmatize his name [by killing him] was the only possible way. After all, essentially, only one thing was important: the cause. The cause that was bringing happiness as quickly as possible to everyone must not perish! This was the only thing that was important . . . and what would happen if they shot him now, and later told everyone that they had killed a very good comrade? How absurd it would be . . . [People] would say: "If he was not guilty, then why did you kill him? Something must be wrong here!" And all would begin to think something quite different from what they should think. And some . . . would laugh slyly, and, like greedy mice, drag fat crumbs of grain caviar to their little holes, and bottles of wine, and make merry with their secretaries as they smeared the mouths of the starving with clay.

Being mostly interior monologues, and most of those set in prison, *Chocolate* has very little in the way of Russian scenery. However, anyone wishing to ponder the complexities of Russian psychology should consider this to be an essential text—particularly since Tarasov-Rodionov was himself later a victim of the same secret police that this novel so passionately defends.

TOPOL, Edward. *Red Snow* (NY, 1987). Topol is an émigré, so there are no cranberries to be feared in any of his books, even if the need to keep rejustifying emigration tends, perhaps, to push events and characters to the extremes of the moral spectrum. This novel, set on the Yamal Peninsula far above the Arctic Circle, is the most exotic of Topol's books, providing as it does a bleak but fascinating view of the havoc that Soviet gas and oil development has wreaked among the Eskimo-like Nenets people. The point of view alternates between that of Anna Kovina, a Soviet militia investigator (unusual for a woman), and that of Siegfried Shertz, an American loan broker who inadvertently gets caught up in a vendetta between Nenets and Russians. There are also scenes at Yuri Andropov's deathbed (where the young Gorbachev cuts a threatening figure), as well as a surprising amount of sex for a plot that basically takes place at 40 degrees below zero.

The cold splendors of Siberia are the best part of this book. As Inspector Kovina says, "Even in my rucksack the bottle of vodka I had grabbed before starting out had 'separated out' into about two hundred grams of pure alcohol and a mat lump of ordinary ice. In other words, the temperature here was below minus forty."

WILLIAMS, Alan. *Gentleman Traitor* (NY, 1974). A "what-if" about British spy Kim Philby redefecting to the West. Most of the book is set in Moscow, with excellent descriptions of what life was like in the Soviet capital in the late 1960s, at least for journalists, diplomats, and tourists. Williams's details are very evocative—the dour matrons on every hotel floor, zealously guarding the room keys; the hard-currency bars full of drunken Kenyans; the slushy, badly lit roads; the hotels without sink stoppers or drinking glasses. As is usually the case in books, the main character, Barry Cayle, is a bit too perfect and resourceful, but Williams captures the gnawing paranoia that foreigners always felt in Moscow—of never quite knowing whom one was dealing with, nor whether to trust what he was saying.

NOTED BUT NOT REVIEWED

ALLBEURY, Ted. *All Our Tomorrows* (London, 1982).

———. *Man with the President's Mind* (London, 1977).

———. *Moscow Quadrille* (London, 1978).

BURGESS, Anthony. *Tremor of Intent* (NY, 1966). Only a bit of this book is set in Russia, but in its entirety the novel shows what would have happened had Vladimir Nabokov written the James Bond series.

COETZEE, J. M. *The Master of Petersburg* (NY, London 1994). The "detective" is Fyodor Dostoevsky, the villain is the anarchist Nechaev, and the "crime" is writing fiction. Weird, but worth it.

DeMILLE, Nelson. *The Charm School* (NY, 1988).

GARVE, Andrew. *Ashes of Loda* (London, 1964; NY, 1978).

———. *Two if by Sea* (London, 1949; NY, 1986).

JACKSON, James O. *Dzerzhinsky Square* (NY, 1986). By a former Moscow correspondent.

KILIAN, Michael. *Blood of the Czars* (NY, 1984). By a former Moscow correspondent.

MALASHENKO, Alexei. *The Last Red August* (NY, 1993).

ODELL, Kathleen. *Mission to Circassia* (NY, 1977). Set in 1837, and concerning a Brit mad to assist Circassian "freedom fighters" in fending off the Tsar, this novel is sui generis, and wonderful.

SOLZHENITSYN, Aleksandr. *The First Circle* (NY, 1968). Sure, this giant novel does lots more besides, but in part this is the story of electronic surveillance in its infancy, as Stalin's NKVD tries to catch the man who has telephoned to warn one of its intended victims.

ULAM, Adam. *The Kirov Affair* (NY, 1988). Interesting, but demonstrates, alas, that total authenticity (Ulam was Harvard's senior Sovietologist) does not guarantee a good read. Filled with dialogue like: "I speak here as a Party member and not your superior. If it is proven that Feinman and Gurevich have slandered the Russian nation, then I shall of course vote for their expulsion. But if the charges turn out to be false, it will be my duty as minister to take appropriate steps against those who by slandering our coworkers impair the efficiency of this organization and thereby do harm to our Socialist Fatherland."

X

THE MIDDLE EAST

*"You look, if you will allow me to say so, so splendidly healthy and full
of common sense. I'm sure you're just the person for Louise."*

*"Well, we can but try, Dr. Leidner," I said cheerfully. "I'm sure I hope
I can be of use to your wife. Perhaps she's nervous of natives and coloured
people?"*

*"Oh, dear me, no." He shook his head, amused at the idea. "My wife
likes Arabs very much—she appreciates their simplicity and their sense
of humour."* (Agatha Christie, Murder in Mesopotamia)

*My mind wandered . . . to my time at Cambridge University, En-
gland. . . . The fact that I was Arab and Iraqi frequently brought suffering due to the deep-rooted racism of my fellow undergraduates. They
firmly believed Arabs habitually bribe and cheat. We do. The racism lies
in the fact that they believed they did not.* (Julian Rathbone, Sand Blind)

*Hafez Najeer, head of Al Fatah's elite Jihaz al-Rasd (RASD) field intel-
ligence unit, sat at a desk leaning his head back against the wall. He
was a tall man with a small head. His subordinates secretly called him
"The Praying Mantis." To hold his full attention was to feel sick and
frightened.*

*Najeer was the commander of Black September. He did not believe
in the concept of a "Middle East Situation." The restoration of Palestine
to the Arabs would not have elated him. He believed in holocaust, the
fire that purifies.* (Thomas Harris, Black September)

*Jalal was waiting for Hoffman in his lair on the third floor. He looked
just as Hoffman remembered him: perfectly groomed and perfectly hor-
rifying. His skin was a creamy brown, without a blemish or a wrinkle.
The beard was like a Seurat painting, as if each hair had been painted
in separately, each with its own particular shade. The eyes were wide
and dreamy from so many years of pleasure and drug use, but the body*

was still trim and well-toned from daily workouts in the gym. He was dressed in fine linen trousers, a silk shirt that, on a woman, would be called a blouse, and a cashmere jacket so perfectly cut that it fit like a second skin. Hoffman extended his hand, but Jalal gathered him in an embrace.

"My dear, my dear, my dear," said the prince, kissing Hoffman once, twice, a third time. He had that soft, silky way with other men that, among Gulf Arabs, was meant to convey not homosexual desire but good manners. (David Ignatius, *The Bank of Fear*)

From Greenmantle *to* Green Monday

By Vicki Barker

THROUGH THE PRISM of Empire, or the spyglass of the Cold War—for most of the twentieth century, British and American writers have seen in the Arab their own prejudices or fears.

To modern eyes Agatha Christie's Arabs seem affectionate, if cringe-inducing, stereotypes: servants to their colonialist masters, they are a source more of humor than of danger; the Middle East, an exotic setting with little relevance to readers' lives. The Arab was more pawn than threat to superpowers whose arena was Europe.

As the last lights of Empire winked out, World War II brought real dangers, and real horrors, and to mystery writers, a fertile field for archvillains. They generally spoke with thick German accents and sported disfiguring scars incurred during their escape from Hitler's bunker. The Middle East was often a setting in these stories, but rarely more than a backdrop to the main action: a confrontation between hero and Nazi villain, between good and evil.

When the years of world war gave way to the decades of the Cold War, however, the archvillains increasingly spoke with a Russian accent. Bonafide Nazi bogeymen began to feel, and in some cases became, geriatric. Some of them turned up in fictional South American jungles, indoctrinating a younger, friskier generation of killers. Others seem to have been reincarnated in sandals, sunglasses, and burnoose.

As Palestinian terrorism against Jewish targets escalated in the 1960s and '70s, Nazis and Arabs seemed interchangeable to many consumers and purveyors of popular fiction. At a time when the stereotypical depiction of Jews and blacks was being abandoned, authors like Trevanian in *Shibumi* could paint Palestinians as sadistic, sex-crazed murderers with virtual impunity.

The 1973 oil crisis inspired a spate of mediocre thrillers involving oil-rich sheikhs, maniacal mullahs, and square-jawed CIA men. This Arab didn't just have a gun—he had money, and the power that goes with it.

In Saddam Hussein, thriller writers found a villain who is both an Arab *and* a Nazi. The much-televised 1991 Gulf War wasn't even in reruns before writers were folding merciless strongmen, mustachioed torturers, and laser-guided missiles into their plots.

But somewhere out there among all those binary thinkers, a more thoughtful breed of writer labored away. Fueled by a genuine knowledge of, and affection for, the region, sobered by the moral ambiguities of modern war, but nevertheless drawn to the comforting conventions of the mystery/thriller, these novelists are less assured in pointing a finger; more interested in the cultural and historical context of all of their characters.

Thus, David Ignatius's Lina Alwan, who works for the evil, powerful, Nasir Hammoud in *The Bank of Fear,* is "descended from the old aristocracy, the people who had once looked with disdain on newly rich men like Hammoud but had learned, in recent years, to make a grudging peace with them."

Thomas Harris's female assassin and John le Carré's Palestinian hard men are terrorists—but they are the logical products of impersonal history and personal pain. As W. B. Yeats wrote of another group of hard men: "Too long a sacrifice / Can make a stone of the heart." They are believable features on a believable landscape.

And what a human landscape is contained between the Red Sea and the Persian Gulf! The urbane gold trader strolling along the corniche in Dubai; the landlocked Shiite peasant; the epicures of Beirut and Cairo (the lucky ones waiting out their exile in Geneva, Paris, London); the Sufi mystic; the Saudi prince leading a convoy of four-wheel-drives out into the desert for a night under the Bedouin stars; his wives, sporting stiletto heels and skin-tight jeans under their long black *abayas;* his middle-class subject, watching the recession nibble away his subsidies and yearning for more freedom; the miniskirted Iraqi undergraduate; her terrified young

brother, hiding from the draft; the ancient traditions, the new money—
if Islam and anti-Zionism are what most of them share, the best writers
understand the fascination that lies in that which makes each unique.

READING LIST

Reeva S. Simon includes an annotated list of more than five hundred
titles in *The Middle East in Crime Fiction: Mysteries, Spy Novels, and Thrillers
from 1916 to the 1980s* (NY, 1989). What follows is a mere sampling of
the crime novels and thrillers with Mideast settings.

BUCHAN, John. *Greenmantle* (London, 1916). "I had just finished
breakfast and was filling my pipe when I got Bullivant's telegram. . . ." Is
there an Anglophile alive who can resist reading on after that opening
sentence? The time is 1915, and the setting quickly shifts from an English country house to wartime Germany and the trenches of occupied
Turkey, but the sensibility is high Victorian; the heroes, two aristocratic
Muscular Christians who wear their accomplishments as insouciantly as
their Jermyn Street shirts.

The narrator, Richard Hannay, is charged with a mission on which the
fate of the war, and the Empire, could hang: to investigate Germany's secret plans to launch a Jihad (an Islamic holy war) in the East, and to thwart
those plans. The last Englishman who tried to penetrate the mystery lived
only long enough to jot down three clues: *Kasredin, cancer,* and *v.I.* Hannay is that archetypal Englishman, the amateur; although his German is
"good enough to pass for a native," he speaks neither Arabic nor Turkish, and knows nothing about Islam. He protests that he has no qualifi-
cations for the job, but is, of course, persuaded to take it on. And then,
when he suggests an old friend for the mission, his spymaster replies:

"Billy Arbuthnot's boy? His father was at Harrow with me. I know
the fellow—Harry used to bring him down to fish—tallish, with
a lean, high-boned face and a pair of brown eyes like a pretty girl's.
I know his record, too. There's a good deal about him in this office. He rode through Yemen, which no white man ever did before. The Arabs let him pass, for they thought him stark mad and
argued that the hand of Allah was heavy enough on him without
their efforts. He's blood brother to every kind of Albanian bandit.
Also he used to take a hand in Turkish politics, and got a huge reputation. . . . You say he's in your battalion. I was wondering what

had become of him, for we tried to get hold of him here, but he had left no address. Ludovick Arbuthnot—yes, that's the man. Buried deep in the commissioned ranks of the New Army? Well, we'll get him out pretty quick!"

"I knew he had knocked about the East, but I didn't know he was that kind of swell. Sandy's not the chap to buck about himself."

The stolid amateur and the Lawrence of Arabia figure take on two other companions: a slow-talking, quick-witted American named John Blenkiron, and Peter Pienaar, a pugnacious Boer and expert tracker. The men make their separate, ingenious ways to Istanbul, which they reach after a series of harrowing encounters with three nemeses: an evil German general, a corrupt Turkish nobleman, and the archvillain of the book, a beautiful and dangerous German noblewoman. To say that all three villains meet their comeuppance in the denouement, and that the plot to launch an anti-English Jihad is foiled, gives away none of the joy of the book's resolution.

The sexually knowing will smirk at the clumsy perplexity with which the English heroes regard women; the politically correct will wince at the offhand bigotry of the characters, who are, after all, very much the products of their time; but students of contemporary Islam will smile ruefully at the words of Sir Walter Bullivant, who sets Hannay on his quest into the Muslim heart of darkness: "There is a dry wind blowing through the East, and the parched grasses await the spark."

CHRISTIE, Agatha, *Murder in Mesopotamia* (UK, 1936; frequently reprinted). At a remote archeological site in northern Iraq, the beautiful, infuriating American wife of the dig's director alternately charms and bullies other members of the expedition. Mrs. Leidner insists that supernatural forces are ranged against her. Her fears and visions are dismissed as neurosis, until she is found dead one afternoon. Her head has been bashed in, but no one has been seen to enter or leave her room. By happy coincidence, M. Hercule Poirot happens upon the scene. His investigations are assisted and chronicled by Nurse Amy Leatheran, "cheerful, robust, shrewd and matter-of-fact," who had been hired by Dr. Leidner as a companion to his wife. The usual delicious Christie ingredients are all in place: the locked-room mystery; the surfeit of suspects, deftly sketched; the puzzles within the puzzle.

Nurse Leatherman's Iraq is "not romantic at all, not at all like you'd think from the *Arabian Nights*! . . . The *dirt* and the *mess* in Baghdad you wouldn't believe. . . . Of course, it's pretty just on the river, but the town itself is just awful—and no proper shops at all." Like the background of a cartoon, the local color is even more broadly drawn than the characters, creating an impression of heat and dust and little else.

Agatha Christie's Iraq was the Mesopotamia of her husband, the archeologist Sir Max Malloran. The author clearly knows her querns, pestles, and stone-axes, even if her narrator does not! Readers of Christie's autobiography may observe that the fictional Mrs. Leidner bears a striking resemblance to the charming, manipulative wife of an archeologist Christie encountered at the Ur excavations. Thus, the consolation of the mystery writer: to commit on paper crimes that one can only daydream about in life! (See also *Death on the Nile* [1937] and *They Came to Baghdad* [1951].)

DAVIDSON, Lionel. *A Long Way to Shiloh* (London, 1966; in the United States *The Menorah Men*, also 1966). The original menorah, symbol of the Jewish faith, has been lost for nearly two thousand years. Lost, apparently, beyond recovery—until the discovery of a scroll fragment sets off a deadly treasure hunt. Jordanian smugglers may have solved the puzzle; Israeli intelligence recruits Englishman Caspar Laing, brilliant but dissolute professor of Semitics, to crack the code before the menorah falls into the enemy's hands.

In this book published one year before the 1967 war, Lionel Davidson's Israel is skittish and well armed, and ringed by neighbors who do not wish her well. Caspar Laing's quest takes him across a biblical landscape whose past and present are evoked with unsentimental zest:

The wilderness of Zin was the southern limit of the territory variously ascribed to the tribes of Simeon and Judah; the northern one of their much-abused neighbors the Edomites. They were all of them quite welcome to it. It looked perfectly hideous this morning, the great rubble-strewn plain coloured a diarrhoeic green by the torrential rains. Away to the left three thousand years ago had appeared the enormous horde of the Children of Israel, whose appalled reaction is well reflected in Moses' plaintive cry in the 17th chapter of Exodus: "What shall I do unto this people? They be almost ready to stone me." The Children had a point, of course.

Much about this book is irresistible: the almost-tactile sense of place; the thrill of solving an ancient mystery; the excitement of the chase. The vanished authors of the scrolls are brought to life in the narrator's imagination: hurriedly hiding their treasured writings ahead of an advancing Roman army, could they not also have stashed away treasures from the Temple in Jerusalem?

The narrator is just the sort of waspish, brilliant professor who packs college lecture halls worldwide: the roué whose drinking and wenching are redeemed—or perhaps inspired—by his infectious love for his subject matter. However, although the evocations of history, geography, and politics hold up well, there's something dated about all that drinking and wenching: the drinking is described in a detail too loving for the generation of readers who grew up with ALANON; the sex is early *Playboy*, featuring as the romantic interest a shapely, highly sexed woman who gives up her virginity with grateful murmurs, and no emotional mess, after token resistance.

EASTERMAN, Daniel. *The Last Assassin* (London, 1984). One of the more briskly paced petro-thrillers, it opens in prerevolutionary Iran where Peter Randall, the CIA's man in Tehran, is sucked into the search for a shadowy fundamentalist sect after his girlfriend is murdered by one of its assassins. The action moves from Iran to New York to Washington, D.C., where Randall foils an attempt on the life of President Carter, but fails to catch the ringleader of the plot. Inevitably, Randall discovers that forces in the Agency have their own reasons for letting sleeping assassins lie; and when he slips back into the Ayatollah's Tehran with a beautiful Iranian companion and a price on his head, it is as a rogue agent.

Easterman teaches Arabic and Islamic studies in England. There is much authentic detail about Islamic fundamentalism, and a convincing depiction of the Haj, the faithful's pilgrimage to the forbidden city. There is also much inauthentic, unwittingly hilarious detail on spycraft (a CIA agent in Tehran telephoning a deep-cover Mossad agent asks, "Is this line sterile?" What if the answer is *"No!"*?), and the shadowy cult is so shadowy that one quickly loses count of assassins. Nevertheless, the rather purple prose (suns, and eyes, are always "burning") keeps the action rattling along, rather like one of those rickety Middle Eastern buses that somehow reach their destination in spite of their defective machinery.

FOLLETT, James. *Mirage* (London, 1988). It's Israel, 1967. Handsome pilot Daniel Kalen is shot down in the final hours of the Six-Day War. He escapes with a crippling foot injury. Invalided out of the Israeli Air Force, Daniel is handed a job with El Al in London as a consolation prize. Then, when the French cancel Israel's order for fifty Mirage jet fighters, he concocts an audacious plan to steal the blueprints so Israel can build her own fighter jets. Reluctantly, the head of Mossad approves the idea: reluctantly because, unbeknownst to Daniel, the head of Mossad is also Daniel's adoptive father.

There is a romantic interest, of course, and no shortage of murderous adversaries: a rogue CIA agent eager to avenge the deaths of friends killed in the Israeli attack on the U.S. spy ship *Liberty,* and a corrupt aircraft dealer who stands to lose $25 million in sales if Daniel's mission succeeds. Based on actual events, *Mirage* manages to sandwich a lively history of the Israeli military between action that moves from Israel to London to Switzerland.

FOLLETT, Ken. *The Key to Rebecca* (London, 1980). The time is 1942; the place is British-occupied Cairo. Rommel is advancing across the desert, pounding the British lines. The fighting men on both sides are hampered by inadequate logistical support and myopic superiors. But Rommel has a secret weapon: a spy in Cairo who has managed to penetrate the British military's inner circle. The only man who can stop him is a British intelligence officer, Major William Vandam.

Throw in a courageous Jewish courtesan, a depraved belly dancer, and a secret code, and all the ingredients of the espionage potboiler are present and accounted for. The German spy Alex Wolff is sexy, cruel, resourceful; his British adversary is clear-eyed, straight-jawed, and honorable. Despite the rather wooden prose, the action zips along, with help from a supporting cast of pickpockets, desert nomads, Egyptian nationalists, corrupt officials, and bigoted, bored expatriates.

GUR, Batya. *Literary Murder: A Critical Case* (NY, 1993, 1994). A famous, philandering poet is found horribly dead in his Jerusalem University office. Across the country, one of his most promising teaching assistants dies in a suspicious scuba diving accident. In the course of his interrogations, the decorative detective Michael Ohayon must consider the nature of literary and critical sensibilities; the place context has in the judgment of literature; and the sources of poetic inspiration. Internecine wars over access to the department secretary; petty professional jealousies; academic feuds lasting entire careers: such things are universal, it appears. The joy, here, is in the specifics and in the opportunity to see Israelis as they see themselves. Thus, the academics' first impulse on discovering the dead poet is to call their local security officer, to make sure there is no terrorist connection. There is virtually no local color on offer: the author clearly assumes her Israeli readership is personally acquainted with all the settings. With her intellectual curiosity and her character-driven plot, Gur is an Israeli P. D. James. (See also Gur's *The Saturday Morning Murder: A Psychoanalytic Case* [1992], and *Murder on a Kibbutz: A Communal Case* (NY, 1994, 1995).

HARRIS, Thomas. *Black Sunday* (NY and London, 1975). The thriller that launched Harris, and nearly did in the Super Bowl, *Black Sunday* is largely set in the United States, but includes an excellent evocation of 1970s Beirut, before the Israelis bombed the PLO out of town. Michael Lander, blimp pilot, Vietnam veteran, former POW, madman, is haunted by demons, consumed with rage and obsessed with fantasies of one final act of revenge: detonating six hundred kilos of plastic explosives over the Superdome. A human time bomb with the presence of mind to set his own timer, Lander forges an alliance with the Black September terrorist group. As he and his Palestinian lover, Dahlia Iyad, rush to complete their bomb, they are hunted by Mossad agent David Kabakov.

Some of the elements that would later make Harris's *Silence of the Lambs* and *Red Dragon* such mesmeric reading are already in place in this early book: his fascination with the hunter's relationship to the hunted; his empathy with monsters physical and monsters moral; and his ability to explain, without excusing, them. A former journalist, Harris brings a meticulous eye to everything from the correct operation of dirigibles to the proper procedures for smuggling hashish. Mossad agents and Palestinian terrorists play cat-and-mouse against the American landscape, largely ignored by federal authorities who cannot or will not see the danger. This America is still two decades away from the World Trade Center bombing and Oklahoma City; it has yet to learn that terrorism can strike at home, and may even be homegrown.

IGNATIUS, David. *The Bank of Fear* (London, 1994). Sam Hoffman is a London-based American financial consultant. His upbringing as the son of the CIA's Beirut station chief has left him with a repugnance for the Cold War cowboys of his father's hard-drinking generation. It has also left him with an affectionate knowledge of the Arab language and culture. When a Filipino butler comes to him begging him to investigate the rape and murder of his wife, Hoffman tries to refuse the job, explaining that he only investigates financial matters. But when the Filipino claims that the murderer is his employer, an Iraqi financier, and that the British police have suspended their investigation, Hoffman's interest is piqued. Like a twentieth-century Theseus, his questions lead him deeper and deeper into the labyrinth, toward an inevitable confrontation with the Minotaur.

Ignatius draws a convincing portrait of "the silent ones," the trusted, Iraqi-born London employees of the mysterious financier, who wear Western clothes and sport the trappings of Western wealth, but who remain as much the prisoners of their thug regime as the loved ones they left back home. Hoffman's ally, and romantic interest, is Lina, one of the silent ones: "Keep your head down; cash your check; spend your money. That was how the silent ones lived. Lina . . . had learned to ask as few questions as possible. She had no idea where Nasir Hammoud's fortune came from and no interest in finding out. Like most of Hammoud's 'trusted employees,' she was frightened of him. She remained with Coyote Investment for the same reason as most of the other Iraqis: the pay was good and she was too scared to leave." But this hair-trigger equilibrium is upset by Hoffman and his inquiries, and Lina is forced to run for her life.

Better than any other thriller that takes Iraq as its theme, *The Bank of Fear* leads us through the circles of hell, Arab style, introducing us to the Saudi, Kuwaiti, and Iraqi billionaires and their finances—the big fish in what Hoffman senior calls the "Sea of Money." Saddam Hussein's Iraq, with its terror apparatus and prisons and torture chambers, is harrowingly evoked, as are the antics of an expatriate intelligentsia alternately spirited and cowed. A jacket blurb compares Ignatius to Graham Greene; Ignatius's characters don't have Greene's ability to evoke a cosmic context in the political. But Ignatius does yeoman service as a Virgil, taking us through the circles of a very real and very particular inferno.

This is the third in Ignatius's trilogy about America and the Middle East. The other two volumes are *Agents of Innocence* (1987) and *SIRO* (1991).

LE CARRÉ, John. *The Little Drummer Girl* (London, 1983). At the height of the terrorist attacks in Europe, Israeli intelligence recruits a radical English actress for the role of her life: infiltrating a Palestinian terror cell.

The world has changed since the time of *Greenmantle*. The English amateur treads less confidently on the high moral ground. Promiscuous, passionate, and ill-informed, Charlie is a half-baked revolutionary ripe for seduction. As she is sucked deeper into the orbit, first of her spymasters and then of her Palestinian targets, she assumes masks upon masks. The reader watches her watching through each successive mask, seeing each side first as victim, then as villain.

Much of the action takes place in familiar le Carré territory, postwar Britain and Cold War Germany (see Chapter V, "Germany"). But when Charlie is sent for guerrilla training in Lebanon, the reader travels with her to a Palestinian refugee camp:

> She thought at first sight that he had brought her to a village, for the terraces of white huts that clambered down the hillside looked quite attractive enough in the headlights. But as the drive continued, the scale of the place began to reveal itself, and by the time they had reached the hilltop, she was in a makeshift town built for thousands, not hundreds. . . .
>
> The narrow street had a candlelit darkness. Open drains ran down the centre; a three-quarter moon drifted above the hills. The tall girl led the way; the boys followed with machine guns and Charlie's shoulder bag. . . . The noise was the night noise of exile. Rock and patriotic music mingled with the timeless murmur of old men.

The Little Drummer Girl marked a departure from le Carré's Cold War espionage novels, and it foreshadowed such later works as *Russia House*. The narrative point of view is still world-weary, unsentimental, and mistrustful of the bureaucrats on both sides. But, for a change, protagonists caught up in the struggle between great powers are redeemed, not destroyed, by love.

LEASOR, James. *Passport for a Pilgrim* (London, 1968). British physician Jason Love is packing for a medical convention in Damascus when one of his patients comes to him for a favor. The patient's daughter has been killed in a car crash in Syria recently; the father asks Love to photograph her grave and learn some of the details of her death. In the course of this innocent mission, Love stumbles across a few not-so-innocent discrepancies—and then quite literally stumbles across the dead girl, very much alive but drugged in a Damascus clinic. Clearly, all is not as it seems. Then again, neither is Dr. Love: when the guns start being waved about we discover that he had been an intelligence operative during the war. Love meets up with a former colleague, and the two of them embark on a James Bond–style adventure, eventually rescuing, not just the damsel, but a couple of kidnapped Albanian medical geniuses along the way. The Cold War backdrop, a fugitive Nazi villain, a sinister desert monastery, and 1960s-era "high-tech" gadgets (homing devices planted in cigarette packs, electronically implanted mind-reading devices) lend this outlandish tale (one of a series) a certain dated charm.

PEARCE, Michael. The Mamur Zapt mysteries. This series is set in turn-of-the-century Cairo, in the waning days of British administration, when the English colonialists still thought the ousted French colonialists were their biggest headaches. Desultory plot development echoes the heat-slowed lives of the books' protagonists: corpses are thin on the ground, but the characters gradually grow on the reader as they develop through the books. The detective here is an English policeman/detective who holds the ceremonial title Mamur Zapt; formerly secret police chief to the sultans, the job description is now more that of a police chief without portfolio. Recommended:

The Mamur Zapt and the Donkey-Vous (NY, 1990). An ancient, proper French gentleman vanishes from the terrace of Shepherd's Hotel. Is there a connection with the abduction months before of a Greek-born merchant from the bazaar? What do the donkey boys know?

The Mamur Zapt and the Spoils of Egypt (London, 1992). The golden age of Egyptian archeology was, in this account, simply legalized looting by foreign adventurers. Who tried to push the annoying American lady under a bus?

The Mamur Zapt and the Camel of Destruction (London, 1993). An Egyptian functionary is found dead at his desk. The Mamur Zapt's investigations take him to a malodorous quarter of the Old City whose residents are being threatened by an unknown hand.

PETERS, Elizabeth (Barbara Mertz). *Night Train to Memphis* (NY, 1994; London, 1995). American Vicky Bliss is a detective for feminists and post-feminists alike: tall, blond, and sardonic, a former art thief turned assistant curator at a Munich museum, at once successful and desired. As she flits across the map solving mysteries, Vicky is usually surrounded by a gaggle of yearning men—but, secretly, her heart belongs to her lover and adversary: the mysterious and elusive "Sir John," con man, thief, and master of disguise. The two play cat-and-mouse with each other through a series of books. In this one, the stakes are murderously high.

The German police persuade Vicky to pose as a lecturer in Egyptology on a luxury cruise up the Nile; her real job is to foil a criminal whose identity is not known to the authorities but whom they know to be on the ship. The suspect, not surprisingly, turns out to be her lover. Rather more surprisingly, he turns up with his new bride on his arm.

Before the various mysteries and misunderstandings are disentangled, there is a murder, a theft of antiquities, abductions and rescues too numerous to count, and a chase across the desert. Oh, and some bad guys from Vicky's past come back to haunt, taunt, and hunt her down.

This sort of story is known as a romp. The Egyptian setting rarely intrudes on the antics.

RATHBONE, Julian. *Sand Blind* (London, 1993). Set in Spain and Iraq in the months leading up to Saddam's 1991 trouncing at the hands of American pinball machines, this thriller is very good on the technology that turned the tide of the war. The author has dextrously interwoven the fictional and the historical. Much of the action takes place in Spain in 1990, where a disillusioned English radar technician is hired to develop some sophisticated antiradar software. By the time he realizes his employers are the Iraqis, he also realizes that they have the power of life and death over those he loves.

Rathbone's Saddam is a believable monster; he is in fact one of the most plausible characters in the book, and some scenes set in the presidential palace have a chilling reality. Unfortunately, *Sand Blind*'s English author commits some howlers in his attempts to capture American slang; the female honey pot/assassin seems cut with another author's cookie cutter; and the sex scenes seem to take place under the light of a naked 100-watt bulb: too much light, too little heat. Nevertheless, for those who watched the war on CNN, it's diverting to watch the fictional characters borne closer and closer to familiar, historical events.

ROSENBERG, Robert. *Crimes of the City* (NY, 1991; London, 1992). Avram Cohen is a Holocaust survivor, "old enough to remember goose-step marches outside his bedroom window in Berlin and yet young enough to be commander of the Criminal Investigations Department for the Jerusalem police, [he] was wise enough to know that ideals can be rusted by politics." Cohen has three crimes to solve: the grenade attack on a group of peace demonstrators; the butchering of two nuns in a Russian convent; and the apparent copycat knifing of a nameless beggar with a concentration camp number tattooed on his arm. Gradually, he comes to feel that, even if there turn out to be three separate murderers, there is only one true culprit: the possessive, religious mania that Jerusalem, city of peace, can inspire in visitor and inhabitant alike. "In America," a psychologist observes, "they have psychosexual crimes. We are beginning to witness psychomystical crime."

Rosenberg's fictional detective spends as much time clashing with Israeli bureaucrats as he does tracking down the truth. He tangles with a prime minister who bears a striking resemblance to Menachem Begin, falls afoul of the intelligence services when he tries to investigate the Russian convent's resident KGB agent, and incenses the religious right when his investigation focuses on one of their leaders. All have political reasons for wanting the investigation slowed or stopped. In the end, the fictional detective tracks down the sickos, without curing the disease. Offstage, the *intifada* is gearing up; but Rosenberg is more concerned with the deeds and the misdeeds of Jews. Four years before the assassination of Yitzhak Rabin, the author of the aptly titled *Crimes of the City* was telling Israelis that how a religious state deals with its fanatics is a test of that nation's soul.

STEWART, Mary. *The Gabriel Hounds* (London, 1967). Christabel Mansel, spirited, spoiled, and rich, is touring the Middle East when she runs into her dashing first cousin, Charles. He suggests that she try to visit their eccentric great aunt who long ago retired, like the legendary Lady Hester Stanhope, to live like a pasha in reclusive splendor in a mountain fortress. When Christy makes her way to the palace of Dar Ibrahim, however, she finds a disturbing ménage in place: a taciturn head servant; a sullen, beautiful serving girl; and an indolent, enigmatic young Englishman. Great Aunt Harriet, when Christy is finally granted a midnight audience, turns out to be a bald and turbaned termagant, lolling among dusty brocades. Although Aunt Harriet seems sane enough, Christy is left with the sense that something is terribly wrong in the pasha's palace. She and Charles decide to investigate—and are quickly caught up in a mystery that threatens their very lives.

Set in Lebanon in the 1960s, *The Gabriel Hounds* features one of the more satisfactory denouements in escapist literature, combining fire and water and a stampede of rodents.

THOMAS, Ross. *The Mordida Man* (London, 1981). When an international terrorist named Felix is snatched off a London street by operatives with American accents, his close friend, the possibly insane ruler of Libya, is displeased. So displeased that a Libyan delegation on a private visit to the United States departs hastily—taking along Bingo McKay, good ole boy, operator, and brother of the president of the United States. Clearly, an exchange of hostages is called for. Unfortunately for Bingo and the president, the CIA didn't take Felix, and they don't know who did. The reader does know: it was a renegade CIA man in the pay of renegade multizillionaire Leland Timble. Timble has everything money can buy, except the luxury of living as a free man in the United States; he hopes that, in exchange for turning over Felix, the federal government will forget all about the embezzled bank funds that financed Timble's self-imposed exile in the Caribbean.

As you may by now suspect, this is a world in which nothing goes according to plan; unfortunately for Timble, Felix proves to be allergic to sedative-tipped umbrellas, and he dies during his abduction. So the kidnapping becomes a con, with Timble attempting to shake down both the Libyans and the Israelis for ransom money.

While the CIA searches frantically for both Felix and Bingo, the president's top adviser quietly enlists help from a less official quarter: Chubb Dunjee, decorated Vietnam War veteran, former one-term congressman and bare-knuckled political operative, who earned the nickname "The Mordida Man" during an extremely profitable stint in Mexico.

A Mordida Man is a social lubricant in a corrupt society: he lives by giving bribes and peddling influence. Chubb Dunjee is also living in self-imposed exile, in Portugal, having tried to declare $251,817 in bribes as a business expense. Like Timble, he, too, would like to go home; so he agrees to take on the case.

The action rockets around England, America, Italy, Malta, and Libya, but Ross Thomas is more interested in bulldozing his way through a human landscape. The CIA men in *The Mordida Man* are the buccaneers who ran wild during the sixties and seventies, wily and corrupt, with spreading beer guts and an eye for the main chance. The possibly insane leader of Libya looks and acts an awful lot like Mu'ammar Gadhafi, although he is rather pointedly described as Gadhafi's successor; possibly because, at the time of writing, author Thomas could not be sure that the real-life supreme leader was going to survive U.S. attempts to vote him out with F-111 fighter jets.

NOTED BUT NOT REVIEWED

AMBLER, Eric. *A Coffin for Dimitrios.* See Chapter IV, "Eastern Europe."

———. *The Levanter* (NY, 1972). An American journalist is caught up in the plots of a Palestinian guerrilla leader.

———. *The Light of Day* (London, 1964). The "Topkapi" caper.

ANGUS, Sylvia. *Death of a Hittite* (NY, 1969). At a remote archeological dig in Turkey, the journalist hero finds a new body in an old tomb.

CHUBIN, Barry. *The Feet of a Snake* (London, 1984). Ordinary businessman Michael Adel is coerced into a spy mission back into the Iran he last knew before the Islamic revolution.

DeMILLE, Nelson. *By the Rivers of Babylon* (NY and London, 1978). Palestinian terrorists blow up the Concorde . . . and that's just Chapter Six!

PETERS, Elizabeth. *The Last Camel Died at Noon* (NY and London, 1991). Egyptologist Amelia Peabody and her husband set out for an archeological dig in nineteenth-century Sudan, only to be drawn into the search for a vanished African explorer. The nineteenth-century Amelia narrates with twentieth-century diction and wit.

ROBBINS, Harold. *The Pirate* (NY, 1974). Ostensibly set in Europe and the Middle East, most of the action takes place inside the pants of its super-rich characters. A tale of greed, lust, and passion. Shockingly dull.

ROBINSON, Lynda. *Murder in the Palace of Anubis* (NY, 1994). Whodunit set in ancient Egypt.

SIMON, Roger L. *Raising the Dead* (NY, 1988; 1989 pb). Moses Wine, Simon's L.A.-based wisecracking Jewish private eye, finds himself in Jerusalem working for Arabs.

THOMAS, Michael. *Green Monday* (NY, 1980). In the wake of the Arab oil crisis, one of the first and best of the oil-fueled financial thrillers. "Green Monday" is the day the stock market goes bananas.

XI

AFRICA

Pointe Noire was a big, sprawled-out, fly-blown, ill-tempered town knocked flat on its back by the heat. (Matthew Head, *The Cabinda Affair*)

She turned to me and said, "Have you decided what you would like to do today? Is it the fetishes? You look dressed for an outing." (Head, *The Cabinda Affair*)

African military officer: "Tell me, Mr. Upshaw, do you really believe that this country of mine is ready for representative democracy?" Upshaw: "I don't know if any country is ready, except Switzerland." (Ross Thomas, *The Seersucker Whipsaw*)

There is a storm in the air and when it breaks the lightning may strike anyone. (John Wyllie, *To Catch a Viper*)

"Afraid I must go, Lisa. It's getting late, and my headlights are not all they should be." (M. M. Kaye, *Death in Kenya*)

Now You See It, Now You Don't

By Richard Lipez

SINCE NEARLY ALL the mysteries set in Africa have been written by non-Africans—or by European immigrants whose connections to the continent are tenuous—in many of these books the place has a mirage-like quality. The topography is described, and the weather is reported, but the continent's humanity is indistinct. This is especially true in colonial-era mysteries, where African men are "boys" who labor in the fields or

turn down bwana's bed, and African women are exotic roadside at-
tractions. The Africans assert their presence from time to time in these
mysteries—most often as petty thieves—but they are mainly strange folk
in the background who practice their superstitions, pad around in the
dark, and forget to serve tea on time. Read enough of these, even the best
ones, and you begin to understand why in East Africa it took the Mau
Mau uprising just to get the white settlers' attention.

Which is not to say that within these serious limitations some fine
mysteries haven't been written for and about the Europeans and other
immigrants and passers-through. Matthew Head (pseudonym for art
critic John Canaday) is witty, Elspeth Huxley observant, and Graham
Greene bleakly eloquent in their preindependence stories. And each in
his or her own way entertainingly, sometimes even movingly, evokes
Africa as the colonials experienced it.

Most of the postcolonial African mysteries have also been written by
non-Africans, and while they, too, tend to center on white people's tribu-
lations, the best of them—and not always the most recent—bring alive
the real Africa in its fascinating human multiplicity. John Wyllie's series
featuring West African detective Samuel Quarshie, a Western-educated
physician who hasn't abandoned his roots, is a mother lode of lore about
traditional African animist religions (see *To Catch a Viper*). Quarshie uses
his knowledge of and respect for "magic" to solve crimes, even those involving Africans who consider themselves modernized but whose heads
are sometimes still full of the old spirit world.

Dennis Casley, in *Death Underfoot,* introduces a Kenyan police detective, James Odhiambo, who must puzzle out the white folks and their
peculiar ways, do the same thing with traditional Africans, and make his
way among the tribal chauvinists and corrupt politicians who replaced
the racist colonials in running so many African nations. (See below for a
separate look at mysteries set in South Africa.)

Of the few mysteries written by Africans, not many are available outside Africa—Ngugi wa Thiong'o's bitter tract *Petals of Blood* is one—but
the MacMillan "Pacesetter" novels can be found in Nigeria and some other
countries. According to an essay in *Mysteries of Africa,* edited by Eugene
Schleh, these are pulpy thrillers in which the African Westernized elite
are chauffeured around in Mercedeses as they try to stamp out violently
superstitious lowlife types. The Pacesetter books provide insights into the

African urban upper classes and their ambivalence toward traditional Africa.

Civil war has been a depressing fact of life in several African regions since colonial rule ended, and some of the most devastating accounts of these wars—which often were fueled by the Cold War superpowers— have appeared in thrillers by, among others, Philip Caputo and Thomas Keneally. (See "Horn of Africa" mysteries, below.) In wars where the bad guys won, the awful results are on display in books such as Gaylord Dold's *The World Beat,* about Mobutu Sese Seko's nightmarish contemporary Zaire, and *Kahawa,* Donald E. Westlake's caper novel set in Idi Amin Dada's Uganda. Westlake is also one of the few mystery writers to take seriously the fate of East Africa's dispossessed Asians.

In most mysteries set there, the real Africa is badly distorted, when it's not missing altogether. Yet the best of these books still manage to reveal a great deal about the immense African continent and its diverse peoples, sometimes inadvertently, sometimes with considerable artistry.

READING LIST

West Africa

HEAD, Matthew (often filed in libraries under his real name, John Canaday). *The Cabinda Affair* (NY, 1949). Insouciant Americans cut through the torpor in post–World War II Léopoldville (now Kinshasa), and in Cabinda, a little, enervated Portuguese enclave at the mouth of the Congo River. Canaday served with the U.S. Board of Economic Warfare's mission to the Belgian Congo in 1943 and later wrote three African mysteries featuring Hooper Taliaferro, a game but credulous young U.S. official, and Mary Finney, a middle-aged missionary M.D. who uses her brain power and her Mack truck personal style to solve murders.

In this one, Taliaferro is investigating a suspicious contract for $4 million worth of mahogany when a British con man is stabbed to death just feet from where Taliaferro is sleeping in the home of a Portuguese logging tycoon. Taliaferro had walked ten miles in the heat that day, after his rental car broke down, so he's out like a light.

Canaday's plot is fine, but it's his wry narrative voice that makes his work exceptional. A young lawyer steps off a small plane: "So this was Cotter. He was green with air-sickness and yellow with atabrine." The

Africans here are barely a presence—they're servants and thieves—but Canaday is sharp and funny on the dessicated colonials, especially the French. (See also *The Devil in the Bush* [1945] and *The Congo Venus* [1950].)

GREENE, Graham. *The Heart of the Matter* (London and NY, 1948; NY, 1967). This is one of Greene's most moving novels of character in moral crisis, but it's also got diamond-smuggling, blackmail, and murder in an unnamed West African British colony (probably Sierra Leone) at the tense height of World War II. Henry Scobie is the police official who is disliked for his rigid probity. His arty wife, Louise, is sick of the heat and the Philistines. To pay her way to South Africa—and to get some peace—Scobie holds his nose and borrows money from a shady Syrian merchant who convinces Scobie that the Syrian's illegal activities do not include smuggling stolen South African industrial diamonds to the Nazis. It's a fatal miscalculation for Scobie. Soon he's hounded by an obnoxious British spy who's got a crush on Louise, by the Syrian, by the erratic young widow Scobie has fallen in love with in Louise's absence, and by his own tortured Catholic convert's conscience.

Greene evokes the time and place masterfully. His West African rainy season all but leaves a fungus on the novel's pages. His dialogue is marvelous—"One needs a long spoon to sup with you, Yusef," Scobie tells the Syrian—and his ending is both morally ambiguous and hair-raising. *The Heart of the Matter* is not by most definitions a mystery, but it is mysterious, disturbing, and memorable.

THOMAS, Ross. *The Seersucker Whipsaw* (NY, 1967, 1992). A West African nation optimistically poised on the brink of independence in the mid-sixties is the setting for this uneasy amalgam of violent African politics and happy-go-lucky American commercial competitiveness. Peter Upshaw and Clint Shartelle are breezy, amoral political operatives hired by Chief Sunday Akomolo, who's running for premier of the fictional Albertia (based on Nigeria?). Neither American knows anything about the local cultures, but southern good ol' boy Shartelle claims voters everywhere will back the candidate who will "cause them the least pain."

Plausibility is not Thomas's forte, but he's intermittently entertaining here. The politicos sabotage opposition parties by linking their candidates with skywriting that causes impotence (according to the rumors the Americans start), and with a blimp that looks like an A-bomb. The saboteurs arrange for the Night Soil Collectors Union to stage a strike and for

Akomolo to settle it, a big boost for his numbers. In the end, violence erupts and the Americans are redeemed when they ally themselves with a cause that Thomas seems to regard as something bigger than revenge. Tacked onto all this is a love affair between Upshaw and Anne Kidd, a sexually spry but otherwise wan Peace Corps teacher, whose apartment looks like "a cross between Barkandu and Grand Rapids."

WYLLIE, John. *To Catch a Viper* (NY, 1977). After all the mysteries where the African continent serves as a backdrop for stories about the woes of the *ferenji*, Wyllie's Samuel Quarshie novels come as a revelation. Before World War II, Wyllie, a Canadian, worked for the West African Red Cross, and later wrote a series of superb mysteries featuring a West African M.D. who solves crimes against other Africans by combining scientific training with insights into African beliefs in magic. In *To Catch a Viper,* Quarshie must find the killer of his brother-in-law so the man's angry spirit won't haunt the neighborhood. Since Abegbayo, a respected school headmaster, died of multiple snakebites, Quarshie regularly consults his Aunt Zumeira. She's both a leader of the market women and a priestess in a snake cult.

Cynical politicians, it turns out, are manipulating local beliefs in the magical powers of vipers in order to change national boundaries nonsensically drawn up by old white men at a table in Paris in 1885. (For Wyllie's fictional Akhana, read Ghana.) The serious, resolutely decent Quarshie has feet planted in both modern and traditional Africa, and the tension produced from this bifurcation alone is terrific. Wyllie's is rich, thoughtful crime fiction and required reading for mystery fans visiting Africa. He's especially good at showing traditional African beliefs in community and how those communities work for the good of individuals. (See also *Skull Still Bone* [1975], *The Killer Breath* [1979], and several others.)

Northwest Africa

SMITH, David. *The Leo Conversion* (NY, 1980). The limp jocularity is reminiscent of an old Hope-Crosby road movie, but Smith's larky tale of a New York lawyer hooking up with a Nigerian judge to track down a priceless religious artifact is worth reading for the desert Northwest African atmosphere and for capsule histories of, among others, the Berbers, the Tuaregs, and the early Hausa nation.

James Stevens and his old friend and colleague Judge Muntaka pursue a thirteenth-century manuscript from Nigeria, where it was filched from a museum, into Niger and on to Morocco. The untranslated parchment is being sought by art dealers and by Islamic, Christian, and Jewish clerics and scholars, each of whom thinks the translation might bolster his faith's claims of having influenced early West Sudan civilizations.

Smith's plotting is artless; people keep drawing guns on one another, firing and rushing away. But the travel adventures and misadventures are fun, including an episode in which a desert village headman instructs the travelers to repair the three flat tires on their Land Rover by filling the tires with camel dung and letting them harden in the sun for three days.

Central Africa

DOLD, Gaylord. *The World Beat* (NY, 1994). Dold's insurance investigator Mitch Roberts wins the prize for the most ghastly intestinal infection suffered by a character in a mystery set in Africa. On a two-thousand-mile journey up the Congo into Zaire's interior, Roberts becomes so spectacularly sick he doesn't know whether the clouds of blue butterflies he keeps seeing are real or not, and he's too wretched to care. Roberts nearly dies but recovers enough of his strength to continue his search for a European physician kidnapped from a mining company clinic. Roberts is to deliver the ransom for her release.

Dold's labyrinthine plot is plausible—the African AIDS epidemic crops up—but what's most memorable is the reporting on life in Mobutu Sese Seko's "Disneyland Hell." In this Central African kelptocracy, bribes are necessary for all official and many unofficial transactions. The chief function of government is preying on the governed. It's not exactly anarchy; travel in Mobutu's Zaire is more like travel in ninth-century Europe: it's negotiable, but it's not for the faint of heart—or stomach.

Horn of Africa

CAPUTO, Philip. *Horn of Africa* (NY, 1980). The movement for Eritrean independence (see Thomas Keneally's *To Asmara*, next page) actually predated Ethiopian dictator Mengistu Haile Mariam by about twelve years; the first shots were fired in the early sixties against the UN-mandated hegemony of Ethiopian Emperor Haile Selassie. The early Eritrean secessionists were all sorts—Muslim fundamentalists, Christians, Marxists, nationalists—and they fought one another before the multiethnic, nonsectarian Eritrean People's Liberation Front came out on top. Caputo's fierce, thoughtful adventure novel is about those early battles and secret efforts by the Cold War superpowers to manipulate the outcome.

Charlie Gage, a Vietnam vet and later a war correspondent in Beirut, is haunted by the horror of war and lives with "a dread without object or sense." He lets himself be recruited by a CIA operative who's arming and training a pro-Western Muslim force in the country Caputo calls "Bejaya." For Gage, "action is freedom from thought." But he is soon repulsed by the corruption of the CIA man and by his fellow mercenaries, one of whom is an American fanatic in love with violence. Gage's moral journey is gripping, as are ghastly scenes of high-tech fighting among low-tech tribesmen in the Horn's desert lowlands, "the ragged edge of the world."

CODY, Liza. *Rift* (NY and GB, 1988; 1989). Cody, who's English, has built a good reputation with her Anna Lee and Eva Wylie PI novels (the startling Wylie is also a part-time professional wrestler). Cody has also published this African thriller, and while *Rift* is often flaccid and confusing, it will interest some visitors to Ethiopia with its descriptions of the Rift Valley. Termite mounds "rose on every side, orange, red, yellow, and grey: some like wasted Giacometti figures, some like stalagmites: a vast hallucinatory sculpture garden."

A young British film wardrobe assistant, Fay Jassahn, is restless in Kenya and decides to drive north and find out "if the Rift is the abyss part of Abyssinia." For Fay, it is. She picks up some rude traveling companions, and it turns out they're connected to a murder back in Nairobi. Also, it's 1974 and revolution is about to devour the Ethiopian upper classes. For Fay, though, her worst travails center on ticks, fleas, dirty water, cramped buses, and bad hotels with smelly outhouses. Murder is the least of it in what feels more like a *National Lampoon's Ethiopian Vacation*.

*KENEALLY, Thomas. *To Asmara* (NY, 1989). The author of *Schindler's List* went to Eritrea as a journalist in 1987 and two years later published this turbulent thriller that's also a passionate endorsement of the Eritrean People's Liberation Front. Because of the EPLF's Marxist origins—largely abandoned by 1987—the West never gave a fig about Africa's most humane outlaw government and its long struggle to secede from an Ethiopia

*vaut le voyage (see page 4).

ruled by the despotic Stalinist Mengistu Haile Mariam. Keneally helped educate the world about the EPLF, which finally won its war of independence in 1991.

Asmara is Eritrea's highland capital. Built by Italian colonizers, it's as inviting to the senses as any town in the Tuscan hills. Visitors there—and a visit is recommended to what may be Africa's most stable and promising new nation—won't find the city in Keneally's novel, for in 1987 it was occupied by the Ethiopian army, and free Eritrea existed only in besieged mountain caves. In the novel, an EPLF official recalls Peer Gynt and tells a visitor, "When we have Asmara, we will remember these bunkers as magic caverns."

The visitor is journalist Timothy Darcy, whose messy personal life recedes as he embraces the Eritrean cause. On his journey to investigate Ethiopian charges that the EPLF is blowing up famine-relief convoys, Darcy is accompanied by several other foreigners (one turns out to be a spy), including a jaunty old British feminist who wants to encourage the EPLF in its campaign to ban female genital mutilation. Keneally is too hard here on Ethiopians as a people; most of them were Mengistu's victims too. He fell for the demonization that was part of the EPLF's war effort. But for the most part, *To Asmara* is superior fiction, both as a thriller and in its beautiful evocation of a unique African people and place.

TYLER, W. T. *The Lion and the Jackal* (NY, 1988). It's not exactly a mystery, but this bitter novel of character and suspense will grab and hold the attention of anybody visiting or mulling over a possible visit to Somalia. Tyler's pessimism seemed extreme when the novel came out, but history has done little to contradict his assessment of the place he calls "Jubba" in his story. To Tyler, it's "a series of seductive social and historical myths created by a people good at telling lies." Tyler's U.S. Foreign Service protagonist, glum Logan Talbot, is stuck in the depressed and depressing Jubban capital—obviously Mogadishu—during what is clearly the 1977–78 Ethiopian-Somali war. Talbot is no fun, but Tyler's Major Jama of the "Jubban" Army is a more compelling creation, a morally complex man who is tempted to stop an idiotic war by committing a small act of treason.

———. *The Ants of God* (NY, 1981). This one is an adventure novel and love story set mainly in Ethiopia, and Tyler is pretty grim here too. But like the later book, it contains some wonderful descriptions, includ-

ing an opening scene at Awash station, possibly the most romantic railway station in the world. It's on the Addis Ababa–Djibuti line, which
drops 8,200 feet to the Red Sea in twenty-four hours. Riders watch the
flora and fauna metamorphose—and all but disappear—as they drop. The
trip is an African microcosm and one of the wonders of the continent.

East Africa

CASLEY, Dennis. *Death Underfoot* (GB, 1993; NY, 1994). Casley's first
novel featuring Kenyan Police Inspector James Odhiambo is as pleasingly
unhurried, exacting and intelligent as its protagonist. Odhiambo is reminiscent of John Wyllie's Samuel Quarshie (see page 149) in his moral rec-
titude and his tendency toward somber reflection that borders on the
morose. But Odhiambo's life is even more complicated than Quarshie's.
He's not only torn between modern and traditional Africa—Odhiambo
fears that his American-educated wife considers him lumpish and out of
it—but he's also a Luo tribesman distrusted by his Kikuyu superiors. And
his Luo relatives in the countryside expect him to lead a Luo resurgence
in Nairobi.

Death Underfoot reinvigorates an old formula by having an African detective investigate a homicide among Happy Valley fast-lane whites. During an outing at Hawk's Nest, "an expensive tourist trap built in a tree"
where visitors go to view wildlife, a white woman with a lurid past is axed
to death, tossed off the deck, and trampled by elephants. Higher-ups want
a quick resolution to the case, however unjust, so as not to interfere unduly with tourism. Odhiambo is bitterly obstinate in pursuing the truth
and barely survives the professional and actual long knives of Kenyan top
officials, including one whose specialty is known locally as "vanishment."
As a take on modern Kenya, Casley's novel is adroit, readable, and unnerving. (See also *Death Undertow* [1995].)

HUXLEY, Elspeth. *The African Poison Murders* (in Britain published as
Death of an Aryan; London and NY, 1939; NY, 1988). She's best known
for *The Flame Trees of Thika* (1959), her memoir of growing up in Kenya,
but between 1937 and 1965 Huxley also published five mysteries set in
the East African country she calls Chania. Her Africans are servants and
farm workers. They're portrayed respectfully, but Huxley sees "the natives" almost solely from the veranda, where the colonials gather for tea.
This can be frustrating. Huxley is acute, however, in her dissection of the

English farmers, who are alternately smug and jolly as they go about their marital and other intrigues.

And there's great power in Huxley's evocations of the African landscape, both its beauty and its perils. In *The African Poison Murders,* which is about internecine battles within the local Nazi bund, an arsonist's fire roars across the plain. Afterward, "every blade of grass and leaf of bush, every grasshopper and spider had perished. . . . Several crested cranes with brightly colored plumage, gobbling fried insects, rose unhurriedly and flapped away, trailing their long legs behind." As a literary conjurer of the African landscape, Huxley is not in the same league as the estimable Isak Dinesen. But she's roughly of the same era and receptive sensibility, and Huxley's mysteries are good reading for visitors to East Africa. (See also *Murder at Government House* [1937], *Murder on Safari* [1938], and *The Incident at the Merry Hipp* [1963].)

KAYE, M. M. *Death in Kenya* (NY, 1958, 1983). Carol Burnett in her heyday couldn't have come up with parodies as nutty as M. M. Kaye's overheated, overripe, over-dumb "romantic" mysteries. This one is set in the "White Highlands" of Kenya at the end of the post–World War II Mau Mau terrorist uprising, which Kaye explains to readers in a note "was an unpleasant business while it lasted."

Lady Emily DeBrett has a farm near Lake Naivasha, where all the women are neurasthenic, all the men are "fatally good-looking," and all the Africans are below average. Her grandson Eden DeBrett once nearly married his cousin Victoria Caryll, but, a relative muses, "Inbreeding never did anyone any good." Now they're both back in palaver-on-the-veranda-land, and Eden's wife, Alice, has been smothered with a "brightly colored" cushion and hacked to pieces with a panga. Gilly Markham, the alcoholic farm manager, dies too—snakebite, or so it seems for five minutes. Are Mau Mau diehards hiding down in the swamps? Don't bet on it. The African continent is incidental here. (See, also, *Death in Zanzibar,* NY and London, 1959, 1983.)

McQUILLAN, Karin. *Elephants' Graveyard* (NY, 1993). For sophisticated understanding of present-day East Africa land-use and wildlife problems, no mystery writer is better than Karin McQuillan. A dedicated naturalist who appreciates the opposing viewpoints of conservationists, farmers, ranchers, and even poachers, McQuillan works these conflicts into the plots of murder mysteries featuring Jazz Jasper, a young American woman who's fled a bad divorce back home and runs safari tours in Kenya.

The second in the series, *Elephants' Graveyard,* has a fine, creepy opening paragraph: "Dead bodies don't last long out in the African bush. There's nowhere to hide under that big, clear sky." The man who's been shot dead is Emmet Laird, the local head of Save the Elephants. His body has been heaped with brush to protect it against scavengers; elephants have covered him up, as they would one of their own. Jasper works in tandem with Police Inspector Ormandi to learn whether Laird's murder was personal or the work of poachers.

McQuillan is a remarkably revealing delineator of the African land and people, but be warned that Jazz Jasper's personal life is often hard to fathom. She's got a whiny American boyfriend, *and* she plays sexual games with Ormandi that are sometimes delightfully erotic and sometimes frightening. Take to her or not, among fictional sleuths in Africa, Jasper is an original. (See also *Deadly Safari* [1990] and *The Cheetah Chase* [1994].)

THIONG'O, Ngugi wa (usually known just as Ngugi). *Petals of Blood* (NY, 1978). Both murder mystery and anticapitalist polemic, this angry, dense, novel by a well-known Kenyan leftist got its author thrown into jail when it first came out. It's heavy going, and Ngugi's call to improve human nature through social engineering—including the abolition of private property—won't quicken the pulses of most contemporary readers. But it's hard to be unaffected by Ngugi's cold rage over government and big business corruption in postcolonial Kenya. One of the three men who die in an arson fire is a Kenyan businessman who made his original fortune transporting the bodies of Mau Mau members killed by the British. The other two are upper-class thugs who abused workers and smashed trade unions. Ngugi's protagonist, a schoolteacher named Godfrey Munira, is one of four suspects detained by police after the fire. It's Munira's spiritual journey from dour, conventional Presbyterian minister's son to calculating revolutionary that drives the novel.

In a sympathetic essay on Ngugi in Eugene Schleh's *Mysteries of Africa,* Steven R. Carter writes: "Just as the Mau Mau remade Christian songs into revolutionary ones, Ngugi turned the classic detective novel with its conservative social values into an anti-detective novel with a radical social vision." Carter quotes East German critic Ernst Kaemmel, who maintains that mysteries generally revere property and the individual and are in that sense reactionary. Whether one shares all, or some, or none of Ngugi's beliefs, *Petals of Blood,* while no page-turner, is distinctive among mysteries set in Africa. It's also one of the few written by an African and published in the West.

WESTLAKE, Donald E. *Kahawa* (NY, 1982, 1995). It sounds like a treacherous combination: Westlake, who specializes in blithe rogues, setting a caper novel about the theft of a coffee train in the hellish Uganda of Idi Amin Dada. But while researching his only African mystery, Westlake read an account of Amin's massacres and decided not to "dance on the graves" of Amin's half a million Christian and other victims. The result is a mordant, dead-on portrait of maybe the most godawful of the postcolonial Big Man African dictators. It's also the suspenseful tale of some white mercenaries ("mercs," in the lingo), anti-Amin Ugandans, and expelled Asians trying—despite the cunning of spies and saboteurs—to put one over on the preeminent African lunatic of the 1970s.

Kahawa means "coffee" in Swahili, the combination of Arabic and Bantu languages that Westlake describes as "the Yiddish of East Africa." In 1977, a Brazilian frost inflates world coffee prices. The caper team figures to make a bundle off the heist and get Amin's goat. When the coffee train vanishes, some Ugandan officials think it's been "magicked," but of course it's clever engineering that's done the trick. Westlake's interweaving of East African political and social history is as deft as the caper itself. His characters are sharper than they are deep, but most are likable—especially Westlake's hero, Lew Brady, who says, pre-heist: "I can always make a living. I'd rather do something interesting."

NOTED BUT NOT REVIEWED

CAMERON, Sara. *Natural Enemies* (Atlanta, 1993). American journalist Sam Hawthorne and his Kenyan naturalist ex-lover, Maya Saito, on the trail of elephant poachers.

FORSYTH, Frederick. *The Dogs of War* (NY, 1974; 1975). Mercenaries topple the government of platinum-rich "Zangaro" and set up a puppet dictatorship.

HALL, Adam [Elleston Trevor]. *The Tango Briefing* (NY, 1973). British agent Quiller on a mission in Tunisia.

INNES, Hammond. *The Naked Land* (NY, 1954). Adventures in Morocco.

MASON, A. E. W. *The Four Feathers* (London, 1902; NY, 1987). The kitsch classic where the Brits storm Khartoum in 1882 and avenge the slaughter of Chinese Gordon by the "fuzzie-wuzzies."

NICOLE, Christopher. *The Happy Valley* (London, 1989). Book jacket: "It was an earthly paradise for the settlers—until scandal and violence divided the colony."

XII

SOUTHERN AFRICA

A thunderstorm of appalling ferocity was inevitable at the close of such a day. Trekkersburg, which lay in a hollow on rising ground like the dent a head makes in a pillow, felt the final stages of the fever coming on just after seven. The weight of hot air pressing down on the town turned chill then hot then chill again. It started moving restlessly from side to side, setting weather vanes spinning. Strange, dislocated sounds were heard. Limbs of trees shivered. A thick, stifling blanket of black cloud was drawn up to blot out the bare bulb of the moon. The hallucinations began: it was as though, far above, a gigantic tin roof was being bombarded with boulders; as if each flash of lightning was a scar of pain through a reeling mind. A shuddering climax was reached. The rain came like a muck sweat. (James McClure, The Caterpillar Cop)

Death with a British Accent
By Robin Winks

A FRICA IS A popular venue for mystery and crime fiction, and even more for spy adventure thrillers, but the southern portion of the continent is not the location of choice.

Southern Africa—comprising South Africa, the two former Rhodesias (now Zambia and Zimbabwe), Malawi, the former Southwest Africa (now Namibia), and the states of Botswana, Lesotho, and Swaziland—is united by having once been colored pink on African maps: all were parts of the British Empire, thus facilitating plots that draw upon the traditions of British spy and thriller fiction and dialogue in which the author need not face the problem of rendering translation credible. Attempted murder at Victoria Falls (Agatha Christie), transplanted English quasi-cosies in the

Transvaal (June Drummond), skulduggery over diamonds (Geoffrey Jenkins)—these all work well enough, though they lack the authenticity that Karin McQuillan has brought to contemporary Nairobi, or Michael Pearce to Egypt at the beginning of the century (see Chapter X, "The Mideast"). There are two tried-and-true themes for criminous fiction in southern Africa: diamond smuggling and Russian/Chicom/Cuban meddling in explosive race relations. Both have produced a plethora of badly written and cliché-ridden books. There are relatively few that can be recommended for a sense of place.

To be sure, almost any novel set in South Africa, at least during the height of apartheid, involves a crime: muggings, casual killings of black laborers, mixed-race sex, bathing in a Whites Only beach as a Colored, etc. The best fiction to read for an understanding of South Africa is by Doris Lessing, Nadine Gordimer, André Brink, Peter Abrahams, Herman Boesman. Few mystery writers can hold their own in such company. Indeed, perhaps only one—James McClure—delivers the authenticity that these "serious" writers do.

In Eugene Schleh's *Mysteries of Africa*, Susan Friedland supplies a list of "South African Detective Stories." Most are quite bad, unobtainable, not in fact set in South Africa at all, or without any sense of place, using one stretch of desert—usually the Kalahari—interchangeably for all sandy wastes. Some exceptions follow.

READING LIST

BLACK, Lionel. *Chance to Die* (London, 1965). Here is a representatively generic yarn, set in Swaziland, and readily interchangeable with a dozen other novels as to plot and yet often effective as to place.

BURMEISTER, John. *Running Scared* (London, 1972). A well-told tale of a botched kidnapping that moves from Cape Town into the countryside with assurance, but is marred by an unexpectedly sentimental ending.

CHRISTIE, Agatha. *The Man in the Brown Suit* (London, 1924). This may be Dame Agatha's worst book. Anne Beddingfeld, too spunky for words, sails on the luxury liner *Kilmorden Castle* for Cape Town, in pursuit of a killer. Half the book is aboard ship; the other half is set in an increasingly unrecognizable southern Africa, from Cape Town to Rhodesia to Johannesburg.

CREASEY, John. *Call the Toff* (London, 1953). For those who like the Toff series, this is vintage stuff, set in Cape Town and Johannesburg. The Honourable Richard Rollinson, sworn enemy of the underworld, ventures abroad to remove crime before it can take root.

DESMOND, Hugh. *The Jacaranda Murders* (London, 1954). Not much real detection, but the use of Natal as a setting is unusual.

DRISCOLL, Peter. *The Wilby Conspiracy* (NY, 1972). Made into an unconvincing motion picture, this book pulls out all the stops on white man–black fugitive symbiosis in South Africa. Diamonds are involved, there are some excellent chase sequences (always a good excuse for observing the countryside), and the high veld is well portrayed.

DRUMMOND, June. *Slowly the Poison* (London, 1975). Set in South Africa in the 1920s, this well-crafted story involves a widow who goes to live with her in-laws and is suspected of having murdered her husband. Social life among the straitlaced whites is well described.

EBERSOHN, Wessel. *A Lonely Place to Die* (NY, 1979). This grim tale introduces Yudel Gordon, a prison psychiatrist in Johannesburg, and is unremitting in its revelations about white-black relations and police brutality.

————. *Divide the Night* (NY, 1981). Johnny Weizman is sent to police psychiatrist Yudel Gordon for treatment, having killed eight blacks serially, the last a fourteen-year-old girl; no court will condemn him, for he has been "defending his property." Gordon must find answers in Soweto, in police records, and among Afrikaner rightists.

HERMAN, Richard, Jr. *Iron Gate* (NY, 1996). Probably the beginning of a trend, this book posits an Afrikaner Resistance movement against all black Africans and all who would cooperate with them. Col. Matt Pontowski, USAF, is sent on a mission against the Iron Gate, a fortress from which the Afrikaners, with the apparent help of Israeli scientists, have developed controlled nuclear cold fusion. There is a lot of flying, and much rapid shifting of scenes.

JACOBSON, Dan. *The Price of Diamonds* (London, 1957). A first-rate work of fiction, often quite amusing. Not a mystery, though it involves some illegal activity.

————. *The Trap* and *A Dance in the Sun* (London, 1968). Two novellas, originally published in the 1950s, which reveal South African rural life with an eye to the lies people tell each other; stories of suspense rather than mystery.

JENKINS, Geoffrey. *A Twist of Sand* (London, 1959). Quite possibly the best thriller set in Southwest Africa, with the Skeleton Coast an almost living presence. Jenkins was a prolific thriller writer.

KOLARZ, Henry. *Kalahari* (NY, 1979). Translated from German, this is a straightforward survival tale set in the desert land of South Africa and Namibia/Botswana.

McCLURE, James. A journalist born in Johannesburg, McClure moved to Britain in his twenties, and in 1971 began to write a series of police procedurals (and brilliantly clued mysteries) about an Afrikaans police lieutenant, Tromp Kramer, and his assistant, Bantu Detective Sergeant Mickey Zondi. Set largely in Trekkersburg, a readily recognizable Pietermaritzburg, these novels quickly won a dedicated following for their scurrilous dialogue, raunchy sexuality, and above all, insidiously revealing commentary on how apartheid shaped human relations. Often the initial "crime"—a sexual liaison, for example—would not have been defined as criminal anywhere else. Then murder is committed to cover it up, and soon the whole of apartheid is at play in defining crime and in the process of investigation.

When alone together, Kramer and Zondi engage in an easy camaraderie, but each slips into a role as soon as a third person is present, in order to keep to the rules of the game. Kramer is crude, prejudiced, yet honest. He believes that everyone should try to get along, but he is not opposed to racial classification and separation. McClure depicts Indians, Coloreds, and the spectrum of black society in South Africa with affection and realism, and while he clearly sees most Afrikaners as Philistines, he is not without sympathy for "the lost tribe." There are no better mysteries to read while contemplating South Africa. Here are some of the standouts:

————. *The Steam Pig* (London, 1971). The debut novel, very tough, not for the squeamish, a cunningly constructed mystery with many compelling characters.

————. *The Caterpillar Cop* (London, 1972). A twelve-year-old boy is found strangled and mutilated near the country club, apparently the work of a sex maniac. Kramer has his doubts, and a series of odd clues, including a sliced caterpillar, lead him to a surprising solution.

————. *The Gooseberry Fool* (London, 1974). A heat wave at Christmas, and the murder of an apparently inoffensive bachelor, mixed with political interference (and hints of espionage), make for a complex story. McClure provides more South African background than usual.

————. *The Artful Egg* (New York, 1984). Some reviewers have felt that McClure's work showed signs of decline after his first three novels; if so, he returned in strength in this amusing, sad, well-told mystery which involves Ramjut Phillay, Asiatic Postman 2nd Class, together with McClure's usual repertory group, again in a first-rate story.

————. *The Song Dog* (NY, 1991). McClure takes a young Tromp Kramer back to 1962, and to Jafini, in northern Zululand, where he is to investigate the death of the town's chief detective. We learn how he meets up with Mickey Zondi. This prequel seems a bit tired.

XIII

———≈«◎»≈———

JAPAN

The Tokaido Express was racing along noiselessly on its endless gleaming twin tracks, and loudspeakers in all carriages were respectfully informing the honorable passengers that Mount Fuji, Japan's highest and holiest mountain, would soon appear and could be viewed through the windows on the right. The message was repeated in English, and the [Dutch policeman] looked up at the little box above the sliding door, as if he were amazed that it could say something understandable. He was getting used to the all-encompassing riddle around him; the signs written in three different scripts, all of them meaningless; the language in which he couldn't recognize a single word; the utter foreignness of the farmhouses and temples, set in the lush green fields or built on hilltops; the outlandishness of the farmworkers wearing vast straw hats and coats made of dry leaves or stalks, and who sheltered under oilcloth parasols, decorated with huge diagrams. He had never been in the Far East before and felt himself wholly unprepared for the jumble of new images which were forced on his brain, asking for explanation and translation. But he had passed the first stage of bewilderment, and his mind now seemed ready to accept the strangeness and even to rest in it, as a show put up for his entertainment and imagination. He was no longer intent on trying to understand, but was allowing his mind to receive the impressions and to enjoy the colors and shapes and sounds. And now the loudspeaker had said something he could understand without bothering to translate: Mount Fuji. (Janwillem van de Wetering, The Japanese Corpse)

WHEN IN JAPAN: Be sure to stay in a traditional inn. With its tatami mats (traditional Japanese rooms are measured in the number of mats it takes to cover the floor), its bedding stored away in a cupboard during the day, its pillow stuffed with rice husks (surprisingly comfortable), and its teapot full of hot water that appears at the appropriate time, the traditional inn exudes age-old hospitality. And since almost every police inspector in a Japanese mystery stays overnight in one while on the track of his murderer, you will be soaking up vital ambience. On checking in, you will be expected to change from your street shoes into sandals or slippers provided by the management (the same drill occurs when you enter a Japanese home). When entering a restroom, you will again change footwear, putting on special toilet slippers. Your inn will undoubtedly offer a hot bath in a communal pool. The protocol here is simple: unlike in a Turkish bath, you're on your own. Just be sure to clean off *before* getting in; the bath's sole purpose is relaxation.

Culture as Mystery

By Dennis Drabelle

MURDER—THE DRIVING force behind the mystery novel—is a rarity in Japan. With about half the population of the United States, in a typical year Japan logs only about one-fifteenth the number of murders. Even the petty crime rate is remarkably low. Bicyclists in Tokyo seldom lock their vehicles, and office workers commonly leave their umbrellas in a stand at the building entrance in full confidence that they will not be stolen. How representative of the Japanese national character, then, can a murder tale be?

Yet mysteries make appropriate entrées to Japanese culture because for outsiders the country itself is a mystery, a literally insular society that plays by arcane rules and rituals, with a famously difficult language encrypted in ideographic code. For that matter, indirection is standard operating procedure for the Japanese: to acquaint oneself with national mores by picking up crime stories instead of sociological studies is to take a fittingly oblique approach.

Japanese mysteries can be divided into two groups: the Technicolor variety and the black-and-whites. The Technicolors, which are invariably written by non-Japanese authors, raise to the level of caricature such stereotypical national characteristics as passion for game strategy, devotion to martial arts, and reliance on ways of knowledge that bypass Western rationality. The best of these are written with a light touch, rather like W. S. Gilbert's text for *The Mikado*: Trevanian and Ian Fleming come to mind. Of lesser interest is Eric Van Lustbader, whose characters pursuing ancient Japanese grace and wisdom are reminiscent of American hippies embarking on Plains Indian vision quests.

The mysteries in black-and-white (proper film *noir* colors) are written either by Japanese (notably Seicho Matsumoto, Shizuko Natsuki, Kyotaro Nishimura, and Masako Togawa) or by outsiders who have spent some time in the country (Fred Hiatt and Janwillem van de Wetering). The Japanese writers, of course, can hardly be expected to spend much time holding up their fellow citizens' foibles for inspection—and probably lack the objectivity to do so in any case. Yet some of their books make ideal companions for the traveler—especially Natsuki's *Murder at Mt. Fuji,* with its perspectives on the great mountain; and, in a country famous for its elegant and precisely timed trains, Matsumoto's *Points and Lines* and Nishimura's *The Mystery Train Disappears.* By and large, these Japanese writers are also better mystery-makers than their *gaijin* rivals. At her best, for example, Shizuko Natsuki writes on a level with Christie and Rendell; one would like to see more of her books brought into English.

Outsiders Hiatt (a reporter) and van de Wetering (a student of Zen) have no compunctions about embroidering their stories with insights into Japanese practices and mind-sets—and frame pretty good puzzles to boot. Falling somewhere between the two color schemes is James Melville, who has lived in Japan, knows it well, declines to sensationalize it, can be most informative about the look and feel of life there, has created well-rounded characters in Inspector Otani and his wife, but as a storyteller is simply unable to quicken a reader's pulse.

The number of mysteries by Japanese that are translated into English is not large. But together with books written in English by visitors and expatriates, they make for an interesting patchwork portrait of a country where crime may be un-Japanese but, by the same token, the urge to read about it may be all the stronger.

READING LIST

COLLINS, Robert J. *Murder at the Tokyo American Club* (Rutland, Vt., 1991 pb). As the title indicates, this comic mystery centers on expatriates in Tokyo. Though mildly amusing, it bogs down in perfunctory plotting and characterization. Also by the same author is *Murder at the Tokyo Lawn Tennis Club.*

EDOGAWA RANPO. *Japanese Tales of Mystery and Imagination,* translated by James B. Harris (Rutland, Vt., 1956). Say this author's name quickly a few times, and you might figure it out—it's a pseudonym (for Taro Hirai) that mimics the Japanese pronunciation of "Edgar Allan Poe." Poe was the originator of the modern mystery tale, Ranpo its pioneer in Japan: until he began writing in the 1920s, Japanese mystery lovers had to make do with stories translated from other languages.

This sampling of Ranpo's short stories reveals a fascination with the grotesque, as well as a penchant for fast-springing, last-minute tricks. "The Human Chair" is characteristic. The title says it all: a kinky carpenter actually fashions a capacious chair in which he can install himself and imperceptibly engulf its female occupants—but there's a surprise ending. No one story is a masterpiece, but collectively they are morbidly disturbing.

FLEMING, Ian. *You Only Live Twice* (NY, 1964). It was surely inevitable that 007 should visit Japan, if only to sample the local women. In this, the penultimate entry in the series, Bondo-san teams up with lissome Kissy Suzuki, who dives for pearls wearing a thong—and nothing else. The plot is strictly comic-book: Bond's nemesis Blofeld has restyled himself Dr. Shatterhand, acquired a Japanese estate, and stocked it with all manner of poisonous plants and animals. Why? To indulge his death-lust by attracting suicide-prone Japanese.

Fleming spices his yarn with standard Japanese quirks, explaining everything from the unluckiness of the number four (one word for it sounds like the word for death) to what ninjas are (see the entry on Van Lustbader on page 174). The book retails stereotypes and beggars credibility (in makeup, Bond manages to pass for a deaf-and-dumb Japanese!). Yet it consistently amuses. Nothing Fleming says about Japan is flat-out wrong (though a lot of it is superficial), and the story holds up as a campy confection. In fact, it can serve as a flashy introduction to Japan's sinister side, after which you can take up more thoughtful writers like Natsuki and van de Wetering.

HOYT, Richard. *Japanese Game* (NY, 1995). Here is a corrective to thrillers populated by awestruck Japanophiles. Hoyt (or at any rate his characters) finds the present-day Japanese to be conformist, male chauvinist, and across-the-board amoral. The plot is far-fetched—the U.S. vice president's incognito daughter is kidnapped on the high seas and sold into prostitution in Japan—but the anti-Japanese raillery can be quite funny, especially an exposé of how *besuboru* (baseball) has been smoothed, by custom if not actual rule-change, to suit Japanese tastes.

LATHEN, Emma. *East Is East* (London, 1991). Lathen's banker-detective, John Putnam Thatcher, heads to Japan on behalf of a client; naturally murder intrudes upon his sojourn. Lathen marshals a good deal of information about MITI, the Japanese trade-regulating agency, and the difficulties experienced by foreigners trying to break into Japanese markets. There is also an engaging discussion of *nichi,* the Japanese habit of finding personal significance in affiliation with a group. Though I myself find Lathen's mysteries styleless and soporific, there are plenty of Thatcherites out there.

MARQUAND, John P. *Stopover: Tokyo* (Boston, 1957). Best known for his novels about New England gentry, notably *Point of No Return* and *Wickford Point,* John Marquand also wrote a series of spy tales in the 1930s featuring Mr. Moto, Japan's top secret agent. Mr. Moto usually operates extraterritorially (see Chapter XIV, "China"), but this one (a later revival of the character) takes place in the homeland metropolis. The spying is low-tech, the slang is period ("rod" for gun), and Japan is fresh from the great rebuilding after World War II.

Marquand seizes upon the superficiality of the country's new Western look of metal-and-stone buildings in place of wood-and-paper ones, of suits and skirts and shoes worn in public instead of kimonos and clogs: At home "the shoes would be left outside. There would be straw matting underfoot. European clothes would be hung away, and there would be kimonos—no chairs, no beds; and still, perhaps, wooden blocks for pillows. There would be cushions beside low tables, a charcoal brazier and tea, and *sushi* made of raw fish and rice, and a porcelain jar of hot sake surrounded by minute cups. There would be the family tub for the hot bath, and now that it was summer, an open window would afford a glimpse of a tiny garden court, with goldfish in a lily pond. This picture would vary with poverty or wealth, but everywhere in Tokyo the pattern would be the same. The old conventions lay just behind the modern curtain and behind the barrier of language. Every stranger, in his own way, was conscious of that older life. It must have been hard to live two lives at once, as people always did in Tokyo."

Mr. Moto teams up with two young Americans to neutralize Skirov, a

Soviet agent who is trying to foment a Communist revolution in Japan. The pace is leisurely, the atmosphere is heavy with intrigue, and the book cries out to be read while sipping a Scotch on the rocks.

MATSUMOTO, Seicho. *Inspector Imanishi Investigates,* translated by Beth Cary (NY, 1989). Two national traits figure prominently in this mystery unraveled by a middle-aged detective who in his off-hours is addicted to gardening and liable to try his hand at haiku. The first is the constant flow of self-effacement that lubricates Japanese interpersonal relationships. Characters are always making excuses for the meals they serve, the artworks they create, the homes they have furnished. The formulaic humility (which is sure to be reciprocated) reinforces a widespread disapproval of puffing oneself up, of standing outside the norm.

The other trait on display here is the insistence on knowing who everyone is, which is institutionalized in official registries of people by house and family. This cataloguing makes it all but impossible to go underground in Japan—you can't live anywhere without registering, and you can't register without supplying your prior registration. Inspector Imanishi begins to zero in on the killer after stumbling on a way in which it just might be possible for a Japanese citizen to beat the system and reinvent himself.

The same author's *The Voice,* translated by Adam Kabat (NY, 1995), is a collection of short mysteries, many of which spring from encounters between strangers. The volume is part of a series, "Japan's Mystery Writers," published in English by Kodansha, which also includes the book that made Matsumoto's reputation: the excellent *Points and Lines,* translated by Makiko Yamamoro and Paul C. Blum (NY, 1995 pb). In this cunning novel, a police detective confirms his hunch that the ostensible "love suicide" of a government official and a waitress was a double murder. The crime-solving depends on demolishing an alibi that relies on the clockwork operation of Japan's magnificent railway system (see also the entry on Nishimura, on page 171). The book's title refers to vantage points available to eyewitnesses in a Tokyo train station.

McFALL, Patricia. *Night Butterfly* (NY, 1992). In this novel McFall, an American who lived in Japan for a year, picks out certain obvious facets of Japanese lowlife circa 1972, including gangsters and love hotels. The book is notable, however, for its glimpse of the profession of hostess at a Japanese bar and for its occasional bursts of insight. For example, "At four P.M., the beginning of rush hour, the Japanese renowned for their politeness were transformed, body against body, into a pushing, shoving, anonymous mob."

MELVILLE, James. *The Chrysanthemum Chain* (NY, 1982, 1986). Englishman Melville's novels featuring Kobe police superintendent Tetsuo Otani are exemplary introductions to Japanese culture embedded in unfortunately humdrum stories. This one, typically, spends less energy on the mystery of who killed a British expat than on the almost clockwork reaction of Japanese officials to the news that some of their colleagues were involved with the dead man in a web of homosexual contacts. The ensuing cover-up becomes virtually an act of state. As a Japanese reporter observes, "Ever notice how often we talk about 'We Japanese'? Apart from China I don't believe there's such a totally integrated society in the world. We're all part of the organism, we're all part of the corruption." (It should be noted that in the fifteen years since this was written, a fissure has opened up between the Japanese people and their politicians, corrupt or not.)

————. *The Ninth Netsuke* (NY, 1982, 1986) has one of the author's better plots. Netsukes are small ivory carvings, originally used as toggles for tobacco pouches, that have become valuable in their own right. Otani's wife is kidnapped out of their house by operatives looking for a netsuke that has fallen into the couple's possession. While Otani unravels that kidnapping and a murder, the author takes the reader inside one of Japan's garish love hotels and to a traditional wedding.

He also provides a telling summary of the obligatory conversational preliminaries. Otani has gone to Tokyo to respond to an allegation that he has mishandled a case. "It took a little time to approach the business of the meeting, for it was necessary first to apologize at some length to Otani for having intruded into his no doubt very busy schedule, and to thank him most sincerely for making the long journey to Tokyo.

"Otani for his part then had to deny strenuously that he had been put to the slightest inconvenience, and counter by apologizing for disrupting the Agency's arrangements at short notice and bothering senior officials with the affairs of a remote and insignificant police force."

Further entries in the series cover a veritable hit-list of Japanese cultural traits, including the urge to court death by eating potentially poisonous blowfish (*Sayonara, Sweet Amaryllis*); Japanese gangsters (*Death of a Daimyo*); and the tea ceremony (*The Death Ceremony*). Other titles include *The Wages of Zen; A Sort of Samurai; Go Gently, Gaijin; Kimono for a*

Corpse; The Reluctant Ronin; A Haiku for Hanae; The Bogus Buddha; and *The Body Wore Brocade.*

NATSUKI, Shizuko. *The Obituary Arrives at Two O'Clock* (NY, 1988), and *The Third Lady,* translated by Robert B. Rohmer (NY, 1987). Natsuki is said to be Japan's best-selling mystery writer, and these two riveting novels go a long way toward explaining why. *The Obituary Arrives at Two O'Clock* centers on the Japanese mania for golf—an especially posh pursuit there owing to the dearth of available flat land.

At the heart of the action lie forms of peculation suited to starting up a country club: siphoning off initiation fees and then, to make up the shortfalls, holding contractors to impossible standards and refusing to pay them for their work. Kosuke Okita, the founder of a small landscaping firm in Tokyo, is a victim of the second practice. When his victimizer, the owner of a golf course in the making, is found bludgeoned to death with a golf club, Kosuke is the prime suspect. His alibi—that at the time of the killing he was out helping a distressed blind woman who had dialed his home number by chance from a phone booth and then disappeared—borders on the preposterous.

Kosuke goes on the lam. His wife receives a package containing his severed finger. A lab analysis shows that the finger was cut from dead tissue, which means that Kosuke himself is dead. Or is he? A figure resembling him is spotted in the neighborhood, and his wife is distraught. On the very last page, Natsuki snaps into place a rousingly clever solution to the puzzle of Kosuke's mortality.

Another masterpiece by Natsuki is *The Third Lady,* a variation on the theme of Alfred Hitchcock's movie version of Patricia Highsmith's *Strangers on a Train.* In the movie, you may recall, the deranged man (played by Robert Walker) suggests to a normal chap (Farley Granger) that they foil motive-hunters by exchanging murders of people they'd like to be rid of. Granger laughs the idea off, only to be flabbergasted when Walker carries out his part of the bargain.

In Natsuki's variation, the pair are a man and a woman with a letch for each other and no qualms about trading kills. The plot hinges on the identity of the female murderer, who commits her murder first, and on the male's feverish efforts to get back in touch with her. As in *Obituary,* Natsuki rounds out her story with a satisfying flourish.

Someone was bound to write a mystery called *Murder at Mt. Fuji* (NY, 1984, 1987; translated by Robert B. Rohmer), and the inventive Natsuki puts the setting to good use in lining up another clever puzzle. After the founder of a pharmaceuticals firm is stabbed to death at the family villa near the fabled peak, his college-age great-niece confesses to having done the deed in a panic over his sexual advances. As Jane Prescott, a young American houseguest, watches, the family enters into a conspiracy to bottle up these unsavory details. Their plan is to make the killing look like the work of an outside intruder, and Jane goes along with them.

The agreed-upon story starts to disintegrate almost immediately, with big, fat clues dropping into the policemen's hands. Jane begins to suspect that one of the family members is subverting the conspiracy. All of this is absorbing until the long last chapter, where the story trails off into a shaggy-dog denouement.

The same author's *Death from the Clouds,* translated by Gavin Frew (NY, 1991), is a pedestrian story of murders among the executives of a family firm that makes mini-calculators. As for Natsuki's *Portal of the Winds,* translated by Robert D. Rohmer (NY, 1990), its highly intriguing question—why do various dead men have the wrong hands and feet when laid out in their caskets?—gets a solution out of science fiction.

NISHIMURA, Kyotaro. *The Mystery Train Disappears,* translated by Gavin Frew (NY, 1990). The ubiquitous and almost tritely reliable Japanese train system is the true hero of this thriller. In an effort to drum up business for its subsidized service, the national railway has introduced mystery trains, destinations unknown, and the public has flocked aboard. One of these, consisting of an engine, twelve coaches, and four hundred passengers, fails to show up at its destination (which is known, of course, only to railroad executives). Shortly afterward the railroad gets a phone call: a gang has hijacked the entire train, whose whereabouts is now unknown (a veritable mystery train), and is demanding a one-billion-yen ransom.

In what amounts to a dual procedural, the methodical police cooperate with the methodical railfolk to pursue the kidnappers. Especially recommended for anyone who travels in Japan by rail pass.

ROWLAND, Laura Joh. *Bundori* (NY, 1996). This is an oddity: the second novel in a series featuring a samurai-detective in Edo, Japan's feudal capital, written by an aerospace engineer living in New Orleans. The characters never quite climb out of the first two dimensions, but the book succeeds largely because Laura Joh Rowland is adept at boxing them inside the rules of seventeenth-century Japanese protocol—and then finding ways for them to break out. A serial killer is loose upon the city, leaving the severed and ritualistically treated head of each victim as a *bundori* (war trophy). Sano, the shogun's personal sleuth, is assigned to stop the killing, a much harder task than it need be due to covert interference from Yanagisawa, the shogun's chamberlain and sometime lover. The encounters between Sano and Yanagisawa have raging subtexts of controlled hostility.

Unlike some western authors, who dwell almost pruriently on "exotic" Japanese mores, Rowland enables the reader to inhabit the feudal code—which, though harsh, has a rigorous beauty—from within. The previous novel in this series is *Shinju*. May there be more.

TAKAGI, Akimitsu. *No Patent on Murder,* translated by Sadako Mizuguchi (Chicago, 1977). A brand-new husband gets a phone call on the first night of his honeymoon. It's the college where he teaches, he tells his bride; they need him urgently to help them correct a foul-up in the grades he has just handed in. He fails to return and, days later, is found murdered. The police learn that nobody at the college made any such call.

It's a tantalizing premise, but the narration is poky and the translation fizzless. The novelist illuminates Japan's tendency toward small-town rigidity writ large when he has one character remark, "A big company . . . is very jealous of its reputation. It would be unthinkable of them to raise to executive rank a man who had a criminal in his family. It's just not done."

TOGAWA, Masako. *The Master Key,* translated by Simon Grove (NY, 1985). A winner of Japan's Edogawa Ranpo Prize (named after the author who took that pseudonym—see page 166), this first novel keeps the reader off-balance with a dizzying series of incidents that seem unlikely to fit together but finally do. The eponymous key unlocks all the rooms in a Tokyo apartment house for maiden ladies, where decorum requires that each male visitor wear a tag indicating that he has passed muster at the downstairs desk.

En route to a perhaps overly elaborate resolution, Togawa sketches the Japanese treatment of women circa 1962 (when the novel first appeared in Japanese). To judge by the denizens of this building, the single urban female must have been a virtual outcast then, unlikely to have much of a career and driven to such follies as withdrawing into debilitating eccentricity, spying on her neighbors, and succumbing to religious fanaticism.

The same author's *The Lady Killer,* translated by Simon Grove (NY, 1986), features a married man who in his career as an extracurricular womanizer—he records his conquests in a "hunter's diary"—becomes a kind of male Typhoid Mary. One by one, the women he picks up are found strangled to death in sequence (the previous one being killed while he is in bed with the newest), and his seductions catch up with him when he is arrested and convicted of murder. His lawyers notice discrepancies in the prosecution's case and set out to overturn the verdict. You may be able to guess whodunit, but not, I'll wager, why.

TREVANIAN. *Shibumi* (NY, 1979, 1980). Roughly a third of this thriller takes place in Japan, but its real interest lies in the protagonist's mystique. Of European ancestry, Nicholai Hel is orphaned at an early age and then raised in Japan by a master of Go, a board game beloved in Japan, where its adepts consider it superior to chess. In fact, the novel's six sections have titles corresponding to Go strategies.

As Hel matures, his creator lets himself get swept up in Japan's ancient traditions and recurrent moments of grace to the point where his normally crisp prose becomes sticky with gossamer. For example, the mentor describes Hel's Go game as "abstract and unkind. Your play is somehow inorganic . . . unliving. It has the beauty of a crystal, but lacks the beauty of a blossom." Among other knacks honed during his long Japanese residence, Hel can feel people's presence before he hears or sees them.

Shibumi is rife with this kind of hooey, but as hooey goes it is first-rate. The best touch comes in a footnote, where the author announces that he will refrain from detailing Naked/Kill, a martial art that Hel uses to dispatch his enemies—and by whose standards "the average Western room contains just under two hundred lethal weapons"—because similar secrets revealed in earlier novels have led to copycat mayhem.

After seeing Japan corrupted by the American Occupation after World War II, Hel forsakes it for the Basque country, on the French-Spanish border. This is a canny move, for there he plugs into another ancient culture with an impenetrable language—and further opportunities for the author to fling hooey.

Its undeniable entertainment value aside, this novel ought to immunize the reader/visitor against the folly of trying to "go native" in Japan.

VAN DE WETERING, Janwillem. *The Japanese Corpse* (Boston, 1977; NY, 1978). The murder of a Japanese expatriate in Amsterdam sends a pair of Dutch policemen to the port city of Kobe (also the sleuthing grounds of James Melville's Superintendent Otani), where corrupt monks are selling and exporting artworks from their temples. Van de Wetering, a native of Holland who writes in English, has lived in Japan and studied Zen. His insights into Japanese mores embellish the plot, which shuttles back and forth between Amsterdam and Kobe. Like the populace as a whole, Japan's gangsters are firmly bound by institutions and rituals, and the parallels between the two milieus make for fascinating reading. One of the Dutchmen is greatly taken with the Japanese custom of the hot bath, and this might be a good book to curl up with after a steamy immersion at your hotel. (For other novels in this series, see Chapter VI, "The Netherlands.")

By the same author is *Inspector Saito's Small Satori* (NY, 1985, 1987), a collection of short stories, many of them originally published in *Alfred Hitchcock's Mystery Magazine.* Typically the solution to the crime involves the inspector's application of gnomic wisdom from *Parallel Cases Under the Pear Tree,* a classical Chinese text on detection and justice.

VAN LUSTBADER, Eric. *The Ninja* (NY, 1980). Here is another writer whose awe of Japanese martial arts borders on fawning. Through the novel prowl modern-day samurai and ninjas (the difference between the two is a matter of class, samurai being top-drawer and ninjas scum), some of whom have acquired a capacity beyond even the fabled sixth sense: "It was akin to having eyes in the back of your head, amplifiers in your ears."

The half-Caucasian, half-Chinese protagonist, Nicholas Linnear, has gone on to sword-wield his way through five more thrillers. Meanwhile, the byline has changed from Eric Van Lustbader to Eric V. Lustbader to Eric Lustbader. Under any name, how sweet the books smell will surely depend on your level of interest in martial artistry.

XIV

CHINA

The sights and sounds of Peking in summer seemed to move on either side of me, unrolling as a scroll painting might unroll, changing with each street corner but never really changing . . . The smell of Chinese cooking came pleasantly to my nostrils. There was a broad tolerance emanating from that conglomeration of sounds and smells that gave me a love for the city of Peking. It was a noble city with its walls and avenues, its hidden temples and its palaces. It was a city of the imagination, a city of the spirit falling into a dreamlike ruin; falling into memories as fantastic as the figures on a Chinese scroll; always changing but never changed. (John P. Marquand, *Thank You, Mr. Moto,* 1936)

Hong Kong invites, entices, accepts, accommodates, pleasures, puts up with, cheats and disgorges several dozen million tourists a year, and almost without exception they all leave their air-conditioned, room-serviced, overpriced glass and concrete cocoons with the delicious feeling that, just below the surface of this bursting town, just around the corner from where they bought their transistor radio or made a good deal on their brand-new stereo equipment, there are sinister, secret and very seedy happenings going on. (William Marshall, *Yellowthread Street,* 1975)

Taiwan . . . Formosa . . . the Republic of China . . . the Taiwan Province of the People's Republic of China—whatever people call it, they all agree on one thing; it's a great restaurant. Some people say that Taipei has the greatest collection of Chinese restaurants anywhere, and I wouldn't disagree. (Anthony Hyde, *Formosa Straits,* 1995)

Here Comes the Judge

By Mark I. Pinsky

DESPITE ITS SIZE and its long tradition of crime stories, China is the setting for relatively few well-written mysteries and thrillers in English; almost as many are set in tiny Hong Kong as in the entire Middle Kingdom. The good news is that this modest selection includes several dozen entertaining novels and represents a respectable geographic spread—sufficient for any three-week visit. Although Chinese mysteries are frequently set in Beijing—Peking in the old spelling—other settings are also from the standard tourist itinerary, including Xian, Guilin, Dunhuang, Inner Mongolia, and Taiwan.

But the quintessential milieu for a murder mystery is Old Shanghai. From the 1930s until the Communists took power in 1949, the city was a legendary and colorful haven for gangsters, gamblers, warlords, high-class White Russian mistresses, tough Chinese streetwalkers, revolutionaries, expatriate adventurers, mercenaries, and spies. The resulting human compost heap fueled a fetid, hothouse atmosphere so strong that it is still a favorite for flashbacks and backstories in novels written today.

Sometime soon Chinese mystery writers probably will emerge to capture this *noir* nirvana, and they will be translated into English. Others may ultimately emerge (or be allowed to emerge) to chronicle crime detection throughout post-"Liberation" China. Until then, Western readers will have to rely on British and American writers on tour or in search of exotic locales. The problem with these "road mysteries" is that China has changed so rapidly that those set in the late 1970s and early 1980s are already hopelessly out of date.

A more serious difficulty with these books is point of view. They see (and describe) China from a bus, a train, or a boat. Occasionally that view is perceptive, as in this passage from Ruth Rendell's *Speaker of Mandarin*: "The mountains that formed the skyline [around Guilin], and in front of the skyline a long ridge, were so fantastic in shape as to resemble almost anything but the karst formations the guidebook said they were. These mountains were shaped like cones, like cypress trees, like toadstools. They rose, tree-studded, vertically out of the plain, their sides straight and their peaks rounded curves. They were the mountains of Chinese paintings that Wexford had until now believed to be artists' stylizations."

But because they are written by visitors, these books focus more on the travelers than on the culture they are encountering. The characters' concerns are those of tourists, as in this passage from Stefanie Matteson's *Murder on the Silk Road:* "Charlotte had already learned not to expect great cuisine in China. Meals they'd eaten in the big cities had been all right, but she'd been told that the farther out you got, the worse the food became." True enough, yet not very enlightening.

The best alternative to these Chinese "road mysteries" is to seek out one of the most interesting cross-cultural collaborations in the mystery genre: the works of a brilliant Dutch diplomat who, writing in English, re-created the world of a Tang Dynasty magistrate.

Insignificant persons, draw near and meet Dee Jen-djieh—Judge Dee—one of feudalism's finest, a fair-minded and quick-witted jurist of the seventh century. Join the parade of vagabonds, concubines, dissolute monks, impoverished students, shady merchants, soldiers, Buddhists, Taoists, innkeepers, thieves, and unfaithful spouses as they intrigue and do away with each other in the most ingenious ways. Taste the noodles and drink the wine in the grimy teahouses in the back alleys. Savor the atmosphere.

The Chinese have been writing crime and mystery stories for more than a thousand years, but until this century few of these have reached the West. When World War II erupted, Robert H. van Gulik was forced to interrupt his diplomatic and scholarly efforts in Peking to flee the Japanese. While on the run in China's interior, van Gulik spent the remainder of the war translating three tales of the historic and celebrated figure of Judge Dee, who lived from A.D. 630 to 700.

A devoted sinophile, the Dutchman had a purpose beyond entertainment in his creation. "As the Chinese have been so often represented—and too often misrepresented!—in our popular crime literature, it seems only just that they themselves be allowed to have their own say for once in this field," he wrote in the introduction to *The Celebrated Cases of Judge Dee* (1949).

Van Gulik was so taken with Judge Dee that in the late 1950s and 1960s, while serving the Netherlands in various Asian diplomatic missions, he brought the magistrate to life in dozens of new mysteries. The tales were released two or three to a book, accompanied by van Gulik's line drawings. Beyond the three original stories he translated and edited, there wasn't much factual material to go on, he wrote, "since official biographies merely state that as a magistrate he solved a great number of puzzling cases and freed many innocent people who had been thrown into prison because of false accusations."

But drawing on his scholarly research into nearly everything Chinese, from poetry to jurisprudence, erotica to the lute, van Gulik chronicled the life and times of Judge Dee, occasionally borrowing from the exploits of other fabled Chinese crime solvers from different periods of history.

No fortune cookie Charlie Chan, the jurist resembles Sherlock Holmes in his deductive powers, his penchant for investigating in disguise, and his resort to a stringed instrument to aid in concentration. However, as van Gulik explains in his essay, Dee's method of operation is closer to that of television's Perry Mason: the crucial action always takes place in the hall of Judge Dee's courtroom, with the guilty party confessing in the face of overwhelming evidence—and sometimes a little torture.

There are other differences, both in protocol and result. Defendants (without lawyers) and witnesses alike kneel before the judge and knock their foreheads on the flagstones before testifying. They are frequently berated by the judge, who—wearing a brocade robe and a black, wing-tipped hat—calls them "dog's head," "lewd woman," and "insolent scoundrel." Some of the accused give as good as they get, dismissing the magistrate as a "brush wielder"—the Tang Dynasty version of a pencil pusher. And, at the conclusion of some of the mysteries, the convicted killers are executed, their deaths clinically described.

The historic Judge Dee is also the central character in *Deception: A Novel of Mystery and Murder in Ancient China* (1993) by Eleanor Cooney and Daniel Altieri. This historic potboiler focuses on the judge's later court life, jousting with the infamous Empress Wu Zetien, a ruler in the traditions of the Dowager Empress Ci Xi and Jiang Ching.

What Judge Dee is to Old China, William Marshall's Detective Inspector Harry Feiffer is to modern Hong Kong. The British Crown Colony of Hong Kong, due to be handed over to China in 1997, is a lot like Rick's Café in Casablanca: sooner or later, everyone comes there. For decades, millions of tourists have dropped—white-knuckled—out of the sky over Kai Tak Airport and landed on that downtown postage stamp, while getting a voyeur's look into the flats that line the short runways.

Over the past twenty years, William Marshall has turned out more than a dozen quirky mysteries featuring Feiffer and the other denizens of the Yellowthread Street police station, making it clear that the Colony is much more than a department store on a rock. In the process, Marshall provides an excellent insight into the combination of predatory capitalism and the Devil-take-the-hindmost social system that has until now fueled Hong Kong's prosperity (coming soon to a North American country near you!). Everything changes, even Kai Tak, which will soon be replaced by a large, modern airport.

For more than a century, Asians in general and Chinese in particular have supplied villains for Western fiction—the venerable Yellow Peril exemplified by Sax Rohmer's "insidious" Fu Manchu. During that period the Eastern evil-doers were found outside their homeland, in cities like London, Honolulu, and San Francisco, a product of run-of-the-mill racism and xenophobia. The end of the Cold War and the resulting change in the geopolitical equation may signal the return of Asian villains. This time around, with China's inevitable emergence as a modern superpower, we can probably expect a less crude form of the sinister Orientals of late-nineteenth and early-twentieth-century fiction.

Like the best detective fiction, tourism in post–Tiananmen Square China carries in its baggage unavoidable moral questions. Chief among them is the endless but necessary debate about whether contact with Westerners and Western dollars facilitates democracy, or props up the authoritarian gerontocracy that has governed the Middle Kingdom for decades. Assuming you resolve or rationalize that issue and decide to go to China, here are some books to take along.

READING LIST

COONEY, Eleanor, and ALTIERI, Daniel. *Deception: A Novel of Mystery and Murder in Ancient China* (NY, 1993). While acknowledging their debt to Robert van Gulik, Cooney and Altieri offer a more complex and historically accurate Judge Dee. Their tale begins where van Gulik's ends, in the latter part of Dee's career as he is elevated from provincial magistrate to government minister. Set in Chang'An, Loyang, and the Grand Canal city of Yangzhou, the story is broadly concerned with the rise of Buddhism in Tang Dynasty China, and the parallel rise of the Middle Kingdom's only empress, the infamous Wu Zetien. Two tenuously connected murders bracket what is essentially a novel of bloody court intrigues from which Judge Dee disappears for long stretches. Empress Wu is reminiscent of Russia's strong-willed Catherine the Great, and she is beguiled by a charismatic Buddhist monk, much as Czarina Alexandra was entranced by the sinister Rasputin.

This Judge Dee remains a sleuth on the Sherlock Holmes model, one who often resorts to disguises. "Curiosity is the force that drives me," their jurist explains. "Puzzles left unfinished . . . are such infuriating things . . . I did much of my life's work for myself—for the simple reason that I cannot tolerate an unsolved riddle." But he is class-conscious as well, sounding a little like U.S. Supreme Court Justices William O. Douglas or Thurgood Marshall. He wonders why it is "that a man is considered more likely to be capable of murder if he is a common sort of fellow, a rough-hewn worker who uses his hands to earn his living? Why does blame attach itself so effortlessly to a man with dirt under his fingernails? What is the source of our suspicion and contempt?" As with van Gulik's Dee, there are anachronisms: Investigators draw outlines of bodies at a murder scene. Seventh-century characters use expressions like "Feh!" and concepts like "ontological," and there is more Buddhist arcana than anyone other than a devotee would want to know. There is far more sex and violence in this incarnation of Judge Dee, but also less humor and warmth than that surrounding the more endearing star of van Gulik's series.

HALL, Adam [Elleston Trevor]. *The Mandarin Cypher* (London and NY, 1975; NY, 1985). British secret agent Quiller, of the similarly named memorandum, is dispatched to Hong Kong to retrieve a Defense Ministry turncoat. The missile expert has gone to work for the Chinese, at the urging of his sex-and-money-hungry wife, helping to build a launch pad disguised as an offshore drilling platform. On the espionage evolutionary scale, author Hall is halfway between Ian Fleming and John le Carré. Alas, like Bond, Quiller has not aged well. He is cerebral and expert in hand-to-hand combat, eschewing firearms. There is even a sly anti-Bond joke: while 007 orders his signature martini "shaken, not stirred," Quiller keeps trying to order Indian tonic without gin—usually without success. But his lengthy, interior monologues are tedious and the abrupt breaks in the action at the start of each chapter are disconcerting. "It was a hundred to one against my getting off this missile base with a whole skin, but I was going to try," Quiller confides. Bet the long shot. (Other Quiller China titles include *The Peking Target* and *The Sinkiang Executive*.)

HIAASEN, Carl, and MONTALBANO, William. *A Death in China* (NY, 1984). Before the success of his *Tourist Season* and *Skin Tight*, Carl Hiaasen coauthored several novels with William Montalbano, then a fellow staffer at *The Miami Herald*. Montalbano, now with the *Los Angeles Times*, apparently provided much of the on-the-ground research for *A Death in China*, based on his reporting assignment in Beijing for the *Herald*. An art history professor and Vietnam vet stumbles into some murderous intrigue while in China on a group tour. At Xian, he reacts typically to his initial look at the Emperor Qin Shi Huangdi's unearthed terra cotta army, in "a skylight-lit hall the size of a football field. His first thought was that it was the cleverest and most awesome museum he had ever seen. To protect the excavation while simultaneously exploiting the discovery as a tourist attraction, the Chinese had simply erected a museum over the dig."

A deadly plot unfolds to steal three of the life-size clay warriors. Hiaasen and Montalbano effectively offer a travelogue of Xian—the ancient Tang Dynasty capital of Changan—along with a sense of expatriate life in contemporary Beijing. The action shifts to the United States in the book's second half and, while not up to Hiaasen's later solo efforts, is quite serviceable.

HYDE, Anthony. *Formosa Straits* (NY, 1995). Nick Lamp, underachieving son of a Chinese-American family, is out to make his fortune in Taiwan. But after stumbling onto the murder of an old family acquaintance, his concern shifts to saving his life and new love, dashing from the streets of Taipei to Hong Kong to Xian and Shanghai. En route, Hyde gives us another variation on one of the juiciest scandals on Chairman Mao's family résumé: wife Jiang Qing's past as a movie actress and party girl, a combination Madonna and Evita Perón. Hyde also provides short courses on Chinese nuclear strategy; the Shanghai film industry in the 1930s; the Emperor Qin's terra cotta army; Lin Biao's abortive attempt to overthrow Mao; and why Hong Kong is such a great place for R & R from the region's authoritarian regimes. The Taiwan sections of the book are best, with culinary recommendations and an excellent retelling of a real-life thriller, the assassination of dissident journalist Henry Liu, who was gunned down by a Taiwanese government hit squad in California in the 1980s. The prose is nuanced and graceful, despite pacing that occasionally accelerates to somewhere between breakneck and breathless. Good insight into traditional family values, Chinese style. Nice naughty bits.

LE CARRÉ, John. *The Honourable Schoolboy* (London, 1977). This is one of le Carré's most complicated novels and, at 543 pages, one of his longest. Sandwiched between *Tinker, Tailor* and *Smiley's People*, the second of the Karla trilogy begins in Hong Kong with a classic turn of media manipulation and the action never stops. Ill-fated journalist Jerry Westerby is pulled in to help George Smiley battle his Kremlin nemesis and Circus rivals. This is the class of the Far East field, by the master. But consider this mischievous question: Where would modern English espionage fiction be without Philby, Burgess, Maclean, and Blunt?

MARQUAND, John P. *Thank You, Mr. Moto* (Boston, 1936, 1985). It is the mid-1930s, and Northern China is in turmoil, with only feuding warlords standing between the invading Japanese Army and Peking, where the book is set. In this excellent, atmospheric tale, Marquand lyrically evokes a charming, walled city that is no more. With the exception of some "hissing" on the part of Asian characters, there is surprisingly little of the era's casual racism and ethnocentrism. Japanese detective Mr. I. O. Moto, always seen through the eyes of Europeans, is subtle and sophisticated and not cartoonish. The rest of the cast is familiar: the diffident American intellectual and the feisty young countrywoman who tries to save him; the dissipated Manchu noble; the cashiered British army officer. Mr. Moto, currently serving as a military intelligence agent, tries to solve a murder and thwart an international incident without unduly upsetting his rivals in the Imperial Army.

————. *Mr. Moto Is So Sorry* (Boston, 1936, 1985). Set in the same period as *Thank You, Mr. Moto,* the characters are nearly identical (with different names), as is the plot. Instead of Peking, the multinational crew is on a train from Korea to Manchuria, crossing Northern China on the way to an archeological dig in Mongolia. This time around, Mr. Moto is trying to solve a murder while dueling with Russian agents and his Japanese Army rivals. At one point, an American character experiences an emotion familiar to the contemporary tourist, feeling "like a slow-witted barbarian who was uncouthly trying to understand unknown complexities."

Mr. Moto patiently explains to his American friend Calvin Gates that he has no problem accepting the need for a political murder, even of Gates. But he tells the Yank that he is "so sorry" because the would-be killer, a Japanese military officer, was unacceptably rude to his intended victim. While not nearly as descriptive as *Thank You, Mr. Moto,* there are nice touches, as in this view from the train, of another vanished fragment of old China: "The waning light softened the harsh outlines and made the walled towns that they passed mysteriously remote in a sort of timeless loneliness, and endowed the whole country with an exotic portentious beauty."

MARSHALL, William. *Yellowthread Street* (NY, 1975). In this debut appearance of Hong Kong's Detective Inspector Harry Feiffer, Marshall sets the pattern for the series: a tightly interwoven, almost frenetic plot. Within the space of a single night and 122 pages, the officers of the Yellowthread Street station house in the fictional Hong Bay section of the Colony have to deal with a pair of dismembered Chinese paramours; a movie theater stick-up involving off-duty U.S. sailors; a dead constable; a large Mongolian with a shaved head and a very sharp Gurkha sword. An empathetic bonus for visitors: one of the plot strands concerns several hapless American tourists in search of lost luggage—and each other. The chaotic climax delivers one of the best floor-by-floor, one-building shoot-outs since both movie versions of *The Getaway*. Great fun.

————. *Perfect Ending* (1981). Stormy weather. Seven novels into the series, Harry Feiffer is growing weary of his life and occupation: "In the mirror facing him [was] a tall, tired looking man who around his eyes seemed to have lost all his dreams somewhere along the line." Senior Inspector Christopher O'Yee, half Irish, half Chinese, is still daydreaming about chucking it all and lighting out for the Old (American) West. "I happen to be American by birth and I've reached middle age and like all true born Americans of middle age I hear the great outdoors calling to me." Outdoors, what calls are the winds of a great typhoon approaching the Colony. Six officers in a nearby station house are found dead by an already deranged umbrella peddler, who claims the killer had the head of a large cat and carried a butterfly in its mouth. No diverting subplots this time around. Feiffer logically works the pieces of the puzzle—police corruption, capital formation, and the Chinese hereafter—as the winds howl. Interesting class tension surfaces between Feiffer subordinates Spenser and Auden. There is a signature Yellowthread climax involving a delirious O'Yee and a determined predator.

————. *The Far Away Man* (1984). The weirdness quotient rises on Yellowthread Street, along with Hong Kong's summer heat. Spenser and Auden, the two officers named for English poets, try to solve the mystery of a man who seems to jump from a fourteen-story apartment house every few minutes, but never hits the ground. Detective Senior Inspector O'Yee teeters on the edge of sanity, standing ankle deep in forty-seven disassembled guns in the basement of the Hong Bay police station. Harry

Feiffer grows frustrated by a serial killer from his past, and yearns for help from another detective series: "I'm only sorry the late Dame Agatha Christie isn't with us anymore or she could have set it all in a house on the bloody windswept moors and, like 'The Mousetrap,' it could have run on stage for thirty bloody years!"

————. *Inches* (1994). Like his characters Feiffer, O'Yee, Spenser, and Auden, author Marshall seems to be coming unhinged as 1997 approaches, and with it the Colony's handover to China. Typically, Auden is the object of repeated attacks by seagulls while standing on a catwalk outside a sanitarium eighteen floors above the street. O'Yee follows cryptic, anonymous instructions to go undercover as a homeless derelict. Feiffer puzzles over nine corpses in a closed bank branch. Angst abounds. In the midst of a postmortem, a coroner considers the future: "He didn't care what happened after the Communists took over the Colony. He had been a government medical officer long enough to qualify for a more-than-adequate pension, and, at home in England, he had a house in the country with enough room to set up a small part-time medical practice, that he had almost paid off." Though fraying, the strands of the various plots are ultimately tied off, but the conclusion is bleak: "Soon the Communists would come. A little at a time, piece by piece, Hong Kong was becoming a dying city, fading in light and brightness like a house bereft of occupants." (Other Yellowthread Street mysteries include *The Hatchet Man, Gelignite, Thin Air, Skulduggery, Sci Fi, War Machine, Roadshow, Head First, Frogmouth, Out of Nowhere.*)

MATTESON, Stefanie. *Murder on the Silk Road* (NY, 1992). Sexagenarian (and still sexy) movie star Charlotte Graham, between projects, goes on the road to China's Far West. Like most Hollywood actresses and multiple Oscar winners, Graham is self-absorbed, but she can break away from her favorite subject long enough to describe some deadly intrigue at a fossil dig in far western Dunhuang. There is a good tourist's-eye view of China train travel in the early 1980s, to an area that still draws only the hardiest of travelers to its fabled Buddhist cave murals. Despite the seemingly odd mix—the politics of paleontology and the *I Ching*—the narrative works, much of the time. Graham's cranky conservatism is a slight irritation, and the killer comes out of nowhere. Matteson's digressions become so long-winded that she feels the need to provide periodic plot summaries, so as not to lose the thread.

NORMAN, James [James Norman Schmidt]. *Murder, Chop, Chop* (NY,

1942). Title notwithstanding, this thriller-mystery combo has a distinctive period flavor without a dated feel. "Chinese names, to be appreciated, should be rolled between the tongue and teeth and gnawed upon carefully," Norman advises. Set in and around Xian (Sianfu) in the late 1930s, its central character is Gimiendo Hernandez Quinto ("G.H.Q."), a gigantic, multilingual Mexican guerrilla who once rode with Pancho Villa, but now trains Nationalist Chinese peasants to fight the Japanese invaders. Quinto has to contend with multiple murders, betrayals, scorned women, and corrupt bankers. The action revolves around Daqing Hot Springs, outside Xian, where Nationalist leader Chiang Kai-shek lost his false teeth and changed modern Chinese history—an incident recounted as the action unfolds. Despite his patronage, Quinto clearly (albeit subtly) admires Chiang's Communist rivals, if you catch his admiring references to the Reds' Eighth Route Army and their celebrated General Chu Teh (Zhu De). At one point, Quinto hums a battle song from the Republican side of the Spanish Civil War, which author Norman reported on. The partisan leader says he nabs criminals "by dialectic. A good system."

Quinto's perspective on the nationalities he encounters is refreshing, including one expatriate adventurer, quick to condemn, who is described as having "a great thickness of New England American ancestry." The British, he observes, "had a tendency to over-do things, particularly bathing, imperialism, exercise and drinking." And especially the Irish. "Cantonese are said to resemble the Irish, who carry a chip on both shoulders—one chip for the love of liberty, the other for the love of a good fight." A pose struck by a young Chinese beauty "hits even the most insensitive Chinese between the eyes with as much ease as Mother Machree in tenor reduces an Irishman to putty." Norman, who earned a Bronze Star and battlefield commission in the South Pacific during World War II, wrote two subsequent China novels starring Quinto—*An Inch of Time* (1944) and *The Nightwalkers* (1946). Based on this one, they are worth pursuing.

RENDELL, Ruth. *The Speaker of Mandarin* (London, 1983, 1988). For such a skilled writer, Rendell gets off to a disturbingly leaden start. In the first few pages, a Chinese government guide is described as "slant-eyed," and given to saying things like "I afflaid you be solly." Such racism would be more understandable (but no less excusable) if this novel had been written in the 1920s or 1930s, rather than in the early 1980s. And it's a pity, because the story of an English policeman on a busman's holiday in

Southern China is otherwise excellent, homing in on the sometimes murderously claustrophobic dynamics of group travel. Rendell's description of the officiousness and petty tyranny of official government guides is dead on. In one instance, which replicated an experience of my own, a hostile guide borrows a tour book one night, memorizes a section, and repeats it the next day as a lecture.

After the standard Hong Kong and Beijing area stops, London's Chief Inspector Wexford manages a side trip to Changsha, the capital of Hunan Province, not included on most itineraries. Along the way, Wexford "wondered, and not for the first time, if there was such a thing as a hundred-watt bulb in the whole of China." Only the critical first third of the narrative takes place in China, including the tourists' inevitable boat ride down the Li River from Guilin. On Wexford's home turf in London, the inspector finds himself trying to solve the mystery of a missing two thousand-year-old corpse, a drowning in China, and a fatal shooting in England by asking "the requisite question that always made him feel like a character in a detective story." Exactly.

SIMON, Roger L. *Peking Duck* (NY, 1979, 1986). Los Angeles private detective Moses Wine, a former Berkeley radical and law school dropout, is coping with middle-aged angst following the successes recounted in *The Big Fix* and *Wild Turkey*. A used Porsche and his face on the cover of *Rolling Stone* have sent him into an introspective tailspin, concerned about the distance he has come from his sixties ideals. "Through a series of rationalizations common to most middle class American males on the way to middle age, I figured if I was going to eat the forbidden fruit I at least ought to take a good bite. Hence the Porsche." Wine's antidote is to accept an invitation from his Aunt Sonya, a lifelong radical, to join "Friendship Study Tour Number Five" to the People's Republic of China. For Wine, it's "a new beginning, a spiritual journey . . . a search for self, a search for values that were waning so fast I wondered if I ever had them."

The tour contains the usual collection of California lefty stereotypes: movie star, congresswoman, encounter group therapist, alternative newspaper publisher, bored wealthy housewife, assorted academics. Author Simon, who recently has devoted most of his time to screenwriting, at least knows the people he caricatures. And he evidently read enough Marx and Mao to understand what he was seeing when he toured China in 1977, as the country was just starting to accept American tourists. The action, set in Hong Kong, Canton, Shanghai, and Peking, tracks Wine's search for a priceless Han Dynasty gold-and-jade duck lifted from a museum in the Forbidden City. At one point, Wine says that he doesn't like detective stories because "they usually sacrifice everything to the plot." But in this case, Wine and the people he encounters are far more interesting than the plot. One tour guide tells Wine, "In three years, China will be capitalist again . . . and people like you will feel totally betrayed." As in many mysteries, the rich narrative foreplay is not equaled by the hurried, ideologically dubious climax.

TASCHDJIAN, Claire. *The Peking Man Is Missing* (NY, 1977). Mystery as memoir. This is by far the most intriguing book of the China lot, and when I spotted it on a remainder shelf years ago I swept up all six copies. The author, an American, was a young member of the anatomy department of Peking Union Medical College in 1941, when the Japanese attack on Pearl Harbor caused foreign nationals in the Chinese capital to dash for safety. Lost in the chaos were two redwood crates containing the 500,000-year-old remains of forty individuals known collectively as Peking Man, destined for the United States for safekeeping. Taschdjian offers an explanation for what happened to the priceless remains that is fanciful but also plausible. One of the fictional characters, the erudite and philosophical Father Lorrain, is based on Pierre Teilhard de Chardin, who was living in China at the time and performed the author's wedding.

TREVOR-ROPER, Hugh. *The Hermit of Peking: The Hidden Life of Sir Edmund Backhouse* (NY, 1986). Oddly, the most compelling modern mystery set in the Chinese capital isn't fiction. This genuinely creepy tale unravels the strange life of Backhouse, an English baronet, scholar, and major benefactor of the Bodleian Library at Oxford. Acclaimed historian Trevor-Roper, a Cambridge don and a veteran of the British Secret Service, turns detective as he examines Backhouse's obscene memoirs and the reclusive man behind them. Crook, secret agent, inventor of a scandalous past, Backhouse fascinates. My only complaint: although Trevor-Roper's descriptions of the salacious sections of the memoirs are titillatingly vivid, he turns coy and offers no examples.

VAN GULIK, Robert H. *The Celebrated Cases of Judge Dee [Dee Goong An]* (Tokyo, 1949; NY, 1976). This is the original—sort of. Although Judge Dee lived in the seventh century (A.D. 630–700), the three tales here knitted together were not written down until the eighteenth century. Van Gulik reconciled and translated several versions of the work, edited and shaped it somewhat, and illustrated the text with drawings in the style of the Ming Dynasty period (A.D. 1368–1644). The result was so effective that van Gulik's version was translated back into Chinese in the 1980s for serialization in the *Peking Evening News*. These three cases involve the murder of a traveling silk merchant in Shandong Province, a crime of passion in a small village, and the death of a bride on her wedding night.

————. *The Haunted Monastery and the Chinese Maze Murders* (The Hague, 1957; Kuala Lumpur, 1961; NY, 1977). In his second effort, van Gulik borrowed plot elements from three sixteenth-century Chinese crime collections—none of which involved the real Judge Dee—and adapted his cast of characters for two stories. In the first, numerous residents of a Taoist monastery, including the abbot and three women, have been dispatched to the hereafter. The judge and his wives have taken refuge from a mountain storm, but remain to solve the murders. In the second story, Dee, en route to a new posting in China's Far West, investigates a serial killer of women, while himself under threat from another ruthless criminal. The solution to one crime is contained in a scroll painting; another in a garden maze.

————. *The Chinese Gold Murders* (London, 1959; Chicago, 1977). Following a successful Chinese military campaign against Korea in 662, the young judge receives his first posting to Penglai in Shandong Province, near what is now Qingdao (Tsingdao), where the beer is brewed. The promising young magistrate must find a missing bride, a war slave, a traitor, and a gold-smuggling ring—plus a murderer.

————. *The Chinese Nail Murders* (London, 1961; Chicago, 1977). At another desolate post, this one in North China in A.D. 676, the judge continues to distinguish himself. But crime strikes his official entourage as a faithful aide is struck down. While a devoted family man, the judge is not immune from temptations of the flesh, nor without a sense of humor about it. In this story, he recalls that he took a third wife at the urging of his first wife, who thoughtfully chose the new addition to the household. "She was a handsome, lively woman," Dee explains, "and it was nice that now there were always four to play dominoes."

————. *The Monkey and the Tiger* (London, 1965; Chicago, 1992). In the second and more interesting of these two stories, "The Night of the Tiger," the judge is recalled from his post on China's northern border to the capital of Changan (just outside present-day Xian) in A.D. 676 to become Lord Chief Justice, a post the real jurist held. En route, he is waylaid in what appears to be Shanxi Province by bandits called Flying Tigers—perhaps a tip of the hat to the World War II flyers van Gulik rubbed shoulders with. The bandits hide out in loess caves not unlike those in Yenan chosen by Mao and the Eighth Route Army in 1935. The first story, "The Morning of the Monkey," is dedicated to van Gulik's pet gibbon, Bubu.

————. *The Willow Pattern* (London, 1965; Chicago, 1993). After you read this, I guarantee you will never again look at the familiar blue-and-white porcelain in the same way. Willow Pattern chinoiserie is one of van Gulik's intentional anachronisms, having originated in eighteenth-century England. In A.D. 677, the Lord Chief Justice Dee, one year into his term as president of the Metropolitan Court in Changan, is appointed emergency governor of the imperial capital. A devastating plague has broken out and order must be maintained, while a number of seemingly unrelated but brutal murders are solved. A clue is in the Willow Pattern. For comic relief, one of the judge's bailiffs marries twins.

————. *Murder in Canton* (London, 1966; Chicago, 1993). One of the last Judge Dee mysteries written by van Gulik, who died in 1967, and the last chronologically, set in A.D. 681. The Lord Chief Justice's duties are now as much political as judicial. In the South China river port, capital of Guangdong Province, the judge has to prevent an uprising by Arab pirates while solving several murders. The historical period is all wrong for Canton, but the narrative doesn't suffer. (Other Judge Dee books include *Poets and Murder, Judge Dee at Work, Necklace and Calabash, The Red Pavilion, The Lacquer Screen, The Emperor's Pearl, The Chinese Lake Murders, The Phantom of the Temple,* and *The Chinese Bell Murders.*)

⟫⟩⦿⟨⟪

XV

MALAYSIA/SINGAPORE/ BORNEO

South Bridge Road was quiet, except for those of the ever-present European and Pacific island tourists who had gotten up early to take in the sights. They were walking in pairs or in groups, talking animatedly, taking pictures the way they do—like giant dolls running through a programmed series of maneuvers. Ever since Singapore became an independent island republic in 1965, the government has made a concentrated effort to lure more visitors and thereby increase the primary contributor to the gross national income. This program, to the bitter disgust of a minority of inhabitants—myself included—has been an overwhelming success. (Jack Foxx, *The Jade Figurine*)

The town [Ayer Hitam, Malaysia] was some shops, the Club, the mission, the dispensary, the Methodist school, my consulate. The Indians lived on the rubber estates, the Malays in neighboring "kampongs," the Chinese in their shops. The town was flat; in the dry season it was dusty, in the wet season it flooded; it was always hot. It had no history that anyone could remember. . . . (Paul Theroux, *The Consul's File*)

The only things which seemed active in that area were the elephants. There were a lot of these, totally uninhibited by man, thrashing around on tracks they make for themselves which tend to run in great fifty-mile loops. We came on three herds of elephants, all minding their own business and expecting us to mind ours, which we did. Minding your own business is the law of survival in the jungle and if you stick to it you can move around in the daytime through the clutter almost as safely as you can in Westminster Abbey. This is, except for the snakes. Snakes have their own regulations and no one seems to have found out what they are. We were always watching for snakes. (Gavin Black, *A Wind of Death*)

*In the garden the fire-flies were flitting here and there. From the earth
rose a scented warmth and you felt that if you stopped you would hear
the growth of that luxuriant vegetation. A white flower of the night gave
forth an overwhelming perfume.* (W. Somerset Maugham, *Ah King*)

The Malay Peninsula, with the climate of a perpetual Turkish bath. (Sir
Frank Swettenham, *British Malaya*)

Generic Jungle and Curry Tiffin

By Robin Winks

THE MALAY PENINSULA, and to a lesser extent Borneo (now divided between Malaysia and Indonesia), often has stood for a kind of generic
jungle in European fiction. Huge pythons, great poisonous sea snakes,
bloodsucking leeches, Malays run amok, Chinese tong wars, and bibulous British rubber planters—all good fodder for fiction—can be set
down in Malaysia and, even if the behavior of the leech is all wrong and
belongs in *The African Queen,* who is to know?

At the tip of the Malay states is Singapore. Until World War II, this
city stood in line behind Hong Kong and Shanghai as a locale in which
all the iconography of the Sinister Oriental stereotype could be put on
display: opium dens, white slavery, militant clans, skulking eavesdrop-
pers with long fingernails. After the Japanese occupation, and well after
the war, Singapore's "economic miracle" moved it up (though still behind
Hong Kong) as the scene for industrial espionage, China-watching, piracy
on the South China Sea, and stolen nuclear secrets. The fact that Britain
conducted an attenuated war in Malaya against Chin Peng and his Communist Terrorists—the C.T.s, as they were called in the headlines—a war
that lasted into the 1960s, provided for an additional overlay between
fact and fiction.

A hundred books about the Japanese occupation, some of them good,
poured out in the late 1940s and for two decades afterward, character
studies or thrillers, local and less successful emulants of *The Bridge on the
River Kwai.* There also was a thriving local industry in novels about ethnic tensions between the largely rural Malays, the industrious Chinese

who often controlled local commerce, the South Asians who had been brought in to work on the rubber plantations and now were small shop-keepers, and the Europeans who managed the plantations or ran the agency houses in Kuala Lumpur and Singapore.

Often a crime figured in these stories, though the crime or its resolution was not the point of the book. Unlike South Africa or Kenya, which produced clue-laden mysteries that, save for their exotic settings, might have been made in Manchester, Malaysia gave rise to markedly little conventional detective fiction, though to a good many thrillers. Many of the books were interchangeable with nearly identically plotted yarns set in Thailand, or New Guinea, or the interior of tropical South America. A dollop of Hobson-Jobson English—calling a shirt a *baju* and having Europeans sit down to a "curry tiffin"—and a passing reference to Singapore's Bugis Street often were all that set these books apart geographically.

READING LIST

AARONS, Edward S. *Assignment—Sulu Sea* (Greenwich, Ct., 1964). Aarons was a key figure in the stable of thriller writers built by the paperback publisher Fawcett in the 1950s to the 1970s. His series figure, Sam Durell, Cajun with a Yale education, was sent all over the world on assignments. Aarons always worked up the backgrounds with care and, though some critics considered his books to be banal, they often stood out in the crowd. Here the main action is in a minor island group off the coast of Borneo, to which the CIA dispatches Durell to keep the Polaris submarine from becoming a Chicom plaything.

————. *Assignment—White Rajah* (Greenwich, Ct., 1970). Aarons's fortieth book, and by now a bit repetitive, but with *tuan* Durell still leaping buildings (or at least small streams) at a single bound, the action continues nonstop. The scene is not Sarawak, as one might expect from the title, so much as Malaya's East Coast. The unlikely plot is about hijacked U.S. naval planes.

AMBLER, Eric. *Passage of Arms* (London, 1959). This is the best thriller set in Malaya, in part because Ambler is the best writer to have used a peninsular setting, but also because he uses scene to supreme effect. (See also his 1956 novel, *The Night-Comers,* set in Indonesia.) Wonderfully cinematic, *Passage* begins when an Indian clerk in Malaya finds a cache of arms and decides to capitalize on it. Interlocking choices made by people unknown to each other lead inexorably to a feared and dramatic conclusion. The use of local terms is masterful, with no hint of their being sprinkled in merely for effect.

BARATHAM, Gopal. *Moonrise, Sunset* (London and NY, 1996). "The Singapore night, warm and damp like a dog's tongue, licks my face and tickles the side of my ear." This is just right, as are many of Baratham's descriptions. A neurosurgeon, he dissects Singapore's multiracial culture with great skill in this political thriller mixed with social commentary and a sly sense of humor. The protagonist, How Kum Menon, is caught up in the police investigation of his fiancée's death.

BLACK, Gavin. Black (a pseudonym for Oswald Wynd, who has written several novels under that name) made Southeast Asia his special province. His protagonists are usually Scots (as was Wynd), thoroughly at home in Asia (Wynd was born in Tokyo), self-sufficient, observant, and tough. He wrote thirteen novels featuring Paul Harris, a businessman with extensive Asian interests who lives in Kuala Lumpur's posh Kenney Hill section. All are good and use local settings accurately. Personal favorites are:

Suddenly at Singapore (London, 1961). The first Paul Harris novel. Harris is getting started as a gun-runner, hoping to jump-start his business into legitimacy, and he falls afoul of some very rough characters. Local color is at a minimum, but dialogue is crisp and Black firmly establishes his character.

A Wind of Death (London, 1967). The sixth Paul Harris novel, with Black now fully in control and much excellent use of local scene. Harris has become a Malaysian citizen. Lum Ping (that is, Chin Peng) is hiding out on the Thai-Malaysian border up on the Kra Isthmus, and Harris gets involved. Much fast action follows.

The Cold Jungle (London, 1969). Harris is mostly in England or on the Scottish island of Mull in this one, but the use of mirror-image scenes (as the title suggests) takes one mentally back to the Malay peninsula, and we learn a good bit more about Harris.

A Time for Pirates (London, 1971). Harris rescues a young woman from an angry mob in Kuala Lumpur and finds himself involved in the oil business. The Malaysian background is particularly effective here.

The Bitter Tea (NY, 1971). Harris is now a rich man with business interests in Scotland and throughout the Far East. He witnesses an attempt to kill a Chinese leader. Local color is unobtrusive and the writing a bit slack, but the book moves beautifully.

CARTER, Nick. *The Cobra Kill* (NY, 1969). Nick Carter books have been turned out by a dozen and more writers, all to formula; this is as good an example as any. Action takes place in Hong Kong, Singapore, Kuala Lumpur, and in the *ulu* (roughly, jungle), and though the places may have been worked up from a guidebook, they serve pretty well.

CORRIGAN, Mark [pseudonym for Norman Lee]. *Singapore Downbeat* (Sydney, 1959). Good smuggling, etc., in Singapore, pitting Corrigan and his Girl Friday, Tucker McLean, against Mr. Sin.

DERBY, Mark. *Malayan Rose* (London, 1951). Published as *Afraid in the Dark* in the United States, this was Derby's first book. Patrick Derrex agrees to track down and kill a war criminal who is working with terrorists. The Malayan scene is well handled.

————. *The Sunlit Ambush* (London, 1955). Derby worked in military intelligence in Malaya, on which he draws for this rapid-fire thriller. The hero travels in Singapore and then upcountry. Regarded as Derby's best book.

FOXX, Jack. *The Jade Figurine* (Indianapolis, 1971). Foxx is Bill Pronzini, best known for hard-boiled American thrillers. Here a charter pilot is grounded in Singapore for smuggling, and is then implicated in a murder.

KYLE, Duncan. *Green River High* (London, 1979). Set among warring guerrillas in Borneo, where the hero tries to find a lost World War II bomber that is the key to a fortune in rubies.

LILLEY, Tom. *The Projects Section* (London, 1970). An authentic, strong thriller set in Malaya during the Communist insurrection known as "the Emergency," by a person who knew the country well.

————. *The "K" Section* (London, 1971). A well-told tale of a British colony on the verge of independence, with the Special Branch combatting a Communist takeover in what may be Sabah, "somewhere east of Singapore."

MacLEAN, Alistair. *South by Java Head* (London, 1957). MacLean's second book, following on *The Guns of Navarone,* and quite possibly his best. He follows the fortunes of the last boat to slip out of Singapore harbor into the South China Sea as the Japanese overrun the city in 1942. Action is incessant, characters are believable, scene is well used.

MAUGHAM, W. Somerset. *Ah King* (London, 1933). Six of Maugham's best stories, subtly evocative of expatriate life among British planters and men of commerce and their bored wives, each tale concealing a mystery, set in a thinly disguised Malacca, in Singapore, and in Borneo.

ROSS, Sheila. *The Perfect Carrier* (London, 1972). Drug smuggling from Singapore to Borneo, Communists, and much authentic local color in Kuching, Labuan, and North Borneo.

SHERLOCK, John. *The Ordeal of Major Grigsby* (NY, 1964). A manhunt in the Malayan jungles, offering ample opportunity to observe the scenery—the Communist Terrorists again, though not as cartoon figures.

SHERRY, Sylvia. *Frog in a Coconut Shell* (London, 1968). An adventure tale, ostensibly for young (teenage?) readers, with excellent local color, set in a fishing village on the East Coast of Malaya during *konfrontasi* with Indonesia.

STEWART, Ian. *The Seizing of Singapore* (Feltham, 1980). A lurid thriller about a plot to kidnap the prime minister of Singapore and install a puppet. The story is nonsense, but Singapore is nicely described.

THEROUX, Paul. *The Consul's File* (Boston, 1977). Interlocking short stories in the manner of Maugham, set in postcolonial Ayer Hitam, a fictional town in Malaysia—with murder, conspiracy, adultery, and other goodies.

THOMAS, Ross. *The Singapore Wink* (NY, 1969). The late Ross Thomas was the master of the international shell game. An ex–Hollywood stunt man searches—from Los Angeles to Washington and Singapore—for a man he believed he had killed two years before. A real page-turner, this is one of Thomas's best.

TREVOR, Elleston. *The Pasang Run* (NY, 1962). Published as *The Burning Shore* in London in 1961, this is a top-shelf thriller about a burnt-out case who agrees to be manager of a tiny airfield in a remote part of Malaya. Trevor flew for the Royal Air Force in World War II, and airplanes play a prominent role in all his books, most particularly *The Flight of the Phoenix*, which was made into a successful motion picture, and his Quiller series, which he wrote as Adam Hall.

YORKE, Susan. *The Agency House* (London, 1961). Two Chinese orphans rise to political and economic power in Kuala Lumpur and become pawns in a terrorist plot. The writing is flat, there is little sustained tension, but the author knows Singapore.

Kim *and the Great Game*

By Robin Winks

A KEY PHRASE FOR spy fiction (and sometimes for spy reality), the Great Game, comes from the high priest of the romantic fiction of empire, Rudyard Kipling. Though E. Phillips Oppenheim had produced potboilers well before Kipling, in 1901, published *Kim*—probably his master work and certainly the finest of his four novels—no one had described so well the life of the covert agent, of the wanderer who sees, and though seen, is not recognized, who through tradecraft and courage, through knowledge of the landscape and much good luck, survives to play the Great Game again.

Kim is not truly a spy novel. It is a novel about friendship, affection, and bonding, about growing up and out, about Pathan horse-trading, local customs, and Buddhist philosophy. Still, the book contains the elements readers came to associate with the type: long overland treks, going to ground, a sense of constant danger and fatalism. As one spy tells Kim, "We of the Game are beyond protection. If we die we die. Our names are blotted from the book. That is all." One might not let down one's guard, spit, sneeze, sit down, cross one's legs, eat, pass water, in a way other than the role one played required; one was always being watched or must assume this was so, must pay attention to the smallest detail. *Kim* is a remarkably cheerful, even sunny, book, but it is underscored by the paranoia so essential to the genre.

Kim is a half-Irish orphan who grows up to become an agent for Her Majesty's Secret Service. Kim is also Kipling's alter ego. Born in India in 1865, sent to school in England, Kipling returned to India as a journalist in 1882 and traveled extensively. He particularly loved the color and vitality of the Punjab, the Land of the Five Rivers, and the unending parade of humanity along the Grand Trunk road. His love for India, his sturdy British patriotism, and his own childhood in Bombay and Lahore led him to create in *Kim* what he called "a labor of great love" and one of his "wiser" works.

The phrase "the Great Game" would come to embrace all spying and all spy fiction, but in 1901 it had a quite specific locus: the term referred to Britain's imperial contest with Russia for control over India's North West Frontier. Tsarist Russia was pressing down on the high mountain ranges that separated the two great powers, hoping for a sphere of influence in Persia, probing for some means of breaking out of the Black Sea to an all-weather port. The Russian Empire was expanding across Central Asia, through forbidding yet romantic mountain valleys filled with mystery, beckoning adventure, and the promise of mineral resources.

Parts of India and the states to the north and west were ruled by sultans, maharajahs, chieftains, mullahs, sheikhs, tokays, and others who were prepared to collaborate with this or that imperial power in exchange for protection, prestige, trade goods, areas, or even, at times, for some benefit to their people. Germany was making motions toward the Balkans, the Ottoman Empire, modern-day Iraq; so were the French, not yet Britain's ally. As Britain mounted one intelligence operation after another, bribing, suborning, planting disinformation, Russia was the primary target at the turn of the century, and thus the most intense field of play was the North West Frontier.

In *Kim*, Kipling shows Indians as fully the equals of Europeans in all respects. The novel teems with memorable figures and brilliantly evoked places; one hears the sounds of the caravans as they creak and jolt across the high passes, the sounds exact in the cold mountain air; one smells the wonderfully pungent manure of the trail, the hint of heat from the lower elevations; one spits out the dust, breathes in the aroma of the bazaar, stares into bright night sky with Kim as he travels with a Tibetan lama in search of the River of Immortality and, in time, captures the papers belonging to a Russian spy high in the Himalayas. Kipling's sense of place was always acute; he was never better than in *Kim*.

This writer tried to read *Kim* several times, as teenager and as adult, and never broke through its now somewhat distant Hobson-Jobson *pukka-sahib* aura until one day, finding himself in modern-day Pakistan, in Lahore, he took the novel up again, this time in a cheap local reprint edition, and read as he sat facing the great gun Zam-Zam, outside the museum of Lahore, with which the book opens, and heard the sound and smelled the smells of that city, and understood just how magnificently accurate Kipling's scenes were, reading the book straight through in a night and the following day.

Here was a land far more real than E. M. Forster had provided. Here, in Hurree Chunder Mookerjee, who teaches Kim how to survive as he plays the Great Game, and in Mahbub Ali, a Pathan horse-trader of narrow gorges, high passes, and redolent caravanserai, Kipling creates some of his most memorable characters. Kim is in search of his identity—Who is Kim? What is Kim? he asks—but he is also at ease in many worlds, Hindu, Muslim, Buddhist, British. He is the eternal watcher in the shadows, the precursor of all those who will play the Great Game over the twentieth century. That Britain's best-known spy and traitor of the century, H. A. R. Philby, was called "Kim" is less a degeneration of the tradition than a tacit recognition of the duplicity always just behind the courage.

CHECKLIST

Other Asian Destinations

Burma

GILMAN, Dorothy. *Incident at Badamyâ* (NY, 1989). Orphaned in Burma, the sixteen-year-old daughter of American missionaries is headed for New York when she is kidnapped by the Red Army.

MASON, F. Van Wyck. *Trouble in Burma* (NY, 1962). U.S. Army Intelligence agent Colonel North and his quaint Thai sidekick go looking for a Voyager satellite somewhere in the jungles of Burma.

India

BLOCHMAN, Lawrence G. *Bombay Mail* (Boston and London, 1934). The governor of Bengal is murdered in his private car on the train of the title in the first of three novels featuring Inspector Leonidas Prike of the CID and a mostly European cast of characters in colonial Bengal.

DRUMMOND, Ivor. *Necklace of Skulls* (NY, 1977). Three ditsy young dilletantes pursue drug-smugglers in India and encounter the ancient cult of the Thugs.

EASTERMAN, Daniel. *The Ninth Buddha* (London, 1988; NY, 1989). The son of a British agent in India is abducted to Tibet where he is welcomed as a reincarnation of Buddha.

KEATING, H. R. F. *The Perfect Murder* (London, 1964; NY, 1965). The first of twenty or so cases for Inspector Ganesh Ghote of the Bombay CID, a series often praised for its portrayal of the many subcultures of the subcontinent.

———. *Inspector Ghote Goes by Train* (London, 1971; NY, 1972). From Bombay to Calcutta on the "Calcutta Mail" to fetch an arrested con man.

MANN, Paul. *Season of the Monsoon* (NY, 1993, 1995). A mutilated corpse in a lake in Film City, India's Hollywood, is the focus of the first of Mann's novels featuring half-breed police inspector George Sansi.

———. *The Ganja Coast* (NY, 1995, 1996). A murder case for Inspector Sansi in the hippy paradise of Goa.

MATHER, Berkely. *The Gold of Malabar* (London and NY, 1967).

———. *Snowline* (NY and London, 1973). Hippies caught up in smuggling drugs from India to Marseilles.

Nepal and Tibet

DAVIDSON, Lionel. *The Rose of Tibet* (London and NY, 1962). A quirky updating of James Hilton's fabled *Lost Horizon*.

HARVESTER, Simon. *The Chinese Hammer* (London, 1960; NY, 1961).

MASON, F. Van Wyck. *Himalayan Assignment* (NY, 1952; London, 1953). Colonel North and the Cold War version of the "Great Game."

MATHER, Berkely. *The Pass Beyond Kashmir* (London and NY, 1960).

WOLPERT, Stanley. *The Expedition* (London, 1967; NY, 1968). To Nepal in quest of the Yeti (a.k.a. "The Abominable Snowman").

Indochina

DIEHL, William. *Thai Horse* (NY, 1988).

GILMAN, Dorothy. *Mrs. Pollifax and the Golden Triangle* (NY, 1988). On vacation in Thailand, part-time CIA agent Mrs. P. mixes it up with drug smugglers and warlords.

GREENE, Graham. *The Quiet American* (London, 1955; NY, 1956). Saigon in the early fifties is the setting for Greene's prophetic novel about an American innocent, CIA agent Alden Pyle, caught up in a conflict he tragically misunderstands.

HARVESTER, Simon. *Battle Road* (London and NY, 1967).

———. *Dragon Road* (London, 1956; NY, 1969).

HEFFERNAN, William. *The Corsican* (NY, 1983, 1984). The drug underworld from Southeast Asia to southern France.

Indonesia

KOCH, C. J. *The Year of Living Dangerously* (London and West Melbourne, 1978). Western newsmen gather in the Mayang Bar in Jakarta during Sukarno's period of *konfrontasi* (confrontation) with whites.

Papua New Guinea

JAY, Charlotte. *Beat Not the Bones* (London and NY, 1952; NY, 1995). The seductive charms of the islands tempt white men to "go native" and "run amok." Winner of the first Edgar for "best novel."

————. *The Voice of the Crab* (NY, 1974). Set in Papua New Guinea around 1954.

Fiji Islands

ARTHUR, Frank. *Who Killed Netta Maul? A Story of Murder in the Fiji Islands* (London, 1940). One of four mysteries featuring Inspector Spearpoint of the Fiji Constabulary.

XVI

AUSTRALIA

The soft, blue, humanless sky of Australia, the pale unwritten atmosphere of Australia. "Tabula rasa." The world a new leaf. And on the new leaf nothing. (D. H. Lawrence, *Kangaroo*)

. . . I ran into my first stretch of bulldust and almost lost control, no feel to the steering, the back tyres spinning and the car lurching wildly. Ahead, round the red shoulder of a hill, loomed a cloud of dust like an explosion, and in the straight beyond, the dust cloud hung in the sky for more than a mile, a glint of glass reflected at its snout. It was the first of the day's traffic, a big refrigerated container truck throwing gravel at me as it thundered past. And then I was into the red cloud that followed in its wake, a sepia opaqueness of nil visibility with dust pouring into the car, filling my mouth, clogging my nostrils. (Hammond Innes, *The Golden Soak*)

We passed Melbourne Travelodge then got onto the freeway through a grey-green Australia of scrawny gum trees and puffy-clouded sky. Gradually the trees were overtaken by builtup areas. In the nineteenth century Melbourne had been the richest city on the continent. It was the establishment city. The gold they'd dug out of the ground had been converted into solid buildings and solid citizens that were going to last forever. There was no convict stain here as there was in Sydney. Citizens were upright, honest. They believed in law and order. I guess that's why they acquitted members of their police force when they shot people. (Marele Day, *The Disappearances of Madalena Grimaldi*)

You know, of course, that the Tasmanians, who never committed adultery, are now extinct. (W. Somerset Maugham, *The Bread-Winner*)

Out on the wastes of the Never Never—
That's where the dead men lie!
That's where the heat waves dance for ever—
That's where the dead men lie.

(B. H. Boake, *Where the Dead Men Lie*)

Way Down Under and Way Out Back

By Robin Winks

R EADERS WHO HAVE never been to Australia tend to view it in one of two ways: as a vast, empty land filled with kangaroos and great red rocks that press down to long stretches of empty beach where husky young men dressed in rather old-fashioned bathing suits rescue embattled swimmers from the sharks; or as one great outdoor barbeque pit with Sydney at its front door and gorgeous sheilas ready for a good time. Actually, until quite recently it was America forty years behind the times. Now it is America ten years into the future. All these images, contradictory as they may be, are true.

Australia has produced one writer of mysteries who is very nearly world class: Arthur W. Upfield, creator of the "half-caste" aboriginal detective named Napoleon Bonaparte, who from the late 1920s until Upfield's death in 1964 dominated the scene. In the 1960s and '70s Upfield's books were dismissed as racist, usually by people who did not read them, though by the 1980s they were returning to favor, both for their quite vivid use of a variety of Australian locales (New South Wales and Western Australia most frequently) and for their observations about the role of race in Australian life.

By the 1990s Australian fiction embraced numerous writers of mysteries, and detective novels reflected North American trends in particular, with private eyes, women detectives, and gay and lesbian themes that, for all their authors' use of Sydney street names, might as well have been set in Los Angeles.

There is, then, a good bit of inconsistency in such fiction when it is considered as travel literature. If set in the Outback, with its distances and dust, its dingoes and dark silences, the books are immediately recognizable as Australian, fulfilling the outsider's expectations; but if set in the great cities of Australia, they convey little that is distinctive except in diction and the occasional throwaway negative line about American influences or lingering British colonial attitudes.

Australia is one of the most urban countries in the world. Most of its population lives in its six major cities. This has almost always been the case since the day in 1788 when Captain Arthur Philip arrived at Port Jackson (Sydney) with the first convict transports. Life was hard and masculine from the beginning, and that life was rooted in the cities, or in the mining camps that depended upon them. Mysteries about the Outback are essentially as romantic as Canadian mysteries set in the frozen North, or American thrillers that look to the cowboy as a central figure. The real action was and is in the cities, and those cities were British, European continental, and increasingly American in their nature.

Most major writers of adventure thrillers have taken on Australia at some point: Hammond Innes, Alistair MacLean, and others have worked up the Australian Outback with considerable accuracy. At times an Australian mainline novelist crosses into thriller or mystery fiction, Nevil Shute (who though born in England lived in Australia after 1950) being the most obvious example. In the 1950s Carter Brown, another transplanted Brit, enjoyed an international readership, though many of his pulp novels were not set in Australia. A genuinely urban voice would not emerge until the 1980s, when Peter Corris introduced his private investigator, Cliff Hardy, a Sydneysider. In 1987 and 1988, respectively, Jennifer Rowe and Marele Day published their first mutedly feminist mysteries. By 1994 Australian crime fiction was so rich and varied that an annotated bibliography of 2,600 titles (many of them distinctly obscure and dated) attested to the health of the genre Down Under. This compilation, John Loder's *Australian Crime Fiction: A Bibliography, 1857–1993* (Port Melbourne: D. W. Thorpe, 1994), is commended to any reader who wishes to find titles set in Canberra, et al., for it faithfully records settings. No such compilation exists for any other nation in the Commonwealth, and the fact that the book is produced in association with the National Centre for Australian Studies at Monash University suggests that crime fiction is now accepted even in the once-cloistered halls of academe.

Still, a traveler hoping to stock up on Australian-written and Australian-set mysteries outside the country will have a problem, for many of the writers who seem to be well regarded in Australia have not been published elsewhere. In fact, some of the most praised authors are not very good or are so drenched in Crocodile Dundee dialect as to be virtually unreadable more than a hundred miles away from Bondi Beach. Yet one doesn't want these writers to merge with P. D. James or Sue Grafton, for the very Australianness of their voices is what makes them interesting. So load up while Down Under, and take their books home with you (tucking a copy of Australia's own mystery magazine, *Mean Streets,* into your pouch) for post- rather than previsit reading.

READING LIST

ANTHILL, Elizabeth. *Death on the Barrier Reef* (London, 1952). Detective Inspector Simon Ashton, of Scotland Yard, helps the Queensland police for reasons that are unconvincing. The Australian flavor is well presented, however, and the Great Barrier Reef plays an important role. One wonders why there has not been more from this writer.

BARNARD, Robert. *Death of an Old Goat* (London, 1974). Barnard's first book, a product of the time he spent as a lecturer in English at the University of New England, in Armidale, New South Wales. This remarkable debut is one of the few mystery novels that are truly solved in the last few lines. Barnard has much to say that is amusing, and even more that is nasty, about his fictional University of Drummondale, and depending upon one's views of academe, one will be either angered or delighted with the result. I fall into the latter group.

BEDFORD, Jean. *Worse than Death* (North Ryde, 1991). Bedford is one of a half-dozen Australian Sisters-in-Crime to win critical recognition. She has written several nonmurderous novels, all in a flat, serviceable prose. Her series figure, Anna Southwood, is a PI with a concern for social issues, which gives Bedford a chance to have her poke about into real institutions—hospitals, adoption agencies, etc.—which provide for an Australian flavor. In this one she investigates a killing she thinks the police have got wrong.

————. *Make a Killing* (Pymble, 1992). Set in Sydney and on the Illawarra coast, this is a crisp inquiry into an apparently accidental death. Unlike her husband, Peter Corris (q.v.), Bedford does not flatten all settings out into a generic city or generic countryside, and it is not her fault that there is a sameness in much of the Australian landscape.

BROWN, Hosanna. *Death upon a Spear* (London, 1986). Brown is the pseudonym of a (male) professor of linguistics in Australia who writes of a (female) private eye named Frank le Roux, who is American, black, very beautiful, and rather irritating. The playfulness in gender switching extends to a parody of academe in which scholars make their name by writing papers on the glottal stop as a syllable prosody. This book, set largely in Canberra, is a hoot, whether poking fun at political correctness or at the way Right Minded People think about Australian Aborigines. The mystery is almost incidental.

CARLON, Patricia. *The Souvenir* (London, 1970). This moving mystery, about small-town crime, focuses on two hitchhikers, one of whom must be a murderer. Recently reprinted, *The Souvenir* is well worth ferreting out. The tone is that of the Canadian writer L. R. Wright.

————. *The Running Woman* (London, 1966). This prolific writer often focuses on children or teenagers, and she deserves to be better known for her portraits of small-town Australia. Here she asks questions about the drowning of a teenager and produces psychologically sound, if stylistically strained, answers.

CLEARY, Jon. *Babylon South* (NY, 1989). Cleary has written more than forty books, many of them about Scobie Malone of the Sydney police. Here Detective Inspector Malone turns back to a case he first investigated over twenty years before, when the head of Australian Intelligence vanished without a trace. The first Malone book, *The High Commissioner* (1966), was set in London, where Malone was sent to act as bodyguard for the eponymous official; it is rightly regarded as a classic. When writing of his native Australia Cleary seems a bit less convincing than when he uses the Himalayas (*The Pulse of Danger*) or Bolivia (*The Liberators*), but even so his Aussie books stand well above the crowd.

————. *Murder Song* (NY, 1990). This book uses Malone as a commentator on the growing corruption in Australian society. A motiveless killing by a sniper leads Malone deep into the Sydney underworld. The writing is becoming a bit careless but the scene is still nicely described.

————. *Winter Chill* (NY, 1995). A return to form, with Sydney in winter made properly unappealing. The president of the American Bar Association is murdered while attending a conference; other murders follow, and Scobie Malone sorts it all out. (Cleary, however, appears to believe Oshkosh is in Indiana.)

CLIVE, John. *Barossa* (London, 1982). This could have been quite a strong book, for its author appears to know what he is talking about—missile scientists working in the Australian desert—and the flora and fauna come across well enough, but the plot sags into the expected un-expectedness.

COOK, Kenneth. *The Man Underground* (London, 1977). Cook appears to be largely forgotten, though his first two books, *Wake in Fright* (1961), set in a small Outback town, and *Chain of Darkness,* were well received. Here Cook takes his readers to an opal-mining town called Ginger Whisker that might well be Coober Pedy and develops both the story and the scene convincingly.

CORRIS, Peter. *The Dying Trade* (Sydney, 1980). This is the book that introduces Cliff Hardy, PI, a man who, as his ex-wife tells him, spends his time among "damaged people." Though often compared to Ross Mac-Donald, the comparison is inappropriate, for Corris neither writes so well nor is as interested in buried psyches. I prefer a comparison to the American Max Byrd who, like Corris, is an academician talking tough. Corris likes violence.

————. *The Empty Beach* (NY, 1983). Possibly Corris's most representative book, with a stronger sense of Sydney than he usually provides. This routine search for a possibly dead though possibly hiding wealthy man whose wife wants him found or proven dead follows all the customary steps. That Cliff Hardy (or Corris?) believes the capital of Oregon is Portland suggests that neither is a geographer.

COURTIER, Sidney H. *The Glass Spear* (NY, 1950). Courtier stands head and shoulders above other Australian mystery novelists for his sense of place and his use of exact, intently described locales. He is rather less good at creating believable plots. Nonetheless, several of his books are just short of outstanding, and one wonders why they are out of print. In this first mystery Courtier mixes anthropology with the squattocracy, combining Arthur Upfield with Dick Francis en route to a creditable conclusion in the Outback.

————. *Death in Dream Time* (London, 1959). This fantastical book both fascinates and repels. Set in an entertainment park based on aboriginal creation myths, with the action spanning just twenty-four hours, the book is a true page-turner. Queensland is the putative locale, though the Dream Time is the truer base.

————. *Murder's Burning* (London, 1967). This well-clued book takes the narrator back to Paladin Valley (fictional) to investigate how the entire valley was destroyed six years earlier. Subterranean passages feature prominently and terrifyingly, and only when the book is back on the shelf will one question the whole business.

————. *Ligny's Lake* (NY, 1971). This was apparently Courtier's personal favorite. A World War II veteran is reported drowned on the day the narrator sees him far away at a prizefight. The narrator-friend sets out in pursuit. That the man who has disappeared is a space-research engineer suggests where the book will go; the conclusion is unoriginal and unconvincing, but the journey is worthwhile.

CREASEY, John. *Murder, London–Australia* (London, 1965). Vintage Creasey, with Inspector "Handsome" (Roger) West pursuing unsolved London deaths to their resolution Down Under.

DALE, John. *Dark Angel* (Sydney, 1995). Teems with Sydney life on the down side, with rent boys, Vietnamese mafia, and burnt-out types. The nearest comparison is Derek Raymond, though cover copy invokes James Crumley.

DAY, Marele. *The Life and Crimes of Harry Lavender* (Sydney, 1988). Claudia Valentine is Australia's first female private eye. Here she looks into the death of a novelist, found at his word processor. The Australian flavor is muted.

————. *The Last Tango of Dolores Delgado* (Sydney, 1992). This was Day's breakthrough book: It won the Private Eye Writers of America Shamus Award as best original paperback. Claudia Valentine is supposed to protect the delicious dancer Dolores, but she fails. Delgado turns out to have been a transsexual; Valentine investigates effectively if belatedly.

————. *The Disappearances of Madalena Grimaldi* (Sydney, 1994) This book isn't calculated to make one want to go to Australia, but once there, it is a compelling read. PI Claudia Valentine is looking for her roots while she also tries to find a missing schoolgirl. The answers are grim, so are Melbourne and Sydney.

DISHER, Garry. *Kick Back* (Sydney, 1991). Disher is Australia's answer to Jim Thompson, and in this debut book, which introduces Wyatt, who robs banks and lifts payrolls, he packs a convincing punch.

————. *Paydirt* (North Sydney, 1992). This is superior crime fiction, not a mystery, but pace and bleak realism keep one turning the pages. Wyatt is a killer and a thief, and he has no redeeming features. The locale is South Australia this time.

DIXON, Jean. *The Climber* (Sydney, 1987). A relatively rare setting,

Ayers Rock, "the oldest rock in the world," makes up for pedestrian writing. A detective inspector and his wife miss a tourist bus and soon learn more about Australia's dead heart than they intended.

FERRARS, Elizabeth X. *The Small World of Murder* (London, 1973). Set partly in Adelaide, this is one of Ferrars's weaker works, as there is little mystery. But the scenes in Fiji, Australia, and New Zealand are well handled.

FRANCIS, Dick. *In the Frame* (London, 1976). Francis is at his weakest when he ventures away from his milieu of English race courses. This book involves art forgery and, of course, horses, and it is a genuine mystery, as Francis's books often are not. Sydney is lightly and pleasingly used with an eye to what a first-time visitor would find intriguing.

GASK, Arthur. *A Secret of the Sandhills* (Adelaide, 1921). Now virtually forgotten, Gask wrote many books about a Sydney policeman, Gilbert Larose, with the later books set in England. Sandhills was Gask's first effort, and it is an execrable mystery but South Australia is well used.

GEASON, Susan. *Sharkbait* (St. Leonards, 1993). A second case for Syd Fish, PI, set in Sydney's Kings Cross area, with a foray into the Hunter Valley. I have not caught up with *Dogfish* (1992), which involves Fish with a transvestite president of the Sex Workers Union.

GREENWOOD, Kerry. *Murder on the Ballarat Train* (Ringwood, 1991). A third novel about Phryne Fisher, fighter in the Resistance during World War II, who is a detective in Melbourne. The train is nicely done.

————. *Death at Victoria Dock* (Ringwood, 1992). Phryne Fisher is definitely over the top, but she is a sound investigator. This book, set in the Melbourne docks, is Greenwood's best, even if her history is at times just a bit woozy.

————. *Ruddy Gore* (Sydney, 1995). A lively tale involving opera, a Chinese magician, and Phryne Fisher once again. She is described as "a woman of surpassing otherness, immensely attractive, supremely alive and shining from head to heel." As Abraham Lincoln is supposed to have said: People who like this kind of thing will like it.

HARDY, Lindsay. *The Nightshade Ring* (NY, 1954). A superior spy story in which MI5 agents pursue a high-ranking Nazi to Australia. Lots of movement.

HOWARD, Tom. *The Last Generation* (Sydney, 1986). Set in Surfers Paradise, along Queensland's Gold Coast, this is a series of connected stories. The locale is nicely depicted.

HUME, Fergus. *The Mystery of a Hansom Cab* (Melbourne, 1886). Usually credited as the first successful Australian mystery, *Hansom Cab* sold a half million copies and launched Hume into a long career. Subtitled "a realistic story of Melbourne Life," this might be just the trick for a long rainy night in that city; one could not possibly read it elsewhere.

INFANTE, Anne. *Death on a Hot Summer Night* (London, 1989). This and other books by the author use Brisbane and the Queensland coast to good effect. They are just good enough to make one wish they were better.

INNES, Hammond. *The Golden Soak* (London, 1973). Innes is famous for his use of exotic locales, which were usually well researched on the spot. The Golden Soak is a mine in a remote part of Western Australia, and Innes delivers his usual fast-moving yarn amidst the heat and dust of the Outback.

KENEALLY, Thomas. *The Place at Whitton* (London, 1964). Keneally is a highly regarded author of "straight" novels; his *The Chant of Jimmie Blacksmith* was a searing indictment of racism in Australia. *Whitton* is a straightforward mystery set in a theological college in New South Wales and is a harbinger of the good things to come.

LAW, Marjorie. *Death in the Spring* (Melbourne, 1965). A nicely turned traditional mystery concerning the death of a gossip columnist in Melbourne.

LINDSAY, Joan. *Picnic at Hanging Rock* (Melbourne, 1967). Well known as a film directed by Peter Weir, this mystery is about the disappearance of schoolgirls on an outing in Victoria.

McNAB, Claire. *Lessons in Murder* (Tallahassee, 1988). McNab introduces Australia's first lesbian detective, Carol Ashton, in this mystery about the murder of a teacher in North Sydney. As Ashton is a detective inspector, her liaisons do not remain secret.

———. *Fatal Reunion* (Tallahassee, 1989). Much the better book, though less concerned with setting, this mystery was her first to attract attention in Australia.

———. *Under the Southern Cross* (Tallahassee, 1994). Australian tourism brings two lesbians together. Carol Ashton is missing, and this is more of a romance, but it uses the Outback to good effect. For more Ashton see also *Copout* (1991) and *Dead Certain* (1992), not reviewed.

MOFFITT, Ian. *Death Adder Dreaming* (Sydney, 1988). Not easy to come by, but worth the effort for its use of Alice Springs and the way in which it handles the murder of a part-aboriginal lawyer.

MUDROOROO. *Wildcat Screaming* (Sydney, 1992). Mudrooroo teaches Australian aboriginal literature. This is his third Wildcat book, Wildcat being an aboriginal wordsmith who has taken to the urban life. Here the reader goes inside Fremantle Prison and learns about the Panopticon Prison Reform Society. Though described as a "revolutionary stylist," the author is quite comprehensible and at times appealing.

NEVILLE, Margot. *Murder of a Nymph* (London, 1949). Neville should enjoy a modest revival, as her books—the work of two sisters—are straightforward, entertaining, and pleasing enough for a hammock. Here we pursue a murderer in a small community of young marrieds north of Sydney.

O'HAGAN, Joan. *Against the Grain* (London, 1987). Much running about in the Northern Territory to protect or obtain a strain of wheat: literate and ultimately pleasing despite some plot problems.

PALMER, Madelyn. *The Whirl of a Bird* (London, 1965). Set at a ski resort on Mount Kosciusko, with a nicely limned detective inspector on the trail.

PEEL, Colin D. *Snowtrap* (NY, 1984). A thriller that rockets from Queensland to Switzerland with little logic, though the opening flying sequence is well done.

ROWE, Jennifer. *Murder by the Book* (Sydney, 1989). Recently "discovered" in the United States, Rowe appeals to those who want a mystery with little blood. The British have taken over an old Sydney publishing firm; murder follows.

———. *Death in Store* (North Sydney, 1991). Verity Birdwood, sent to research a TV show on how a department store deals with Christmas, handles this and seven other mysteries. The Australian flavor is nil.

———. *The Makeover Murders* (North Sydney, 1992). Set in a New South Wales country house, this is the book that confirmed Rowe's bid to be "the Australian Agatha Christie."

THOMPSON, Estelle. *Death by Misadventure* (NY, 1992). The first American publication by a well-regarded Australian writer with many books to her credit. Here a daughter looks for her father in Queensland and New South Wales.

UPFIELD, Arthur W. Upfield is by far the best-known Australian writer of crime fiction, and his creation of the part-aboriginal detective Inspector Napoleon Bonaparte (usually called Bony) brought Outback Australia into the living rooms of thousands of readers. Born in England, Upfield went to Australia when he was twenty-two, and he never lost his outsider's ability to see what was unusual in the Australian landscape. Every book is rich in scene, and while the total body of work is somewhat uneven, at least twenty of his twenty-nine novels still repay a reading. I cite here some particular favorites:

The Bone Is Pointed (Sydney, 1938). A horse returns riderless; twelve years before, the owner's father was found dead in a riding accident. Set in western Queensland, in the Diamantine country, this book is possibly the best Upfield depiction of the bush.

Death of a Swagman (NY, 1945). Set near Broken Hill, NSW, this moving story explores the quintessential Australian icon.

The Widows of Broome (NY, 1950). Two widows have been murdered in a western Australia fishing village. Local color is superb.

The New Shoe (NY, 1951). Often singled out as Upfield's best book, as Bony is fully in stride by now, this being his fifteenth story; set on the coast of Victoria.

Death of a Lake (London, 1954). Jacques Barzun and Wendell Taylor declare this "a complete success" (high praise indeed), and they are right. An inland lake is drying up in a drought that has gripped all of New South Wales.

The Will of the Tribe (NY, 1962). A corpse is found in a meteor crater in Western Australia, and Bony puts his tracking skills to their most difficult test.

Bony's World

A CCORDING TO Ray B. Browne's study of Upfield's novels, many are set in fictitious small towns and on homesteads whose locations can be inferred. The following list is based on Browne's inferences, grouped roughly by area. Asterisks indicate fictitious place-names.*

---

*Ray B. Browne, *The Spirit of Australia: The Crime Fiction of Arthur W. Upfield* (Bowling Green State University Popular Press, 1988). Used with permission.

New South Wales
Bony and the Kelly Gang, Bowral, near Sydney
The Bachelors of Broken Hill, Broken Hill, in the west
Winds of Evil, Wirrigatta Station, near Broken Hill
House of Cain, Melbourne and the northwest
Death of a Swagman, Merino, in the west
Bony and the Black Virgin, Mindee on the Darling River
Murder Must Wait, Mitford
Death of a Lake, Porchester Station, Lake Otway
Madman's Bend, White Bend
The Sands of Windee, Windee Station
The Barrakee Mystery, Barrakee Station, River Darling Basin

Queensland
Venom House, Answerths Folly, Edison
Wings Over the Diamantina, Coolibah Cattle Station, in the west
The Bone Is Pointed, Opal Town, St. Albans

South Australia
The Lake Frome Monster, Lake Frome, in the east
Bushranger of the Skies, McPherson Station, 80 miles N.W. of Shawo's Lagoon
Bony Buys a Woman, Mount Eden, Lake Eyre
The Battling Prophet, Mount Gambier
Man of Two Tribes, Nullarbor Plain, in the southwest

South West Australia
Mr. Jelly's Business, Burracoppin

Western Australia
Widows of Broome, Broome
Bony and the Mouse, Daybreak
The Beach of Atonement, Dongerra
A Royal Abduction, Eucla
Breakaway House, Murchison Breakaway, in the west
Bony and the White Savage, Rhudder's Inlet, Leeuwin Lighthouse
The Will of the Tribe, Wolf Creek Meteor Crator
Sinister Stones, Agars' Lagoon, 240 miles south of Wyndham

Victoria
* *The Mountains Have a Secret,* Dunkeld
* *The Devil's Steps,* Wideview Chalet, Mannon, Mount Chalmers
The New Shoe, Split Point
An Author Bites the Dust, Yarrabo (near Melbourne)

The Tasman Sea
The Mystery of Swordfish Reef, Bermagui on the Tasman Sea

WHITE, Osmar. *Silent Reach* (London, 1978). A former British intelligence officer is working undercover on a vast ranch in northwest Australia, where gangs of night raiders are attacking mines and homesteads. The temperature reaches 129, which helps blind us to the stiff writing.

WRIGHT, Steve. *A Drop in the Ocean* (Sydney, 1991). A London PI, living in Australia, is hired by a conservationist who then drowns. Sydney's suburbs are canvassed.

YARBOROUGH, Charlotte. *Murder on the Long Straight* (Hong Kong, 1979). Murder on the Perth-to-Adelaide train, with Malaysian students involved. Not very good, but a nice curiosity from its place of publication to its descriptions of the train journey across the Nallabor plain.

XVII

NEW ZEALAND

It is easy to talk—for it is the first impression which one receives—of those two 'little islands of New Zealand lost in the immensity of the Ocean.' But they are little only beacause of the almost fearful solitude which surrounds them. (Andre Siegfried, *Democracy in New Zealand*)

> *Always to islanders danger*
> *Is what comes over the sea . . .*
>
> (Allen Curnow, "*Landfall in Unknown Seas*")

New Zealanders are all the time standing on the edge of these seas. They spend their lives wanting to set out across the wide oceans that surround them in order to find the rest of the world. (John Mulgan, *Report on Experience*)

It is no uncommon thing to get five or six samples of weather in almost the same number of hours, each vieing with the other which shall be the most unpleasant. It is a strenuous climate, and it breeds strenuous folk. . . . (F. T. Bullen, *Advance Australasia*)

As always early on a fine morning, the mist lay across the lake like a fragile curtain and the surface of the water was flat and unbroken except for the quiet lap along the shore. Everything was still, and all that moved was Dougherty as he dragged a small dinghy down from its hiding place, pushed it out into the lake, and sprang in. . . . He rowed steadily for an hour, not being able to forget that the Maoris had called the lake Wawiwhiu, whistling waters. As soon as the sun had been up for a while it would stir the wind in the mountains and send it whistling down to the lake, making it dangerous for small craft. By that time he'd need to be safely at the head of the lake. (Jack McClenaghan, *Moving Target*)

Little Islands in a Big Sea

By Robin Winks

U NTIL RECENTLY NEW Zealand has been remarkably free of crime, especially of the kind that shows up in fiction. Consisting of two islands 1,200 miles from Australia, the nearest continent, New Zealand enjoyed a high standard of living, political stability, and—relative to the rest of the world—a low level of social or ethnic unrest. Escape into a crowd was difficult. Even car thieves could do little, not being able to transport their booty off the islands. Nor did New Zealand figure prominently in anyone's fantasies about espionage (despite a tightly run and efficient intelligence operation that, until a spat with the United States, helped to keep Americans informed about various Pacific island developments). Little crime, little crime fiction seemed to be the story, with the important exception of Ngaio Marsh, who set most of her mystery novels in England. She did not forget her native land, however, and the little that most mystery readers knew of New Zealand came from her work.

Much has changed in New Zealand in recent years. A rising crime rate, greater ease of travel, and sharp Maori-*pakeha* (as the "white" population is called) conflict, as well as higher unemployment and the almost universal problem of teenage angst turned dangerous may provide for a more criminous literature. Certainly, novels that turn on a criminal act have increased substantially, but New Zealand writers seldom use the mystery genre to tell their tales. Now and then a roving thriller writer passes through, uses New Zealand as a setting, writes off a trip on taxes, and moves on. There is still no large body of crime literature set in New Zealand.

What there is, however, is of high quality, at least where use of locale is important to story, for New Zealand is a remarkably beautiful and diverse land. It is also small enough that travelers feel they have grasped the whole of it in three weeks or so and confidently write when they might better have remained silent. Just as Canadians do not speak as Americans do, New Zealanders do not speak as Australians or the English do, but many a passing writer has failed to listen well, and there are numerous short stories buried in collections that purport to tell of a New Zealand mystery and then get their first adverb wrong.

This is too bad, for the country deserves study. It is one of the world's most literate societies, with a high rate of book consumption, but the market is too small to sustain local writers, and the locales are not sufficiently generic to translate into worldwide interest. One can imagine Philip Marlowe walking the mean streets of Sydney; Auckland, for all its petty crime and ethnic tensions, is simply too sunny or too wet.

READING LIST

ATLEE, Philip. *The Kiwi Contract* (Greenwich, Ct., 1972). Atlee's series figure, Joe Gall, "the government's ace nullifer," hops around the world cleaning up improbable situations, and on this occasion he impersonates an oil geologist while traveling through New Zealand. The story is garbage, but surprisingly, the New Zealand locales are intelligently used and often well described.

BAGLEY, Desmond. *The Snow Tiger* (London, 1975). Bagley was one of the best writers of generalized thrillers in the manner of Hammond Innes and Alistair MacLean, though unlike MacLean, he never stopped doing his research. This humdinger is set in a small mining town that is destroyed by an avalanche; a court of inquiry follows, with each survivor telling a version of what happened.

BALL, John. *The Kiwi Target* (NY, 1989). The creator of *In the Heat of the Night* also wrote routine thrillers set in exotic places. Here an American-born businessman goes to New Zealand to save his firm from being taken over by a multinational enterprise and stumbles into murder and a good bit of inexplicable and ill-explained hugger-mugger. New Zealand is badly used: this is the tourist quickie in a nutshell.

BENNETT, Margot. *That Summer's Earthquake* (London, 1963). Bennett is being reprinted these days, though this one hasn't shown up again. Work on a sheep station and a major earthquake figure in this quasi-thriller; no mystery.

BOSWELL, John. *The Blue Pheasant* (London, 1958). A thriller that involves Hong Kong, New Zealand, and Australia, all well observed, though not well heard.

JAY, Simon. *Death of a Skin Diver* (NY, 1964). An appealing book set in and near Auckland, with likeable people, a complex plot, and excellent use of real places presented realistically.

———. *Sleepers Can Kill* (NY, 1968). Jay shifts from mystery to espionage, still in Auckland, with the same excellent use of setting, but here the story is unconvincing even as the action is well described.

JOSEPH, M. K. *A Pound of Saffron* (London, 1962). A novel about ambition, lies, and justice in a New Zealand university, this is not a formal mystery though it has some of the elements, as does C. P. Snow's classic, *The Masters*: intrigue, endless plotting, and revenge. As usual academics are twitted—often without compassion—for devoting their lives to "Some Unexplained Marginalia in Spanish Peruvian Texts of the Seventeenth Century."

McCLENAGHAN, Jack. *Moving Target* (London, 1966). A superior tale of going to ground in the face of overwhelming pursuit, this first novel rivals the best of Geoffrey Household. A deserter eludes capture for more than a year, helped by roadmen and farmers; he is then presumed dead in an avalanche. The South Island in World War II is beautifully described.

MANTELL, Laurie. *Murder in Fancy Dress* (NY, 1981). This competent New Zealand writer deserves a wider following, as she creates good puzzles and plays all the cards of the traditional cosy very well. On this occasion a dogged policeman in a small New Zealand town investigates the death of a local policeman. Petone—the setting—is no longer a small town, but all else is right.

————. *A Murder or Three* (NY, 1980). Despite a dust jacket that identifies Lower Hutt as being in Australia, this book is redolent of New Zealand flora and fauna, some of the latter criminal. Mantell is much influenced by Dick Francis, though she doesn't follow the horses.

————. *Murder and Chips* (NY, 1982). Quietly competent police work set against small-town Hutt Valley politics provides for genuine insights into New Zealand society.

MARSH, Ngaio. Marsh is by far New Zealand's best-known writer—not only of mysteries, but in any form (though no doubt Katherine Mansfield and Janet Frame might be cited by some). A Dame of the British Empire, for her contributions to the theater rather than to genre fiction, Ngaio (pronounced, please, *neigh-oh,* the name of a distinctive New Zealand flower) Marsh is in the grand tradition of the English cozy and ranks with, or very nearly with, Christie, Sayers, Allingham, and James. Most of her books are set in the United Kingdom and involve Scotland Yard's Roderick Alleyn and his wife Troy, but New Zealand figures in some. The most entertaining and instructive are:

Vintage Murder (London, 1937). Inspector Alleyn is on vacation in New Zealand, where he investigates murder involving a traveling theater troupe from England. The mystery is sound and the setting, most likely Wanganui, nicely described.

Surfeit of Lampreys (London, 1941). The Lampreys are a titled family with roots in New Zealand, in which only the opening chapter is set, though Marsh tells the reader a good bit about society in New Zealand in her few precious pages.

Colour Scheme (London, 1943). The New Zealand local color is extremely well done, though readers have debated for years precisely where in the North Island this mystery—in which a victim, being color-blind, is led by misplaced guide flags to fall into a boiling crater of mud—takes place. The time is World War II, and the Maori play an important role at Wai-ata-tapu Springs.

Died in the Wool (London, 1945). A sheep station owner is killed by a German spy and his body is hidden in a bale of wool. Barzun and Taylor pronounce the tale "grim," which it is, but the description of work on a station (or ranch) is very good.

Photo Finish (London, 1980). Marsh's last book, and if not of the highest, certainly of a high standard. A diva, whose portrait Troy is painting, is murdered. This is Marsh's best use of the New Zealand scene since the 1940s, and her description of the South Island, of Christchurch, Arthur's Pass, and the country around Hokitika, is vividly real.

MESSENGER, Elizabeth. *Dive Deep for Death* (London, 1959). Caving in New Zealand, with good suspense and interesting characters.

MULGAN, John. *Man Alone* (Auckland, 1939). This is a true classic of New Zealand literature, though it qualifies for a place here only in that a crime is committed and Johnson, the protagonist, is caught up in the Auckland riots of 1932 and must flee. New Zealand attitudes between the two great wars are brilliantly reflected in terse dialogue and fine description.

PEEL, Colin D. *Bitter Autumn* (London, 1973). Illegally mined gold on the Coromandel peninsula and some Northland action provide for a sound travelogue within a standard thriller.

PRIESTLEY, Brian. *Makariri Gold* (London, 1977). An expert in counterinsurgency, wounded in Cambodia, comes to New Zealand to visit his brother—to find that the man has vanished. Lots of action and very able descriptions of South Island landscapes, somewhat in the terse manner of Dick Francis, make this a good introduction to both the genre and the land.

SALTER, Elizabeth. *Death in a Mist* (London, 1957). A woman is witness to a murder, imperfectly seen through the mist of a geyser in full spout. An Australian detective investigates the murder. There is an attractive love story and some sound ratiocination.

SLATTER, Gordon. *A Gun in My Hand* (Christchurch, 1959). That rare thing, a New Zealand entry in the Graham Greene look-alike contest. Slatter describes the events of a single day in Christchurch. This is not a mystery but the gun is important to it.

XVIII

MEXICO

COATZACOALCOS: As he descended from the plane, he breathed the hot humid air laden with the scent of laurel and vanilla. He removed his jacket and hailed a broken-down taxi. Swift glimpses of coconut-palm forests, zebu cattle grazing on brick-colored plains, and the Gulf of Mexico whipping up its early-evening thundershower yielded to a view of a port city with low, ugly buildings, their windows blasted out by hurricanes, and dirty neon signs, unlighted at this hour, a whole consumer society installed in the tropics, supermarkets, television-sale and -repair shops, and in the foreground the everlasting Mexican world of tacos, pigs, flies, and naked children in mute contemplation. (Carlos Fuentes, The Hydra Head)

MEXICO CITY: The city unleashed an army of humanity onto its streets. The city gave no quarter, made no allowances for lack of sleep, the encroaching cold, frigid limbs, bad moods, breakfasts caught on the run, acid indigestion, halitosis, upset stomach.

Every morning, in the same way, the city sent its soldiers out to do battle. She sent some out with power in their hands, and the rest with the everyday blessings of the street.

The city was a holy mess. (Paco Ignacio Taibo II, An Easy Thing)

WHEN IN MEXICO CITY: Go to Sanborn's café-cum-"American drug store," where fashionable Mexican ladies once met for tea and where generations of homesick North Americans have sought consolation in a *hamburguesa.* Just be sure to go to the *right* Sanborn's, because the venerable café has become a chain of restaurant/drug stores/bookstores. The one you want, which figures in several novels reviewed below, is just a block off the Zócalo on Madero St. Once a great colonial mansion, it is known as *La Casa de los Azulejos* ("House of Tiles") for its unusual blue-tiled façade. Inside, the restaurant courtyard and the Orozco mural are also worth a look.

Good-Bye, L.A. . . . ¡Hóla, México!

I_T IS TEMPTING_ to imagine Philip Marlowe and the other California tough guys of the thirties and forties packing up their bags of hard-boiled tricks and heading for Mexico in search of seedier hangouts, meaner streets, more outrageous injustices. If ever a city seemed in need of a tough but honest private investigator, it is teeming Mexico, with its many layers of corruption both individual and institutional, its extremes of elegance and squalor.

The right man for the job didn't show up for decades; the North American masters of the hard-boiled, with one notable exception, stayed closer to home. True, Marlowe crosses the border in Raymond Chandler's _The Long Goodbye_ (1953), but he ventures no farther south than Tijuana. Several key events in the novel, however, take place offstage in a small Mexican resort town Chandler calls Otatoclan. Chandler also treats us to Marlowe's observations on things Mexican: e.g., "There is nothing tougher than a tough Mexican, just as there is nothing gentler than a gentle Mexican, nothing more honest than an honest Mexican, and above all nothing sadder than a sad Mexican."

James M. Cain, the exception noted above, makes Chandler sound like a sentimental fool. Cain's portrayal of Mexico City and its denizens in his 1937 novel, _Serenade,_ is nothing short of vicious. Here is his narrator on Mexico's Indians: "An Indian, he's about eight thousand years behind the rest of us in the race towards whatever we're headed for, and it turns out that primitive man is not any fine, noble brute at all. He's just a poor fish."

In Ross Macdonald's _The Zebra-Striped Hearse_ (1962), Lew Archer looks for information about an unhappy heiress's unsuitable lover in the chic village of Ajijic on Lake Chapala near Guadalajara. In the process, he also takes a quick look at the life of expatriate North Americans in Mexico: "This is our fifty-first state," one says. "We come here when we've run through the other fifty." But murder beckons elsewhere, and Archer is in and out of Mexico within twenty-four hours.

There is, however, no lack of English-language mysteries with Mexican settings. In the fifties and early sixties, Suzanne Blanc and Bruce Buckingham wrote novels with Mexican detectives. Margaret Millar dispatched her Chicano detective Tomas Aragon to Baja California in a scenically memorable 1976 novel. And the Florida MacDonald, John D., sent Travis McGee on several Mexican adventures. The Cold War, the drug trade, and Mexico's oil reserves—all have brought spies and other government agents to Mexico over the years. The infamous E. Howard Hunt's first fictional foray south of the border, *Maelstrom,* dates from 1948; his most recent is *Mazatlán* (1993). Donald Hamilton's Matt Helm also found his way to Mexico to tangle with *The Menacers* (1968), *The Retaliators* (1976), and *The Frighteners* (1989).

Another source for distinctive mystery plots is Mexico's pre-Columbian ruins and their sometimes lurid lore: human sacrifice, ancient curses, magic mushrooms. And, of course, unscrupulous archeologists and artifact smugglers. For mystery novelists, Chichén Itzá in the Yucatán is the hands-down favorite among ancient sites and Quetzalcoatl (Kulkulcan to the Mayans) the favored ancient god. Contemporary Mayans or part-Mayans have become quite chic as detectives (see Gary Alexander, and Aaron Elkins, on pages 223 and 224, respectively). There is a definite progression in both interest and political correctness from Bruce Buckingham's pure Spanish, Poirot-shaped Don Pancho to Suzanne Blanc's educated Aztec anomaly, Inspector Menendes, to Gary Alexander's Mayan single father, Luis Balam.

According to Amelia S. Simpson's *Detective Fiction from Latin America* (NJ, 1990), "the detective story has been regularly, although not extensively, cultivated in Mexico since the 1920s." Among the characteristics of Mexican detective fiction: satire, social criticism, and the use of Mexican settings. One seminal title in the recent development of the Mexican mystery, mentioned both by Simpson in her book and by Mexican crime novelist Mauricio-José Schwartz in an interview, is Rafael Bernal's *El complot mongol* ("The Mongolian Plot," 1969), a tough, hard-boiled story that incorporates elements of the spy novel and the thriller while offering a critical look at Mexican society.

Mexico City ultimately found its bard in Paco Ignacio Taibo II, born in Spain but a resident of Mexico since childhood and a citizen since 1980. In Taibo's books the influence of Dashiell Hammett and other North and Latin American writers is filtered through a sensibility at once distinctively Mexican and totally individual. His novels deliver strong doses of social criticism, portraying a country where corruption is endemic and the police are the worst offenders. But the stories also are enormously entertaining: sometimes Marx Brothers zany, sometimes playfully self-referential in the best postmodernist fashion.

READING LIST

ALEXANDER, Gary. *Blood Sacrifice: A Mystery of the Yucatán* (NY, 1993). Luis Balam, the protagonist in this first of a series, is a part-time detective, a full-time Mayan, and a thoughtful guy. When an American evangelical missionary is arrested as the serial killer of four beautiful women stabbed with an ancient Mayan sacrificial knife, Balam is initially relieved that no Indian is involved. Unfortunately, he can't believe that the evangelist is the killer. A well-written book about the seedy side of Cancún. (See also the second Balam mystery, *Dead Dinosaurs*.)

ANGUS, Sylvia. *Dead to Rites* (NY, 1978). The Indian police detective in this classic archeological mystery is no match for Mrs. Wagstaff, a large, self-confident American of a certain age who makes it her business to know everybody else's, including the ancient Mayans'. Mrs. Wagstaff is part of a tour group visiting Chichén Itzá (staying in what sounds like the Mayaland Hotel) when the corpse of a dangerously flirtatious young member of the group is found in a *cenote* (a deep well where the Mayans once tossed sacrificial victims). A witty and intelligent novel.

BLANC, Suzanne. *Green Stone* (NY, 1961). Inspector Menendes of the San Luis Potosí police is an anomaly in his time and place: an educated Indian who speaks four languages, he has a "machinelike" brain and the face of "a grim Aztec idol." As the series detective in three Blanc novels, Menendes both experiences and reflects on the complex racial prejudices of the mixed-blood Mexicans. The central character in this interesting tale is an American woman in flight from a collapsing marriage. (See, also, *The Rose Window* and *The Yellow Villa*.)

BUCKINGHAM, Bruce. *Three Bad Nights* (London, 1956). This is one of two Buckingham novels featuring Don Francisco de Torla Saavedra, Marqués de Langurén y Orendaiin (Don Pancho for short), "the most famous detective in all Latin America." His chief identifying characteristic is the Indian *guaraches* he wears even on formal occasions, though he claims pure Spanish blood. At the behest of a friend, Don Pancho goes to a luxurious resort called Quinta de las Rosas. There he is faced with three murders in as many nights. The setting purports to be Mexican but the situation is classically English: an isolated group of wealthy hotel guests, served by a variety of acute (or merely cute) peasants. Don Pancho's personal servant, Crisanto, for example—his "mozo-butler-valet-cum-confidant"—refuses to accept a salary and has other dumb ideas. (See, also, *Broiled Alive*, 1957.)

CAIN, James M. *Serenade* (NY, 1937, 1978). The narrator, an opera singer whose voice has failed, is down to his last three pesos in Mexico City when he becomes obsessed with a beautiful Mexican-Indian prostitute. When they make love (actually, it's more like rape and it takes place in a church), his singing voice returns. He and his Juana head for the States and another doomed try at success. Cain's sketches of Mexico City lowlife and of peasant poverty are as powerful as they are unpleasant. He is an extraordinary stylist. But even when due allowance is made for the time and the place, the misogyny, racism, and homophobia in this novel verge on the pathological.

ELKINS, Aaron. *Curses!* (NY, 1989, 1990). Gideon Oliver, an anthropologist known as "the skeleton detective," is called to the Yucatán to take a look at some ancient bones excavated at a Maya ceremonial center called Tlaloc. Five years earlier the excavation site was closed by the Mexican government after its director disappeared with a priceless Maya codex. Now it turns out there's a four hundred-year-old curse on those who disturb the place. Someone tries to kill Oliver; someone succeeds in killing a sleazy journalist. With the help of an elegant half-Maya police chief, Gideon uses his knowledge of physical anthropology to solve the case.

Though it belongs to a subgenre of archeological mysteries that goes back at least as far as Christie's *Murder in Mesopotamia* (1935), *Curses!* is full of up-to-date information about the Mayans, mostly elicited by Gideon's wife, whose function is to ask leading questions ("Just what *is* a codex?"). The fictional Tlaloc is next door to the very real Chichén Itzá, and the book also borrows from the history of other Mayan sites, including the Balankanche Caves and Palenque. Read it during the siesta hour at the Hotel Mayaland at Chichén Itzá, where the Olivers also stayed.

FUENTES, Carlos. *The Hydra Head* [Mexico, 1978], translated by Margaret Sayers Peden (NY, 1979, 1993). One of Mexico's most celebrated writers here tries his hand at a spy novel—the "first adventure of the Mexican secret service," as one character puts it. After a series of Kafkaesque encounters, Felix Maldonado, mid-level bureaucrat in the Ministry of Economic Development, wakes up in a hospital bed to learn that his name and face have been appropriated for a very public assassination attempt on the Mexican president and that he has been given a new face in exchange. Oddly, however, there is nothing in the newspapers about the attack on the president—just a brief story about the brutal murder of a woman Felix has loved since their university days.

Then things start to get complicated. This is one of those plots in which nothing—absolutely nothing—is what it first seems to be. At the heart of the mystery are Mexico's vast national oil reserves, which during the oil crisis of the early seventies took on global import. The interested parties here include Israeli, Arab, and Mexican agents and double-agents and triple-agents, most playing their roles with B-movie flourishes. (Fuentes dedicates the novel to the memory of Conrad Veidt, Sydney Greenstreet, Peter Lorre, and Claude Rains.) Fuentes's descriptions of Mexico City are detailed and memorable. Chapter 2, for example, is a wild ride in a one-peso cab—from the Cathedral over to the Paseo de la Reforma and down Reforma to the Cuauhtémoc statue. The driver insists on adding more and more passengers: a pair of giggling nuns, a flirtatious nurse, two students, a fat lady carrying a basket of peeping yellow chicks. The results are hilarious (except for the doomed chicks), and all the cab's human passengers have roles to play later in the novel.

GARCIA, Guy. *Obsidian Sky* (NY, 1994). Brian Mendoza is a Mexican-American grad student doing research at Mexico City's "Templo Mayor," the ruins, unearthed only in 1978, of the sacred center of the ancient Aztec city of Tenochtitlán. Brian has a theory about Aztec ritual sacrifice and what really went down with Cortés and Montezuma and the god Quetzalcóatl, the Plumed Serpent. His search for proof takes him to Cabo San Lucas in Baja California and to Mérida and Chichén Itzá in the Yucatán; it roughly parallels the journey of a sixteenth-century priest of Quetzalcóatl as recorded in a recently discovered codex (parts of which appear in the novel).

Much of this is interesting. The problem is that there is so much of it; there is simply too much *stuff* in this book: great chunks of Mexican politics, rebellion in the Yucatán, a political assassination, threats of a U.S. invasion, a love affair between Brian and a Mexican journalist, abject poverty and fabulous wealth, Brian's unhappy childhood, mariachis in the Plaza Garibaldi, a funeral in L.A., details of every meal consumed and every cigarette lit . . . All this and much, much more in a style that is at best serviceable, at worst clotted with clichés. A disappointment.

HEBDEN, Mark [John Harris]. *Pel Among the Pueblos* (London, 1987; NY, 1988). Hebden's Burgundian series character, Chief Inspector Evariste Clovis Desire Pel, is sent to Mexico in pursuit of a contemporary murderer and a historical mystery. The latter involves the French "intervention" in Mexico in 1861, the short, unhappy life of the Emperor Maximilian, and the whereabouts of some priceless correspondence. Pel's quest takes him from Mexico City to Tula, Tepotzotlan and San Miguel de Allende. Predictably, the cranky, xenophobic Pel doesn't much like Mexico, especially when he runs out of Gauloises. Though the French historical material is interesting, don't use this as a guidebook. Hebden confuses Tepotzotlan, the town with the great church of San Francisco Javier, and Tepoztlan (near Cuernavaca, many miles to the south). And he several times refers to the ruins at Tula as Maya; they are Toltec. Has he confused Tula with Tulum, a Mayan site in the Yucatán?

HIGHSMITH, Patricia. *A Game for the Living* (NY, 1958; GB, 1988). Lelia, a beautiful and fiercely independent Mexican painter, is the lover and friend of both Theodore, a well-off German-born artist, and Ramón, a poor but strikingly handsome furniture repairer. She also has encouraged a somewhat ambiguous friendship between the two men. Nonetheless, when Theodore finds Lelia brutally murdered, raped, and mutilated, he immediately suspects Ramón, a devout Catholic who has been tormented by Lelia's rejection of his marriage proposals. The evidence in the case clears Ramón, but not before he has become convinced of his own guilt and "confessed" to the crime. Theodore determines not to believe the confession and takes the deeply disturbed Ramón under his wing. They join forces with a sympathetic police detective in an effort to find the real killer. This is a superior psychological thriller focusing on the nature of guilt and innocence, sin and redemption, and on the powerful grip of Roman Catholicism on its believers. The main setting is Mexico City's art world, but there are also some splendid scenes in Acapulco and in Guanajuato, where Ramón and Theodore visit the famed mummies, dead for several hundred years but grotesquely preserved by the dryness of the climate.

IBARGUENGOITIA, Jorge. *Two Crimes* [Mexico, 1979], translated by Asa Zatz (Boston, 1984). Falsely accused of an act of terrorism, young radical Marcos flees his bohemian life in Mexico City for the fictional provincial town of Muerdago in the state he calls Plan de Abajo ("Lower Level"), where his rich and ailing uncle lives. There Marcos becomes enmeshed in family plots and counterplots, and is accused of a second crime he hasn't committed. Meanwhile, a crime he does commit goes undetected. The novel blends broad satire of Mexican petit-bourgeois mores and endemic bureaucratic corruption with a sort of Baja California *noir* and a hot, sudden, yet almost puritanical sensuality. Powerful and reminiscent of both Friedrich Dürrenmatt and Leonardo Sciascia. See also Ibarguengoitia's *The Dead Girls* (NY, 1983), based on the real-life murder of six prostitutes and also set in Plan de Abajo.

MACDONALD, John D. *Dress Her in Indigo* (NY, 1969, 1992). When a rich invalid's hippy daughter dies in Mexico, he hires Travis McGee, Florida boat bum and busy amateur dick ("I do favors for friends"), and his economist sidekick Meyer to find out about her last days. This permits them to travel first-class to Oaxaca, where McGee gets to have sex with a kinky British aristocrat as well as a local bimbo or two. The descriptions of Oaxaca and environs are fine; MacDonald has done his homework. But the McGee mixture of athletic sex, graphic violence, smug self-satisfaction, and bad Hemingwayesque prose was hard to take when this novel was new and has not improved with age. Other Travis McGee novels with Mexican scenes include *A Deadly Shade of Gold* (1965, "Puerto Altamura" on the Pacific coast), *Cinnamon Skin* (1982, Yucatán), and *The Lonely Silver Rain* (1985, Yucatán).

MILLAR, Margaret. *Ask for Me Tomorrow* (NY, 1976, 1991). Chicano lawyer Tomas Aragon is hired by very rich Gilly Decker to find her first husband, B.J., who disappeared in Mexico eight years earlier. Gilly has bad luck in husbands; her second one is busy dying from a stroke. Her motives for wanting to find B.J. are not very clear, but the pay is good enough to send Aragon off to Baja California, where he encounters mosquitoes, sand, corrupt officials, and a few people who knew B.J. Those people start getting killed. Millar is an admirable writer; her sketch of Mexican jail culture is particularly vivid. But the plot ambles aimlessly until the next-to-last page, where it takes a sudden and quite preposterous turn. An earlier and better Millar novel, *The Listening Walls* (NY, 1959, 1986), also includes some Mexico City scenes and makes good use of a hotel maid's observations of two rich *gringas*. But the Mexican setting is largely irrelevant in this novel of character.

PETERS, Elizabeth [Barbara Mertz]. *The Night of Four Hundred Rabbits* (NY, 1971, 1989). Carol Farley, the resourceful college-girl heroine of this romantic suspense novel, is lured to Mexico City by a series of enigmatic messages about the father who disappeared when she was twelve. She finds him, but his household is full of sinister secrets—most involving drug smuggling and what used to be called "the drug culture."

Peyote trips may seem a bit dated as a plot device, but Peters is a splendid explicator of things archeological, in this case the pyramids of Teotihuacán. And who can resist the book's title, which refers to an allegedly Aztec gauge of one's state of inebriation? "Four hundred rabbits" is roughly equivalent to "shitfaced." (Peters was not the first mystery writer to be taken with this bit of arcana. See Aaron Marc Stein's 1953 title, *Death Meets 400 Rabbits.*)

STARK, Richard [a.k.a. Donald E. Westlake]. *The Damsel* (NY, 1967; Vt., 1990). Wisecracking professional thief Alan Grofield is holed up in a Mexico City hotel with a bullet wound and $63,000 in ill-gotten gains when a distressed damsel climbs in his window. Both of them are in big trouble and both lie like crazy. But eventually they team up on a mission to Acapulco—via a very roundabout route that takes them to San Miguel de Allende, a nearby spa called Hacienda Taboada, San Luis Potosí, and Taxco. Fast-paced, funny, and very scenic.

TAIBO, Paco Ignacio II. *An Easy Thing* [Mexico, 1977], translated by William I. Neuman (NY, 1990). Taibo's series character, Mexico City private investigator Hector Belascoarán Shayne, got his "certificate in detection" from a correspondence school. "Every city gets the detective it deserves," he thinks. A lonely man whose lover recently left him, Hector shares a squalid office with a plumber, a sewer engineer, and an upholsterer—engaging eccentrics all. But most of his time is spent on Mexico City's streets, working his way through a "three-pronged labyrinth" of cases: a young girl who seems bent on suicide, the murder of a homosexual engineer, and the haunting possibility that Emiliano Zapata, the peasant hero of Mexico's failed revolution, may still be alive. Full of the sights, smells, and sounds of the city—with a strong subtext of social criticism—the book makes especially effective use of the music and patter of a late-night call-in radio show. (Other translated novels in the Belascoarán series: *Calling All Heroes, Some Clouds, No Happy Ending, Return to the Same City*).

———. *Life Itself* [Mexico, 1990], translated by Beth Henson (NY, 1994). In this out-of-series novel, Taibo imagines a precarious socialist utopia, a mining town in north-central Mexico where the citizens have freely elected a radical city government. The town has no beggars, a first-rate bookstore, and enemies everywhere—local crime bosses, corrupt state agents, political thugs. After its first two municipal police chiefs are killed, the town leaders persuade a famous mystery novelist, José Daniel Fierro, to take the job. Fierro's notes for a history of the town alternate with third-person narration of his adventures there trying to solve a series of murders. This novel is full of literary and film allusions, as well as such in-joke touches as characters named after Taibo's real-life friends.

　*———. *The Shadow of the Shadow* [Mexico, 1986], translated by William I. Neuman (NY, 1991, 1992). Set in Mexico City in 1922, this reads like a collaboration between Carlos Fuentes and Ross Thomas. It's unique and it's wonderful. The four main characters, who meet every night to play dominoes, are tough/romantic outsiders: a failed poet who fought with Pancho Villa and now survives by writing ad jingles; a crime reporter; a streetwise lawyer who works for prostitutes in defiance of his aristocratic background; a "Chinaman" born in Sinaloa, who speaks Spanish with a Chinese accent but knows no Chinese, and who is a dedicated union organizer. Though the four represent various segments of Mexican society in the tumultuous postrevolutionary years, they also are vivid individuals. By fate or coincidence, they are caught up in a series of murders tied to a conspiracy between U.S. oil companies and Mexican generals to make an oil-rich region of Mexico into a U.S. dependency. The domino players must solve the mystery to save their lives. Historical figures make cameo appearances, and an afterword sorts fact from fiction.

　WALLER, Robert James. *Puerto Vallarta Squeeze (The Run for "el Norte")* (NY, 1995). From the author of *The Bridges of Madison County*, but—according to esteemed *Washington Post* reviewer Carolyn See—not half bad. It's a thriller about a down-and-out writer in Puerto Vallarta who witnesses a killing and then, with his Mexican girlfriend, is persuaded by the shooter to drive him north to the United States with the *policía* and the *federales* in hot pursuit. Waller, writes See, has "at least the surface of Mexico down pat: the light in the plazas, the dusty Permex stations, the way time stretches out when you're on the road, the unexpected little Eden you can find when a hotel happens to have a pool, the tolerant disdain of a whole village when you drive in hot, dusty, and in every way uncool, at the end of a late afternoon of hot travel."

---

vaut le voyage (see page 4).

NOTED BUT NOT REVIEWED

CARTER, Nick. *The Mayan Connection (Killmaster #194)* (NY, 1984). One of a series of male fantasies starring Superagent Carter and his stiletto named Hugo that began with a short story in 1886 and has given dozens of writers gainful occupation. This prophetic episode involves an Indian uprising in Chiapas.

CASSIDY, John. *Assassination on Maya Bay* (NY, 1989). CIA agent Paul Grant is sent to an international conference at a Gulf Coast Mexican resort to foil a KGB plan to foment a revolution in Mexico.

DEIGHTON, Len. *Mexico Set* (1985, 1986). The second in a trilogy about British agent Bernard Samson, this Cold War thriller is set in Mexico City.

RICHTER, Robert. *Something in Vallarta* (Sag Harbor, NY, 1991). Something *(Algo)* is the nickname of a gringo hippy living *la vida dulce* on Mexico's Gulf Coast. In need of money, Algo's hired by a rich American to trail his girlfriend—right into big trouble.

XIX

CANADA

There is a quiet horror about the Great Lakes which grows as one re-visits them. Fresh water has no right or call to dip over the horizon, pulling down and pushing up the hulls of big steamers; no right to tread the slow deep-sea dance-step between wrinkled cliffs; nor to rear in on weed and sand beaches between vast headlands that run out for leagues into haze and sea-fog. Lake Superior is . . . a hideous thing to behold in the heart of a Continent. (Rudyard Kipling, *Letters of Travel*)

MONTREAL: *Not fifty paces off the Main, down Rue Napoleon, the bustle and press are gone and the noise is reduced to an ambient baritone rumble. The narrow old street is lit by widely spaced streetlamps and occasional dusty shopwindows. Children play around the stoops of three-story brick row houses. Above the roofline, diffused city-light glows in the damp, sooty air. Each house depends on the others for support. They have not collapsed because each wants to fall in a different direction, and there isn't enough room.* (Trevanian, *The Main*)

TORONTO: *Days were perceptively longer now, something only northerners can fully appreciate. The long darkness of our winters is hard to take sometimes. More than anything it's the length of daylight which marks the ending of winter here. In southern Ontario the amount of daylight is a better indicator of changing seasons than temperature. . . . By the time I found the nearest beer store, bought a twelve-pack of Brick Bock Ale in the traditional long brown bottles to celebrate spring . . . dusk was settling in.* (Eve Zaremba, *Uneasy Lies*)

The best that anyone could say of the place was that it was a "sportsman's paradise," which only means a good place to drink whiskey in. (Stephen Leacock, *My Discovery of the West*)

The peaty soil was matted with berries, though a foot or two beneath
was eternal ice. The breeding season was over and the migration not
begun, so there was no bird life on the shore; the wild fowl were all in
the swamps of the delta. The dead level of land and sea made the arc
of sky seem immense, the "intense inane" of Shelley's poem. . . . This
was a world not built on the human scale, a world made without thought
of mankind, a world colourless and formless, but also timeless; a kind
of eternity. It would be a good place to die in, he thought. . . . (John
Buchan, *Mountain Meadow*)

Murder in a Cold Climate

By Robin Winks

W HEN STEPHEN DEDALUS in Joyce's *A Portrait of the Artist as a Young*
Man sets out to become a writer, he takes in his defense "the only
arms I allow myself to use—silence, exile, and cunning." Canadian writers of mystery and detective fiction appear to have thrived on the first
two qualities, for few are well known, and those who have done well financially seldom write about Canada. Only one Canadian-authored and
Canadian-set book, L. R. Wright's *The Suspect,* has won an Edgar Award,
and fully half the winners of the Arthur Ellis Awards, given since 1984
by the Crime Writers of Canada for best novel and best first novel, have
used non-Canadian locales. (John Lawrence Reynolds, who lives in Ontario, sets his books in Boston, which is just marginally within the Canadian orbit, since Nova Scotians traditionally have called the United
States—or at least New England—the Boston States.) There are perhaps
as many as 350 books of mystery and detection set in some significant
measure in Canada, but most are known only to bibliographers who care
about such things.

The problem is obvious enough. Americans think Canadians are just
like them, though with snowshoes on. The British share this belief. Thus
the two largest markets think little about Canadian distinctiveness. Even
many Canadians, outside Quebec province, appear to think they are
rather like Americans and fail to realize just how different Canada really
is. Robert Ludlum once furnished one of his inexplicable novels with a

French-Canadian heroine (thus we said in those distant days) who spoke Swiss French rather than French-Canadian French, the author apparently thinking it not worth the candle to bone up on the difference. There is some truth in the notion of similarity, of course: spy and adventure yarns set in the Canadian Far North, the Yukon, Alaska, or the nether side of the Arctic tend to seem alike, for unless one has Smilla's sense of snow, all those cold wastes are interchangeable.

Books set in Seattle (Earl Emerson and J. J. Jance), Detroit (Loren Estleman and Jon Jackson), or even Minneapolis and Boston sometimes have a Canadian scene or two, since flight and pursuit often ignore international borders. Sometimes, if film rights are in question, stories originally set in the Pacific Northwest or the Great Plains are moved to British Columbia or the Prairie Provinces since shooting costs have been so much lower north of the border. Check out the illogical action in the 1990 Gene Hackman film *Narrow Margin* and then look at the exchange rate. Such movies tell one absolutely nothing about Canada.

Trends in Canadian crime fiction have tended to mirror general North American trends, which is to say, what Americans want to read. There are superior Canadian-based police procedurals (Laurence Gough's stories of Vancouver cops Willows and Parker), hard-boiled backwoods shoot-'em-ups (Ted Wood), urban Jewish private eyes (Howard Engel's Benny Cooperman), and lesbian rent-a-cops (Eve Zaremba's Helen Keremos). The quieter English school is present too: Ruth Rendellian dysfunctional families (L. R. Wright) and sensitive, even plodding chief-inspector-types (Eric Wright's Charlie Salter). There are distinctively Canadian voices here, but one would not know it from book jacket copy alone.

Perhaps most obviously, there is no Canadian James Bond, no Smiley, no Nick Carter, no Matt Helm. At first glance, this seems quite surprising: after all, the defection of Igor Gouzenko from the Soviet Embassy in Ottawa in 1945 was virtually the first Cold War authentication of Soviet espionage in North America, and one might have expected dozens of books to have been spawned in the weeks the young cipher clerk was kept under protection and interrogation at the Canadian intelligence training school in Oshawa. Almost nothing happened.

There are distinctively Canadian themes, of which the most obvious is the tension between French- and English-speaking Canadians and the rise of the separatist movement in Quebec. High-security matters along the Distant Early Warning Line, infiltration into the United States via Canada, the rising drug trade in Vancouver, abetted by the Hong Kong connection, and myriad adventures in the Far North in which the Royal Canadian Mounted always get their man have become staples of Canadian crime fiction, usually without any sense of local color, of a different social structure, even of a subtly different use of language. Most of those 350 and more books are pure action and might take place almost anywhere. The one body of writing in the mystery field that might be expected to be clearly distinctive—French-language novels set in Montreal—is slim and seldom translated.

Still, there are some books that the traveling reader might wish to take along when venturing to Canada, and some of them are very good about lifting the veil on this oft-misunderstood country. Here is a sampler:

READING LIST

BAGLEY, Desmond. *Landslide* (London, 1967, 1969). At the top of his form Bagley was far superior to the better-known pair, Hammond Innes and Alistair MacLean; his books have narrative drive, convincing dialogue, real characters, and genuine surprises. He, Gavin Lyall, and Berkley Mather gave the international thriller new life in the 1960s and '70s, when early Cold War certitudes were breaking down. Bagley is best known for his inverted middles: halfway through a book, everything is turned on its head, allowing for two distinct denouements. *Landslide* is representative: A tough geological engineer with a past best forgotten finds himself caught up in a corporate plot deep in British Columbia. The landslide helps rather than stops the action, the motivation is convincing and quite frightening, and everyone acts with great authority and skill. From the opening line, as the protagonist gets off a bus in tiny Fort Farrell, northern B.C. and the Peace River country are beautifully described. Bagley has an eye for an unfolding highway, and he takes the reader with him, dust clouds and all.

BARNAO, Jack. *Time-Locke* (NY, 1991). Barnao is the pseudonym for Ted Wood (q.v.). His protagonist, John Locke, is ex-Harvard, ex-Cambridge, with seven years in the elite SAS; he works in personal assurance (i.e., as a bodyguard) in Toronto. Locke drinks Bushmills, listens to Mozart, and is the most convincing hard-nosed personal security man in literature, even better than Spenser. His wants are simple, or so he tells us on our first meeting (*Hammer Locke,* 1986): "excitement, travel, good food and beautiful women."

Barnao delivers on all promises, though the Canadian portions of the books are all preliminaries: in *Time-Locke,* the action moves to Provence after fifty pages, in *Hammer Locke* to Florence in forty, and in *Locke Step* (1987) to Mexico in thirty. But those few Canadian pages are rich in local observation, and the stories get better and better. Locke is less Canadian but better company than Ted Wood's Reid Bennett. Barnao gives us clients who are more difficult to like than either Rachel Wallace or Paul Giacommin—Robert Parker fans, sit up straight now!—and makes John Locke even more convincing than Spenser and Hawk together.

BOWEN, Gail. *The Wandering Soul Murders* (Toronto, 1992). Set in the Canadian prairies, with the Saskatchewan lakes and small towns around the Qu'appelle Valley brilliantly used, this novel focuses on a center for runaway youngsters in Regina. The sleuth, Joanne Kilbourn, is engaged and convincing. I have not read two previous Bowens and regret it.

BUCHAN, John. *Mountain Meadow* (Boston, 1941; first published as *Sick Heart River,* London, 1940). Buchan—Lord Tweedsmuir by the time he wrote this stunningly introspective book about the ultimate challenge of death—virtually invented the spy thriller with *The Thirty-Nine Steps* (1915) and gave us the ultimate in resourceful men who could go to ground within the landscape to elude pursuers. Buchan wove local color into his plots with extraordinary charm, and he excelled as a nature writer, capturing the smell and look of changing weather with a rural Scot's intensity basic to this kind of travel literature. Richard Hannay was his all-action hero, with the barrister Edward Leithen providing a more thoughtful backup.

Mountain Meadow is Leithen's (now Sir Edward's) last adventure: Given a year to live and determined to "die on his feet," Leithen accepts an invitation to go to New York to find a prominent banker who has disappeared. The trail soon leads to Quebec, and then across the Canadian wilderness to the Arctic Circle. No one has brooded to the flicker of firelight more effectively than Buchan, as Leithen pursues his "noble frosty egoism" through Manitoba, over the Great Slave Lake, and finally to the Rivière de Coeur Malade, in the Yukon watershed. This is one of the few classics on any Canadian reading list.

BUELL, John. *The Pyx* (NY, 1959). Set in Montreal, and turned into a real turkey of a movie (with Christopher Plummer), this book stirs quite varied reactions. Barzun and Taylor found it "unreadable"; anonymous jacket-copy reviewers thought it variously "eerie" and "remarkable"; this reader thught it compelling on the first occasion and still good value on the second. A pyx is the ecclesiastical vessel in which the Host is reserved, and the novel is heavily burdened with religious symbolism as it unveils a prostitute's background. Montreal is as murky as the plot, but both are intriguing.

————. *Four Days* (NY, 1962). Buell is a kind of tough-guy Morley Callaghan, distinctively Canadian, as concerned with moral worth as Graham Greene, and the echoes of *Brighton Rock* are perhaps a bit loud. Montreal is more clearly seen here than in *The Pyx*, the moralizing is kept under control, and the central and brutish crime and the events set in motion by it are plainly told. *Four Days* made less of a splash than *The Pyx*, but it is the better book.

CALLAGHAN, Morley. *The Loved and the Lost* (NY, 1951). Callaghan wrote compassionate novels about Canada's Irish, labor tensions, and lowlifers, but he also knew how to put together a good crime novel. This one, about an interracial love affair in Montreal, is not precisely a mystery, though it contains most of the usual elements, and it is remarkably good in dealing with the feel of the city and its ethnic divisions.

DAHEIM, Mary. *Foul Play* (NY, 1991). The action takes place in a historic hotel in British Columbia—an ill-disguised Vancouver—but it might be almost anywhere, this being "a bed-and-breakfast mystery" in which food matters more than place. Still, the yarn rollicks along and often is rather amusing.

DISNEY, Doris. *The 17th Letter* (NY, 1944, 1945). Doris Disney wrote straightforward thrillers, usually focusing on a self-reliant woman who finds herself in danger. This is perhaps her best-known book, filled with action and nasty Nazi spies. An American couple, Paul and Mary Strong, receive a strange communication from a friend who is on a news assignment in Iceland: they are to wait for and "understand" a seventeenth letter they will soon receive from him. When the letter contains only a theater program, city unidentified, they naturally go in search of the place, realizing their friend is in danger. The place proves to be in Halifax, Nova Scotia, and there is a good bit of slipping onto and off of boats, and worrying about wartime convoys, until all comes clear. Halifax is nicely present without overwhelming the action.

ENGEL, Howard. *Murder Sees the Light* (Toronto, 1984, 1986). Engel has a good claim to being called the doyen of Canadian crime writers, and this book, which won the Crime Writers of Canada award for best mystery in 1984, introduces Benny Cooperman, an already established private eye who looks for excuses to stay away from Toronto. Here he is on assignment at Petawawa Lodge baby-sitting a TV evangelist. Complications soon show up when an Indian (this is 1984, remember) guide is found dead, and soon there are rumors of a satanic cult and a hidden gold mine. Canadian speech is well rendered, and the lakes seem real enough, but Engel crowds his pages a bit much for my taste. I wish he would stay in Grantham, his hometown, where life surely is simpler.

————. *Murder on Location* (Toronto, 1982, 1986). Some reviewers liked this Benny Cooperman book and others found it unsatisfying as a mystery. I vote for it, especially because it captures so well the scene around Niagara Falls. Characters are nicely developed, movie types are pleasantly ribbed, no doubt drawing on Engel's years as a CBC producer, and Grantham—the "Port Said of the Great Lakes"—is a more palpable presence. For Grantham, read St. Catharines.

————. *The Suicide Murders* (Toronto, 1980, 1985). This is my favorite Engel, perhaps because the Hammett/Chandler parody is so lightly done, perhaps because the theme of revenge and retribution funnels so nicely into the slightly melancholic mood. There is a well-placed quasi-acrostic as a clue, and the women, of which there are several, come across as individuals. Toronto and Grantham provide the settings.

————. *A City Called July* (Toronto, 1986, 1988). Engel cannot have been happy to have Penguin call him Engels on the spine of my reprint, but maybe it will be worth some money one day. The story is the most intriguing of the Benny Cooperman tales, and the most explicitly Jewish-Canadian, as Benny tries to track down the man who has made off with $2 million from members of the local synagogue, while keeping the investigation all in the family, without alerting the police. The nature of a small city is well described, and the mystery is genuine but a mite transparent. (See also *The Ransom Game* [Toronto, 1981; 1986]—everyone is away in Florida and the local color is a bit washed out.)

FRANCIS, Dick. *The Edge* (London, 1988). This is possibly Francis's poorest book, but since a weak Francis is still a strong read, it ought not to be missed. Tor Kelsey, undercover security agent for the British Jockey

Club, is sent across Canada on the Great Transcontinental Mystery Race Train, looking for trouble, of which he gets an unreasonable amount. The motivation is unconvincing, but the train trip is entertaining and well described.

GODFREY, Ellen. *Georgia Disappeared* (Toronto, 1992). Godfrey has written several mysteries, each better than the previous one, though none yet to the first rank. Set in Toronto, where Georgia Arnott, head of a computer team, disappears from a poolside party, this one is well written though marred by irrelevancies and interchangeable locales.

GORDON, Alison. *The Dead Pull Hitter* (Toronto, 1989). Given my intense dislike for baseball, this is a remarkable book, for I read it at a sitting. Sultan Sanchez, designated hitter for the Toronto Titans, stands his team up when they take on the Boston Red Sox. Kate Henry, sportswriter for a Toronto paper, investigates a double murder; this is a tale well told.

———. *Night Game* (Toronto, 1993). The best of Gordon's books, though largely set at the Toronto Titans' spring training camp in Florida, where a sportswriter is found dead and a rookie member of the team is charged with the crime. Kate Henry solves it all back home.

———. *Striking Out* (Toronto, 1995). Major-league baseball is on hold in the summer of 1994, and Kate Henry finds herself involved with the homeless, feminism, pornography, racist police, and the wounding of her lover. This is a complex story with believable dialogue, though Toronto is less clearly identifiable than in Gordon's early books. (Not reviewed: *Safe at Home,* 1990).

GORDON, R. L. *The River Gets Wider* (NY, 1974, 1975). This civilized mystery has been compared to the work of Louis Auchincloss and John P. Marquand, although James Gould Cozzens comes more readily to my mind. The reader is skillfully led to close-up views of John Andrews, Chief Justice of the Canadian Supreme Court, charged with the murder of his wife. We see Andrews as a child in Edmonton, Alberta, as a war hero, a brilliant lawyer, a well-read and scholarly man who is also cold, determined, even ruthless, and we see all this through the even-handed prose of his defense lawyer. Every sentence registers, and the growing melancholy draws the reader into a personal regard for Andrews. The sense of place is remarkable, and the whole is distinctively Canadian. (See also *The Jesus Boy* [NY, 1975], which is equally compelling though set in the United States more than in Canada.)

GOUGH, Laurence. *The Goldfish Bowl* (London, 1987, 1990). Here

Gough introduces Jack Willows, a veteran detective newly teamed up with Clair Parker, and shows that Vancouver's mean streets have nothing to learn from Los Angeles. A police procedural about an apparently random sniper takes on complex psychological layerings. The street directions are all Vancouver but we might as well be in any rather wet city.

———. *Silent Knives* (NY, 1988, 1990; London, 1988, as *Death on a No. 8 Hook*). The English title is better, since the action takes off when series figure Detective Jack Willows, on vacation, puts his fishing hook into the hand of a dead young woman. Back in Vancouver his partner, Clair Parker, comes upon the body of a mutilated boy. The two cases are linked by tattoos. The reader knows the murderer from the outset, and that there are to be at least three killings. The hard-edged and deeply cynical style that has come to mark Gough's more recent work, which is not set in Canada, is already evident.

———. *Hot Shots* (London, 1989, 1991). Willows and Parker take on a major drug dealer, and Vancouver comes through more clearly in this Arthur Ellis Award winner. The ending is meant to be full of action but it is simply flat. Willows and Parker are now lovers, which is a bad idea. The Ellis Award is a mystery, but either of the earlier books might well have won it, so perhaps the awards committee was just playing catch-up. Basketball accounts for the title.

HAMILTON, Donald. *The Terrorizers* (Greenwich, Ct., 1977). The late Anthony Boucher, who long reviewed for *The New York Times,* was very high on Hamilton, and so am I. He knows how to pace a book, he doesn't mistake movement for action, and he knows boats, guns, and landscape. Agent Matt Helm works for one of those shadowy Washington agencies that can rearrange his life with a phone call, and he usually is to be found escorting someone through a thicket of gunfire, acting as a stalking horse to draw out some right- or left-wing loonies, or simply being a paid killer. Less whimsical than Donald E. Westlake's Alan Grofield, without Travis McGee's soft spot for women, Helm is the thinking man's operative. Here he is fished out of Hecate Strait, off the coast of British Columbia, in a heavy fog, his memory wiped clean, and he has to discover who he is and what he has been while people try to befriend him or kill him. The plot device is an old one, but Hamilton knows how to make it fresh. All Hamiltons are paperback originals and sometimes hard to find.

———. *The Ravagers* (Greenwich, Ct., 1964). Matt Helm spends a lot of time driving cross-country, often in the American Southwest, and Hamilton has an acute eye for the telling detail that sets New Mexico apart from Texas. He is equally good with Canada, as the contrivances of plot take Helm from Regina to Brandon and along the Trans-Canada Highway eastward to Montreal (two dead) and toward Cape Breton Island. It's a good tour in the capable hands of Hamilton/Helm.

————. *The Interlopers* (Greenwich, Ct., 1969). Here Matt Helm wanders about in small-town Washington state, not far from the Hanford Atomic Energy Reservation, playing decoy for his mysterious agency, acting friendly and slow-witted. Soon he is on the road again, from Pasco to Seattle, and across the British Columbia border at Sumas. One can blame Fawcett, the publisher, for the Frazer River (for which read "Fraser"), but otherwise one can tell that Hamilton has driven every inch of Helm's route. The action carries right on up to Alaska, and very nicely too. This is vintage Hamilton.

HARTLEY, Norman. *The Viking Process* (NY, 1976, 1977). A correspondent for the *Toronto Globe & Mail,* Hartley specializes in big business skulduggery. His heroes are not very nice people, and open to blackmail for some sexual indiscretion, and his plots tend to repeat themselves. He gets past their questionable logic by having one person or another say something in a convincing voice. The central action is not in Canada, though here he provides a good opening sequence in Montreal, while telling us that people really don't care about "little nationalist groups" or whether Quebec separates from Canada or not. Bigger issues—like corporate survival—are at stake. Not my single malt.

HENDERSON, James. *Copperhead* (Toronto, 1971). This headlong thriller involves the intelligence forces of Canada, the United States, and Britain, and uses Montreal and Toronto brilliantly before an interlude in Barbados and final action in Alberta. The premise is an interesting one: twelve people, each infected with a strain of bubonic plague, are sent to strategic points in North America. The plague remains inert as long as they treat themselves with an inhibitor carried on an ordinary copper penny. Then Russians pick up two of the carriers and accuse the West of having initiated the plot. Henderson handles the variables well, and both dialogue and place ring right.

HERRON, Shaun. *Miro* (NY, 1969, 1971). Herron writes of a tough agent, Miro, who usually operates in Ireland or Spain. Here, after twenty-five years of isolation and death, he believes himself to be on his last mission. Herron lived in Winnipeg when he wrote his Miro books, though—or so the dust jackets tell us—he summered in Cork. His Ireland seems more real than his Quebec. Still, this world-weary look at an agent who wants to come in from the cold would be singularly bleak wherever it was set.

INNES, Hammond. *Campbell's Kingdom* (NY, 1952, 1986). At their best Hammond Innes and Alistair MacLean produced rattling good yarns excelled by few. Tough men (and sometimes tough women) wrestled with each other, with their consciences, and with the elements in settings clearly seen at firsthand. Innes remained in top form nearly to the end, while MacLean sadly declined in his final books, which were poorly researched and illogically plotted. But in the 1950s and '60s Innes and MacLean led the way.

Innes specialized in books about the sea, and the land that fed off it, and his early book, *The Wreck of the Mary Deare,* is as good as they come. *Atlantic Fury* laps upon Canadian shores, but *Campbell's Kingdom* takes us inland, into mining territory high in the Rockies. Bruce Wetheral inherits a jinxed plot of land fifty miles from Jasper, and he sets out to make it pay against all odds. The action is claustrophobic once Wetheral moves beyond Calgary, and Innes's research—he spent three months in the region—is put to effective use.

———. *The Land God Gave to Cain* (London, 1958, 1971). The title, as every Canadian knows, refers to Labrador, to which Innes made two lengthy trips to research the building of the "Iron Ore Railway" from the St. Lawrence River four hundred miles into the interior. Here he celebrates the men who built it, showcasing his remarkable sense of place and person in a classic thriller that is "much taken up with the conditions of travel," for reasons made obvious by Innes's superb descriptions of the land. This is perhaps the best northern wilderness novel in the genre.

———. *High Stand* (NY, 1986). Innes, from 1978 a C.B.E., returned to his beloved Canadian northland in this fine book, which combines elements from John Buchan's *Mountain Meadow* with Innes's own *Campbell's Kingdom*. The playboy owner of the finest stand of western red cedar in the world disappears, and his English solicitor sets out for Canada to investigate. From the edge of Kluane National Park, through the Yukon, down the Alaska Panhandle, and to the waters of coastal British Columbia, the solicitor pursues his mission. Innes has devoted good portions of his income to reforestation in Wales, and he writes of trees and the land from which they grow with knowledge and affection.

LAW, Alexander. *To an Easy Grave* (NY, 1986). Richard Cane's old college teammate Sean Denby, star quarterback for the Toronto Metros, is murdered, and Cane, stunned by the accidental death of his wife, plunges into the world of drugs and violence to regain his life. This is a first novel, and uncommonly good, especially since the resolution comes as a surprise. Toronto society is well described.

MacLEAN, Alistair. *Athabasca* (NY, 1980, 1982). Alistair MacLean writes good, old-fashioned page-turners. By the 1980s he had grown careless, but his earlier books, and especially those that evoked the bitter ice and snow of the further reaches of the Arctic, achieve the cliché status of books almost impossible to put down. Though he is widely thought to have written extensively about Canada, he did not. *Athabasca* is the only book unquestionably set in Canada—in the rich tar sands of the Canadian North—and even then much of the action, which involves an attempt to hold hostage the Alaskan oil pipeline from Prudhoe Bay to Valdez, takes place in Alaska. *Night Without End* (1960) tells of an airplane's crash somewhere west of Thule, in Greenland; *Ice Station Zebra* (1963), perhaps second only to *The Guns of Navarone* in the MacLean canon, takes place at a British drift ice station closer to Norway than to Canada; and *Bear Island* (1971), listed in various Canadian bibliographies, is clearly somewhere south of Norway's Spitzbergen. There is little on-the-spot research in these books: *Athabasca,* for example, was written in Dubrovnik.

MALING, Arthur. *From Thunder Bay* (NY, 1981). Maling usually writes business-related thrillers, often featuring one Brock Potter, but here he tells us of the destinies of two brothers. One, weak and panicky, kills a Canadian policeman, and the other, successful and admired, risks his career to help him. The action is around Thunder Bay, on the Canadian side of Lake Superior, and at Kenora. The resolution is entirely predictable.

MALTESE, Martin. *North to Toronto* (NY, 1978). A famous sax player is caught by customs officials with heroin in his horn while on a Canadian tour. There follows one long chase scene. The writing is brisk and pointless.

MANTHORNE, Jackie. *Ghost Motel* (Charlottetown, 1994). Harriet

Hubbley is an amateur sleuth and a lesbian who lives in Montreal but is visiting Cape Cod. There is little of Canada here except the speech patterns, which are authentic. The book is a mixed bag, some of it good, a lot of it quite unconvincing.

MILLAR, Margaret. *An Air That Kills* (NY, 1957, 1985). Margaret Millar was Canadian-born and her husband Kenneth Millar (who in time became John Ross Macdonald and then simply Ross Macdonald) was Canadian-educated. Between them they practically patented the Santa Barbara psychological tale in which the solution to the crime in time present lay in trauma of time past. In his early work Macdonald made passing reference to Canada—easy to do when he wrote of Detroit—but Margaret Millar was more faithful. Here we learn how a wealthy man winds up dead in a lake instead of with his friends at a lodge outside Toronto, and though there is not much mystery to the unhappy story, it is quite compelling.

————. *Fire Will Freeze* (NY, 1944). This forgotten early Millar shows her in her worst manic phase, with much so-called humor that is either nasty or obscure. The action takes place around a snow-lodge in Quebec, north of Montreal, and though there is a lot of snow, one cannot tell the Laurentians from the Poconos. After she moved to California, Millar's mental health was said to have greatly improved, and in *Beyond This Point Are Monsters* (1970) she produced a southern California classic, but she could never be bothered with the complexities of clues and actual detection, as *Fire Will Freeze* all too clearly reveals. I've never met a Millar character I really cared about. (Millar's *The Iron Gates* [1945] also is set in Canada.)

NOLAN, Frederick. *The Oshawa Project* (London, 1974). Largely set in Europe, but with a short, realistic chapter in Ontario, this tightly written spy story is about an assassination attempt that seems all too real.

PERRY, Thomas. *Vanishing Act* (NY, 1995). The core action in this taut thriller takes place in the Adirondack Mountains, but there are key scenes on the Canadian side of Lake Erie and in Vancouver. The story is about a Seneca woman who helps people escape from their past, usually in the form of drunken or abusive husbands, and how she takes on an uninvited visitor, John Felker, who says he is running from a crime he did not commit. She is very good at her job, so she observes details, including details of place, acutely. She helps Felker to a new life in Oregon, via her

Canadian lifeline, only to find that all is not as it seemed. This is an excellent example of the stalker stalked plot, so well developed by Geoffrey Household. The subtle differences between Canada and the United States are nicely observed.

REILLY, Helen. *Compartment K* (NY, 1955). How do you make people isolated and defenseless? Snow them into an Adirondack mountain cabin; maroon them on an island off the Cornwall coast; strand them on the sixtieth floor of a skyscraper with no functioning electricity; put them on a transcontinental train. Compartment K is on the Montreal-to–British Columbia passenger train; and having ridden it myself, I can attest that Helen Reilly has the train and the sights from the window (including the long night stretches) down pat. But there isn't much detection here.

RITCHIE, Simon. *The Hollow Woman* (NY, 1987). The hero is John Kenneth Galbraith Jantarro, a one-armed Toronto detective who muffs a ransom drop-off and is nearly killed for his trouble. There is a lot of talk about pain and memory and some old-time Nazi business, and for all one learns of Toronto the Ferris wheel might as well be in Vienna. There is a great deal of detail that counts for nothing.

ROHMER, Richard. *Ultimatum* (Toronto, 1973). Here is an unusually bad book with a crystal clear message: Canadians should fear the United States. Canada's best-selling novel in 1973, the book begins with an ultimatum delivered by the president of the United States to the prime minister of Canada. The year is 1980, and Canada is told to give up its Arctic gas to a United States desperate for energy resources. The good thing about this bad book is that one learns plenty about Canada, especially about Canadian perceptions of their neighbor to the south. Rohmer followed it with *Exxoneration* (Toronto, 1974), a clumsy pun on an energy-hungry and, as the continent was to learn at Valdez, not very socially conscious corporate giant. Here the American president has announced that he intends to annex Canada. When the Americans invade they are soundly defeated, and then the Canadians launch a raid on Wall Street. Dismissed by all reviewers in Canada as pure drivel, *Exxoneration* immediately became a best-seller.

SALE, Medora. *Murder in a Good Cause* (NY, 1990). Possessor of a Ph.D. in medieval studies, Medora Sale won the Arthur Ellis in 1987 for her first novel, *Murder on the Run*. She writes of Inspector John Sanders of the Toronto police and his companion Harriet Jeffries, an architectural photographer. Her first two books (*Murder in Focus* was the next) are solidly plotted, but they are thin on local color and the solution to the mystery is telegraphed well ahead of time. In *Murder in a Good Cause*, Ms. Sale has improved her craft, and Toronto emerges with greater clarity. There is a tendency to overload her plots, however, as here with some nonsense about a terrorist underground.

———. *Pursued by Shadows* (NY, 1992). Sale apparently grows bored with Toronto. *Sleep of the Innocent* (NY, 1991) took her lovers to Martha's Vineyard, and in *Pursued by Shadows* we wander into New York. Still, the action is Toronto-based, and the premise, that Harriet's ex-lover, Guy Beaumont, who shows up at her door, will make Inspector Sanders irritated is well demonstrated, until Beaumont winds up dead in Harriet's living room. This is the best of the Sale books, and quite superior to *Detour to Santa Fe,* which comes next, a farrago of poor research and illogical action.

SAUM, Karen. *Murder Is Relative* (Tallahassee, 1990). Set in Quebec and Maine, both described carefully if somewhat stiffly, this novel tells how Brigid Donovan is hired to write a history of an interfaith community and to look into an unexplained death. There is a good bit of driving back and forth past dark stands of trees.

TREVANIAN. *The Main* (NY, 1976, 1977). The author of the highly popular *Eiger Sanction* and *Loo Sanction* moved on to new territory with *The Main,* set in Montreal's polyglot central district. There is a solid opening that invokes the Main's vitality and that led one reviewer to call Trevanian a Canadian Balzac. A tough and very human police lieutenant is introduced, working on a stabbing in a back alley, and slowly the reader meets the other figures—prostitutes, priests, Chinese restaurant owners, Jews—who give Montreal its special character. This is an unusually good book, full of life and well-observed detail. For years reviewers had tried to guess Trevanian's identity, and in *The Main* he captured Canadian speech so well, the hounds decided he had to be a Canadian. Maybe.

WALKER, David. *Ash* (Boston, 1976). David Walker is a "straight" novelist who has written three backwoods thrillers, of which *Black Dougal* is the best known, *Mallabec* the most Canadian, and *Ash* the most compelling. Nigel Ash is a bush pilot who has lived alone for too long a time. When recuperating from an illness, he discovers his love for friends and his affection for the Canadian woods. Walker cares most about his settings, and he closely observes the landscape, the birds, the animals, and the weather. He is less good with people, but he tells a good story. The scene is New Brunswick.

WESTLAKE, Donald E. *The Black Bird* (NY, 1969, 1990). Originally published under Westlake's hard-boiled pseudonym, Richard Stark, this appealing romp through the Canadian north is close to parody, mixing in apparent Quebecois separatists, Chinese Maoists, Albanian Mao-liners, and the leaders of several minor Third World countries, all meeting at the Château Frontenac in Quebec City. Alan Grofield, a part-time actor and thief, is blackmailed by an agency that looks rather like the CIA into infiltrating these heavies in order to find out what they are up to. The action is constant, the quips often quite good, and the sense of place minimal.

WOOD, Ted. *Dead in the Water* (NY, 1983). In this debut novel Ted Wood (who also writes as Jack Barnao, q.v.) introduces Reid Bennett, the one-man police force of Murphy's Harbour, Ontario, a composite of several small lakeside towns. Bennett has put the grim realities of Toronto policing behind him, hoping to spend his days doing a little hunting, a little fishing, and a little snoozing, but he soon learns that crime knows no boundaries. Bennett is resourceful and tough, and he takes the prescribed punishment, sustaining more falls, attacks, just-missed rifle shots, etc., than any real cop encounters in a career. This is formula fiction, but Wood makes it work well, and Murphy's Harbour, despite the mayhem, seems inviting. This won the 1983 Scribner Crime Novel Award.

————. *Murder on Ice* (NY, 1984). Murphy's Harbour is snowed in, and Reid Bennett is trapped in his own town with members of the feminist Canadian League of Angry Women, who have just kidnapped the newly crowned Queen of the Ice Festival. There is much snowmobile action, and plot twists abound. Wood manages to give the location some particularity, suggesting that not all towns respond to ice and snow in quite the same way.

————. *Live Bait* (NY, 1985). Reid Bennett returns to Toronto to work for a security firm that wants him to catch whoever has been attacking their night watchmen. Bennett discovers that he has been put out as bait, and with the help of his German shepherd dog, Sam, he resolves everything with dispatch and reasonable violence.

————. *Fool's Gold* (NY, 1986). Reid Bennett goes to a gold strike on the northern edge of Lake Superior to investigate the death of a man reportedly mauled by a bear. The action winds up in Montreal.

―――――. *When the Killing Starts* (NY, 1989). Perhaps Reid Bennett's best case: He goes off into the north woods to bring back a twenty-year-old who has joined up with some mercenaries called Freedom for Hire. Bennett knows he will be up against old SAS hands—people like John Locke, of Jack Barnao's books (Wood in his other guise)—and Bennett's comments on casual violence are interesting and pointed. The movement in the north woods is well described, but Bennett comes back to Toronto too soon.

―――――. *On the Inside* (NY, 1990). Reid Bennett goes to the tough northern mining town of Elliot to investigate police corruption. Under cover, he gets a job as a constable. Action is unceasing. (Not reviewed: *The Corkscrew* [NY, 1987]—mad bikers on the rampage—and *Snowjob* [NY, 1993], set mainly in Vermont.)

WRIGHT, Eric. *The Night the Gods Smiled* (NY, 1983, 1985). Wright is the most consistent Canadian writer of Canadian-set mysteries, producing one a year with metronomic regularity. This debut novel introduces Toronto's Inspector Charlie Salter. The formula is tried and true: a crusty policeman must interrogate the rather arch members of a college English department when one of the faculty is murdered while attending a conference in Montreal. This provides a chance for social commentary. We also get a good bit about Salter's married life. The clues are laid down fairly and Toronto seems real if a little boring. Wright will get better with each book. Even so, with this one Wright carried away the John Creasey Prize for Best First Mystery in 1984.

―――――. *Smoke Detector* (NY, 1984). This is perhaps the most Canadian of Wright's books. Inspector Charlie Salter of the Toronto police is in a stalled career and an unhappy domestic situation, and his inquiry into the death of a secondhand furniture dealer doesn't look like it's helping much with either problem. Doggedness pays off.

―――――. *The Man Who Changed His Name* (NY, 1986). After taking Charlie Salter off to the Old Country in his 1985 book, Wright returns to Toronto for his most complicated plot yet. Charlie's ex-wife Gerry, gone from his life for twenty-five years, shows up in his office shortly before Christmas to ask him to find a murderer for her. Charlie does. His relationship with his second wife, Annie, is put in some doubt, but all comes right in the end.

―――――. *A Question of Murder* (NY, 1988). Wright brings the Yorkville section of Toronto to life in this uncomplicated mystery concerning security measures taken to protect a royal princess visiting Toronto and a feud between street vendors and the owners of Yorkville's boutique shops. The mystery is satisfying, and Charlie Salter's relations with his wife and two teenage sons are sympathetically described.

————. *A Body Surrounded by Water* (NY, 1987). The clever title takes Charlie Salter and his family to Prince Edward Island, Canada's smallest and perhaps most provincial province. People are suspicious of off-islanders, even fellow Canadians. A string of burglaries on the island intrigues Salter. Both character and place are well realized here.

————. *Buried in Stone* (NY, 1996). Wright gives us a new series figure, a sixty-five-year-old retired Toronto cop who has built his own log cabin in the summer cottage country north of the city. The local scene is deftly handled, the mystery is genuine, and the town of Larch River comes through in all its off-season tacky charm. (Not reviewed: *A Final Cut* [NY, 1991]; *A Sensitive Cast* [NY, 1990]; *A Fine Italian Hand* [NY, 1992], listed in ascending order of Canadian interest.)

WRIGHT, L. R. *The Suspect* (NY, 1985, 1987). The only Canadian mystery to win an Edgar, this extraordinary story of why one elderly man picks up a bookend and beats another elderly man to death is full of compassion for past mistakes, aging, dysfunctional families, and the vagaries of memory. Wright, who has lived on Canada's Sunshine Coast— the wet, succulent district northwest of Vancouver, where one travels by ferry between the sparse roads—describes the area brilliantly. Her series figure is Sergeant Karl Alberg of the RCMP. While romancing the local librarian, Alberg keeps an eye on his fellow citizens in Sechelt, a small town of 1,300 people, which really exists and is lovingly described. "Psycho-suspense" is the easy label for *The Suspect,* but it is far more than that.

————. *Sleep While I Sing* (NY, 1986, 1987). This is that rarity, a second book that sustains the promise of the first. A woman is knifed to death just off the Sunshine Coast Highway. Albert finally finds out why. The atmosphere is Rendellian and the rain nearly constant.

————. *A Chill Rain in January* (NY, 1990). One does grow tired of the rain, but then, that's half the point, as the lives of two women, one escaped from a nursing home, converge. Albert thinks about his two daughters from his failed marriage, who live elsewhere, and contemplates age and solitude. There is little cheer here but plenty of humanity.

————. *Prized Possessions* (NY, 1993). The rainy and isolated British Columbia coast is home to any number of damaged souls, and Wright shows us how the lives of three of them intersect. Though reviewers compare her to P. D. James, more appropriate similarities are to be found with Ruth Rendell and Elizabeth George. Wright understands people, and that they are best interpreted within the landscape that has shaped them. Poverty and stunted lives are just below the surface in the tourist-attractive small towns along the Strait of Georgia.

————. *A Touch of Panic* (NY, 1994). This is Wright's most complex story yet. It is about power and presence, bullies and victims, all in a land of "blue-edged islands tumbling across the seascape, mountains rising from dense coastal forests, and a climate that is the most congenial in Canada." Given all the rain in earlier books, this comes as surprise, but then, this is May. (Not reviewed: *Fall from Grace* [NY, 1991]. The least good of the Sunshine Coast series.)

YOUNG, Scott. *Murder in a Cold Climate* (Toronto, 1988). The book that gives this Canadian wrap-up its title, *Cold Climate* introduces Mountie Matteesie Kitologitak, an Inuk, and draws us into a well-told tale about ethnic relations, possible drug smuggling, and life in the Northwest Territories along the Mackenzie River. This is one of the best of the "cold North" books.

ZAREMBA, Eve. *Uneasy Lies* (Toronto, 1990). The fourth in a series about Helen Keremos, a lesbian private eye, published by a feminist house and praised by Margaret Atwood, this basically routine account of murder in a luxury condominium in North Toronto moves along a predictable path. It is competent, and social issues (including environmentalism) are woven in nicely. Rye and ginger—a fading Canadian preference—is drunk and the feminism rides easily over the pages. I have not seen the earlier Zaremba books so I cannot judge the trajectory.

CLOSE-UP: DYING LIKE A NATIVE

In the hypothesis that you propose, chance intervenes copiously. Here we have a dead rabbi; I would prefer a purely rabbinical explanation, not the imaginary mischances of an imaginary robber. (Jorge Luis Borges, "Death and the Compass")

Dying Like a Native

THE ABOVE TITLE is a trifle misleading since very few people—native or otherwise—die from the ingenious causes perpetrated by mystery novelists. But in many mysteries, the mode of death is made to reflect its setting—a local poison perhaps, such as unripe Jamaican ackee fruit in Joan Hadley's *The Deadly Ackee,* or manchineel apples in another Caribbean mystery, A. H. Z. Carr's *Finding Maubee* (both discussed in Chapter XX), or the East African arrow-poison in Elspeth Huxley's *The African Poison Murders* (Chapter XI). Native weapons such as the machete have proved irresistible to other writers, including Patricia Moyes in *The Coconut Killings* (Chapter XX).

In some murder mysteries, however, authorial ingenuity and scenic idiosyncrasy conspire to produce marvels. Here are a few baroque examples:

DEATH BY MAYAN RITUAL SACRIFICE: Though both Gary Alexander *(Blood Sacrifice)* and Sylvia Angus *(Dead to Rites)* favor antique Mayan obsidian knives as murder weapons, Angus's Chichén Itzá murderer goes several steps further and cuts out the heart of his victim before placing the body on a "Chac Mool," a typically Mayan stone figure, associated with human sacrifice, of a supine man with raised knees and a bowl on his stomach (Chapter XVIII).

UNNATURAL DISASTERS: Murder by manmade avalanche. In Larry Beinhart's *Foreign Exchange,* set in St. Anton, Austria, the victims ski for their lives . . . and lose. Another difficult-to-arrange exit is murder by the inrushing tides of Mont-Saint-Michel (Aaron Elkins's *Old Bones,* Chapter I).

HOT ENDINGS: Murder by galvanic bath at a Romanian spa in Barbara Wilson's *Trouble in Transylvania* (Chapter IV). Murder in a crater of boiling New Zealand mud in Ngaio Marsh's *Color-Scheme* (Chapter XVII).

GOING DUTCH: Attempted murder by windmill in Patricia Moyes's *Death and the Dutch Uncle,* and successful murder by hanging from the gable pulley typical of Dutch seventeenth-century architecture in Alistair MacLean's *Puppet on a String* (both Chapter VI).

FEARSOME FAUNA: Death by blowfish, the always potentially deadly gourmet treat of Japan (James Melville, *Sayonara, Sweet Amaryllis,* Chapter XIII). Murder by multiple snakebites in a book featuring the lore of West African snake cults, John Wyllie's *To Catch a Viper* (Chapter XI).

A FATE WORSE THAN DEATH?: Torture by forced ingestion of spaghetti in Attilio Veraldi's *The Payoff* (Chapter III).

XX

——— ⟩•(《●》)•⟨ ———

THE CARIBBEAN

I thought I was going to land in the Garden of Eden, but I'm too late. The Fall has already taken place. (Jocelyn Davey, Murder in Paradise)

The place looked like an earthly paradise. With its sunshine, its coral reef, its music, its dancing, it seemed a Garden of Eden. But even in the Garden of Eden, there had been a shadow—the shadow of the Serpent. (Agatha Christie, A Caribbean Mystery)

Every Eden had its serpent, and the serpent in the Bahamian Eden was the proximity of America, with its hunger for drugs. (Bernard Cornwell, Crackdown)

"I think we're dealing with coke smugglers, and I don't mean Coca-Cola. . . ." (Desmond Bagley, Bahama Crisis)

Trouble in Paradise

PERHAPS BECAUSE MANY Caribbean mysteries grow out of their authors' one-week fun-in-the-sun vacations, which leave little time for research, they tend to be set in fictional island paradises with names like Santana and Grand Flamingo rather than in the real-life demi-paradises of Jamaica and Trinidad and Sint Maarten. With some important exceptions, they depict a homogenized "Caribbean" culture of piña coladas by the sea and calypso bands playing "Yellow Bird." The serpent in the island Eden may be politics, race, or drugs—but more likely it's just unregenerate human nature, easily uncovered by a vacationing detective.

A second type of generic Caribbean country is the brooding dark island ravaged by colonialism and/or a homegrown dictatorship—of which Bill Granger's St. Michel is a fictional example and pre-Aristide Haiti the real-life prototype. (Cuba is another matter. The Pearl of the Antilles and the sty in the U.S. government's eye, Cuba defies most Caribbean generalizations. The focus of any number of anti-Communist American thrillers, Cuba has also produced a distinctive body of mystery fiction of its own. See *Cuba* section of reading list, below.)

In reality, of course, the Caribbean islands reflect a wide variety of cultural influences—French, Dutch, Spanish, British, American, African, and combinations thereof, though the indigenous Arawaks and Caribs are virtually extinct. The topography is also varied. The tiny Dutch-speaking island of Saba, an extinct volcano covered with lush vegetation, bears little resemblance to the bustling urban sprawl of Spanish-speaking San Juan, Puerto Rico. To glimpse how vivid such differences were in the days before mass tourism, take a look at T. S. Stribling's 1929 book, *Clues of the Caribbees.*

Desmond Bagley's *Bahama Crisis* demonstrates how mass tourism has tended to homogenize the distinctive qualities of the islands so that an absent-minded visitor, safe within the confines of his resort hotel complex, would be hard put to tell whether he was in Jamaica or Virgin Gorda or Grand Bahama. (The Bahamas and Bermuda, incidentally, are not even *in* the Caribbean. But they are very much a part of this generic Caribbean culture.)

Though drug-smuggling and sailing/diving adventures are flourishing subgenres, the archetypal Caribbean mystery plot goes like this: A prominent white American is murdered at a luxury resort; a black native is the leading suspect; the tourist trade is threatened. But things are never as they seem. See, for examples, A. H. Z. Carr's *Finding Maubee,* Patricia Moyes's *The Coconut Killings,* and Marshall Jevons's *Murder at the Margin.*

READING LIST

Bahamas

BAGLEY, Desmond. *Bahama Crisis* (GB, 1980, 1981). This book begins splendidly—with a succinct and lively history of the settlement and development of the Bahamas in the form of a prologue by the book's narrator, Tom Mangan. Mangan, a rich white Bahamian whose loyalist ancestors immigrated to the island of Abaco after the American Revolution, is an enlightened entrepreneur. He intends to make another fortune in the tourist business but he's also concerned that his black compatriots get their fair share. All's going smoothly until Tom's wife and daughter mysteriously disappear during a boat trip to Miami. Other disasters follow: a riot in Nassau, an outbreak of Legionnaires' disease, a fire that takes 80 tourists' lives, a sabotaged baggage carousel that destroys 108 tourists' luggage, a kidnapping . . . The alert reader will have gathered by now that someone is out to wreck the Bahamian economy, but it takes another 150 pages or so of hyperactivity for Mangan to twig. Thin plot, flat characters, but lots of valuable background information.

BUFFETT, Jimmy. *Where Is Joe Merchant?* (NY, 1992, 1993). Given that this overlong best-seller is laced with New Age hooey (talking dolphins, bossy constellations) as well as a more traditional variety (magic wands), given that the plot is preposterous and the characters cartoons, it's not bad. Buffett, the singer/composer of the anthem of beach-bound Baby Boomers ("Wasted awaaay again in Margaritaville . . ."), seems to know his Caribbean—especially the more raffish of the Bahamian Out Islands (some real, some fictional). There are also brief stops in Cuba and Haiti. The protagonist, a laid-back seaplane pilot named Frank Bama, is persuaded by his ex-girlfriend to undertake a search for her brother, famous rock singer Joe Merchant, presumed dead but recently sighted in Havana. There's a host of curious characters; lore galore about the Caribbean of "cutthroats, contraband, drug-smuggling, and corrupt government officials"; and a lot more plot, some of it centered on the sunken treasure ship of King Henri Christophe of Haiti.

CORNWELL, Bernard. *Crackdown* (NY, 1990). The evil that the drug trade hath wrought is the theme of this sailing adventure. The narrator, Nick Breakspear, the rebellious son of a great British actor, is a former Royal Marine and a would-be "gypsy sailor." While working as skipper of a charter schooner out of Freeport, he and the ship's cook, a gorgeous runaway professor of women's studies, are hired by an American senator to take the senator's two coke-addicted kids on a cruise intended to rehabilitate them. The kids and some heavyweight drug dealers have other plans. After a promising start, the novel turns lurid—and very violent. Take heed: if you're going to the Bahamas, steer clear of Norman's Cay.

Cuba

A note on the Cuban mystery: In her useful study *Detective Fiction from Latin America* (NJ, 1990), Amelia S. Simpson describes how in the 1970s and '80s, encouraged by a government prize, the mystery flourished in

Cuba. Writers were expected to follow an ideological line, however, at odds with many of the conventions of the genre, such as the individualistic detective hero. Some writers such as Juan Angel Cardi and Arnaldo Correa found literary strategies to avoid overt propagandizing. The insistence on a rigid political correctness reportedly has eased in recent years; no Cuban mystery novel, however, has yet made it into English translation—unless one stretches the genre to include Alejo Carpentier's 1956 classic novella, *El Acoso* ("The Chase").

Among the many Cold War melodramas set in Cuba, there are a couple of standouts:

BUCKLEY, William F., Jr. *See You Later Alligator* (NY, 1985, 1986). In this clever mix of fact and fiction, Buckley puts his CIA hero, Blackford Oakes, in Cuba in the weeks leading up to the Cuban Missile Crisis of '62. While Castro, Khrushchev, and JFK play the most dangerous game of the Cold War, Oakes is busy negotiating with Che Guevara for an agreement that would keep the Soviets out of Cuba in exchange for an end to the American embargo. (He's also busy screwing Che's lovely lady translator, but that's to be expected of Oakes, a preppy James Bond, 007's equal in libido and daring if not in high-tech gadgetry.) Buckley's portrait of Che is unexpectedly ambiguous, complicated, and, up to a point, sympathetic; Che even gives Oakes a personal guided tour of the Sierra Maestre. Things get out of hand toward the end, however, when Oakes must single-handedly save the Free World once again. The jaunty title comes from Oakes's code name, *Caimán* (alligator), and the phrase with which Che ends each of their negotiating sessions: "*Hasta luego, Caimán.*" (See also Buckley's *Mongoose R.I.P.* [1988], which involves a CIA plot to assassinate Castro.)

*GREENE, Graham. *Our Man in Havana* (London & NY, 1958, London, 1971). Greene labeled it "an entertainment," but *Our Man in Havana* is also high art and required reading for travelers to Cuba. The protagonist, Wormold, is a sad little Englishman, an ineffectual vacuum cleaner salesman and a longtime resident of Havana. His wife has left him; his adored fifteen-year-old daughter, Milly, has expensive tastes. So when a blundering spymaster offers him three hundred dollars a month to be British Intelligence's man in Havana, Wormold accepts and soon finds he has talent—not for spying but for making up plausible stories about

---

*vaut le voyage (see page 4).

weapons and recruits. Then his stories start coming true. . . . This is a comedy with poignant undertones, and a brilliantly sinister portrayal of Cuba on the eve of Castro's triumph.

One unexpected side effect of Cuba's three decades of economic struggle is that much of the old Havana Greene knew survives superficially unchanged—including Lamparilla Street where Wormold lived over the store (No. 37 never existed, however). The Floridita still touts its daiquiris; the grand prospect from the waterfront promenade known as the Malecon remains much as Greene described it. The Hotel Nacional and the Seville-Biltmore (now the Sevilla) have been restored to their former glory (without the gambling).

KAMINSKY, Stuart M. *Hard Currency* (NY, 1995). Kaminsky's series of police procedurals featuring Inspector Porfiry Rostnikov is often praised for the books' depiction of the Russian scene. In this one, however, a member of Rostnikov's team is left to cope with a serial killer on the loose in Moscow, while Rostnikov himself is sent to Cuba to deal with a touchy diplomatic problem for the post-Soviet government: a Russian citizen is about to be tried by a Cuban court for the murder of his Cuban mistress. Rostnikov's orders are to avoid an "incident" by quickly confirming the Cuban government's case.

The Moscow and Havana plots are developed in alternating chapters—neither very satisfyingly. Though there are some nice post-Soviet ironies (a Cuban explaining totalitarian justice to a Russian, for example), the depiction of Havana is skimpy and marred by small errors (for example, the former presidential palace is now the Museum of the Revolution, not the Museum of History). Bringing in Fidel ex machina at the end is a sloppy way out of Kaminsky's plot problems. Disappointing.

LOCKRIDGE, Frances and Richard. *Voyage into Violence* (Philadelphia, 1956; NY, 1976). In this "Mr. and Mrs. North" tale, New York publisher Jerry North, his deceptively ditzy wife Pam, and their chums New York police captain Bill Weigand and his artist wife Dorian take a cruise to Havana and Nassau. Also on board is a ceremonial sword and, inevitably, someone gets murdered with it. Instead of heading for the nearest port, the ship captain puts Bill on the case. The plot's silly, but the North circle has a certain period charm. The women wear fetching gowns; everyone reads Wodehouse, quotes Cole Porter, smokes, makes witty and/or languid remarks, and drinks lots of martinis. In Havana they spend most of their time at an elaborate suburban nightclub, known as the Castle

Club, which offers gambling, a huge replica of Havana's Morro Castle, and seminaked dancers.

Curaçao

VAN DE WETERING, Janwillem. *Tumbleweed* (See Chapter VI).

Guadeloupe

FRENCH, Michael. *Club Caribe* (NY, 1977). For "Club Caribe's La Caravane Hotel, Sainte-Anne, Guadeloupe," read Club Med's Caravelle, Ste. Anne, Guadeloupe. But read no further unless you harbor nostalgia for the days when "singles" was paired with "swinging." Published in the same year as Patricia Moyes's *Coconut Killings, Club Caribe* also involves the murder of a U.S. senator on a West Indies resort, racial unrest, and dirty dealings on the development front. But compared to this piece of trash, Moyes reads like Graham Greene. The sex and violence give new meaning to the word "gratuitous."

Haiti

STRIBLING, T. S. *Clues of the Caribbees: Being Certain Criminal Investigations of Henry Poggioli, Ph.D.* (NY, 1929, 1977). Five bizarre tales, alternately comic and lurid, each with a different Caribbean setting: Dutch Curaçao, sinister Cap Haitien in the "Black Republic" of Haiti, sophisticated Martinique, veddy British Barbados, and an East Indian enclave in Trinidad. The islands' distinctive physical and racial/ethnic characteristics are vividly evoked—the latter rather too vividly. It's hard to get beyond the pervasive, casual racism of the surface to the author's more complex recognition of the evils of exploitation and the virtues of what we'd call diversity.

Stribling's traveling protagonist is Henry Poggioli, professor of psychology at Ohio State, a vain young man specializing in "racial psychology" and crime detection. At each stop he gets involved in solving a mystery. He occasionally makes a clever deduction or an enlightened political observation, but as often as not he's baffled. "The Governor of Cap Haitien" is the longest and best of these tales. The eponymous governor hires Poggioli to pose as an American "voodoo inspector" with the aim of exposing a political rival as a charlatan. In the course of some fantastic goings-on, Stribling manages to impart a good deal of information about the grandeur, terror, tragedy, and muddle of Haitian history. Impossible to read it without longing to see for oneself the monumental Citadelle, constructed at the cost of thousands of lives for King Henry Christophe, the slave who became an emperor.

Jamaica

FLEMING, Ian. *Doctor No* (London & NY, 1958). In which James Bond is issued a new gun (in tedious detail) and sent to Jamaica to take on what should be—but, of course, isn't—an easy case. He gets help from his Cayman Islander sidekick, Quarrel, and a blond child of nature named Honeychile. His enemies are the Chinese monster of the title and his half-breed "Chigroe" thugs (who, we're told, have "some of the intelligence of the Chinese and most of the vices of the black man"). There are a few nice sketches of the local scenery but Bond spends most of his time deep under a mountain of guano. (Other Bond mysteries set in the West Indies include *Live and Let Die*, 1954, and *Man with the Golden Gun*, 1965.)

HADLEY, Joan. *The Deadly Ackee* (NY, 1988, 1990). Theo Bloomer, horticulturist/former spy/amateur sleuth, chaperones his obnoxiously upscale niece Dorrie and her chums on a one-week holiday in a hillside villa outside Montego Bay. If your idea of fun is the spring break activities (puking, talking dirty, bickering) of spoiled Ivy League preppies with names like Trey, Biff, and Bitsy, this may be just your cup of rum punch. If not, you will find yourself eager for a murder to take place. The local color comprises the standard tourist sights: a day trip to Dunn's River Falls and Ocho Rios, a visit to Rose Hall, the Governor's Coach Tour. The murder weapon is the fruit of the title—deadly when unripe.

Virgin Islands

HIGGINS, Jack. *Thunder Point* (NY, 1993). Thunder Point is a dangerous reef off St. John in the U.S. Virgins, where a wrecked German U-boat carrying a dark secret has lurked since 1945. In 1992 a nice amateur diver finds the wreck, but before he can show it to the good guys (the head of a supersecret British agency, a sometime IRA terrorist turned mercenary, and the owner of the Caneel Bay diving shop), he is accidentally killed. Meanwhile, the bad guys (a Cuban exile zillionaire and a British aristocrat) find out about it. So the race is on to find the wreck and its precious contents—Martin Bormann's briefcase containing, among other tricky items, a list of British secret sympathizers with Hitler and plans to keep the Nazi cause alive. Pacing is the key here: if Higgins slows for even a second, the holes in the plot gape. Mostly he doesn't, getting us from Hitler's Berlin bunker in 1945 to a Serbian dungeon in 1992 to the Virgin Islands in a mere thirty-seven pages. Though Higgins seems very precise about names and places (he even includes a map of the Virgins), his idea of vivid detail is "every kind of tropical plant imaginable." The deluxe Caneel Bay resort gets a four-star plug.

JEVONS, Marshall [William Breit and Kenneth G. Elzinga]. *Murder at the Margin* (1978; Princeton, 1993). Once again the setting is St. John's elegant Caneel Bay Plantation (here called Cinnamon Bay—confusingly, because there is a Cinnamon Bay Plantation, a low-rent camping resort). The plot's the Caribbean standard: Two prominent vacationers (a retired general and a former Supreme Court justice) are murdered at the resort against a background of racial unrest. Two black radicals are accused. The gimmick here is the amateur detective, a very short economics professor named Henry Spearman (based on Milton Friedman, the authors acknowledge), who uses economic theory to solve the mystery. The authors have worked up the local color quite enjoyably, and the economics lessons provide some insights into the island's problems. But the irrational principle of "least likely suspect" works just as well in solving this case.

Invented Islands

AMBLER, Eric. *Doctor Frigo* (NY, 1974). The narrator, a physician named Castillo working on the fictional island of St. Paul-les-Alizes in the French Antilles, has earned the nickname of the title for his emotional detachment, perceived by his colleagues as coldness. He has a lot to detach himself from. Twelve years earlier his father, a liberal politician in an unnamed Central American nation, was assassinated—perhaps by the ruling junta, perhaps by rivals in his own party. Now the fate of that country has become important to any number of greedy people because of the discovery of offshore oil. The narrator is drawn unwillingly into a plot to overthrow the junta.

Julian Symons has called this Ambler's finest novel. Its great strengths are its political acumen and its depiction of character. Setting plays a lesser role, though Ambler does a fine job on the kind of resort hotel he calls the "five-star automat." (Incidentally, a passing reference to Lafcadio Hearn's 1880s residence in the town where Dr. Castillo lives would seem to pinpoint the principal setting as St. Pierre, Martinique. The only problem is that St. Pierre was destroyed in the eruption of a volcano in 1902. Tricky Mr. Ambler.)

CARR, A. H. Z. *Finding Maubee* (NY, 1971) [a.k.a. *The Calypso Murders*]. A prominent white American is murdered at a luxury resort (Mango Beach) on the island of St. Caro (an American territory based loosely on one of the Virgin Islands?). All evidence points to David Maubee, a charming native thief who has fathered any number of illegitimate babies and become a local legend. The black police chief, Xavier Brooke, a boyhood friend of Maubee's, is ordered to bring him in dead or alive by the ambitious and nasty white governor. But Brooke, a man of character and education, is more interested in finding the truth than in capturing his old pal. Rich in local color (including lots of calypso lyrics and an introduction to the rituals of obeah), this novel is unusual for its consistent and uncondescending use of a native point of view.

CHRISTIE, Agatha. *A Caribbean Mystery* (NY, 1964, 1966). Standard-issue Miss Marple, only this time the percipient spinster is vacationing on the Caribbean island of "St. Honore." She might as well be in Brighton. A garrulous British major dies, and Miss M suspects murder. She's right, of course, and other murders follow. The focus quickly narrows to a half dozen residents at the Golden Palm Hotel. The setting has nothing to do with the plot, and except for some unfortunate racial references and Miss M's distaste for steel bands, it rarely makes itself felt.

CHRISTMAS, Joyce. *A Perfect Day for Dying* (NY, 1994). An old-style mystery in a New World setting. Life on the tiny island of Boucan (probably based on one of the Grenadines) is still dominated by the aristocratic British family in the Big House. The main characters are languid English types out in the noonday sun, with a sprinkling of Eurotrash houseguests—an Italian princeling, an aging "professional Latin lover," and "one of those Pacific Rim femme fatales." The first two murders involve poisonous oleander, a local "cutlass," and an obeah spell. ("Many perils lurk among the palm trees.") The amateur detective, who wangles an invitation to the house party, is Lady Margaret Priam, who combines a ditzy style with considerable competence. Mildly amusing fluff.

DAVEY, Jocelyn. *Murder in Paradise* (NY, 1982). Let's see now: we have a Hong Kong drug-smuggling ring, several double agents, a U.S. military installation with big missiles, an American millionaire with a private army, offshore oil, and an impending Marxist revolution. (Here's a twist: the rebels are the descendants of Dutch settlers with a grudge against con-

tinuing British dominance—even though the island is now independent.) All this and it's Carnival week on the isle of "Santanna" (near
Trinidad). The detective is visiting Oxford *don vivant* (to steal a *Time*
coinage) Ambrose Usher, who spouts Milton and Meville when he's not
making inspired guesses.

DICKINSON, Peter. *Walking Dead* (NY, 1977). Set in the "Southward
Islands," a former British colony turned nasty dictatorship, this is an odd-
ball tale pitting science against magic. It stars a researcher named Foxe
who progresses from running rats through mazes to engineering the escape of a group of mystical zealots from the "mad and evil tyrant"'s dungeon. Unfortunately, the magic has only a remote relationship to voodoo
or Santeria, and the setting of this thoughtful fantasy is only nominally
Caribbean.

GRANGER, Bill. *Hemingway's Notebook* (NY, 1986). Granger's CIA
hero, Devereaux—a.k.a. The November Man—has many fans. Include
us out. This outing is mostly set on a generic Caribbean isle (corrupt, fran-
cophone subdivision) named St. Michel. "Think of Haiti on its worst day
and then you got some idea of St. Michel at its best." It involves decadent and/or corrupt and/or vicious white men, funny and/or sinister
blacks, slaughtered nuns, CIA, Mafia, Castro, voodoo, rape, Swiss bank
accounts, and an exhausting number of double- and triple-crosses. Plus
the eponymous notebook, written in code by Hemingway in his Cuban
days, pointing the finger of blame for the Bay of Pigs and other disasters
in Cuban-American relations. From time to time Granger also tries to
write like Hemingway, and that is a bad thing.

MOYES, Patricia. *Black Widower* (GB & NY, 1975; NY, 1977). This is
the first of Moyes's Henry Tibbett mysteries to involve the fictional British
Seaward Islands, which sound a lot like the nonfictional British Leeward
Islands—perhaps St. Kitts and Nevis. This one begins in Washington with
the murder of the wife of the ambassador of the newly independent island of Tampica. Complicating matters is the fact that the brilliant
Oxford-educated ambassador is black and his beautiful, wayward, and
vulgar wife is English and white. Chief Superintendent Tibbett of Scotland Yard (and wife Emmy) are imported by the Tampicans to conduct
a discreet investigation, which takes them eventually to the island paradise.

————. *The Coconut Killings* (GB & NY, 1977, 1985; a.k.a. *To Kill a
Coconut*). Anyone who has ever returned to a beloved Caribbean island

after it's been "discovered" by the tourist hordes will resonate to the mixed feelings of the Tibbetts when next they see Tampica. This time they're en route to the even smaller island of St. Matthew's (still a crown colony) to investigate the brutal machete murder of an American senator at an exclusive resort, a crime that is creating serious racial problems. The West Indian locals are not particularly convincing, and all the "good" white characters have impeccably correct racial attitudes slightly tainted by paternalism. It's no surprise that the murder turns out to have more to do with corrupt dealings among U.S. senators and lobbyists than with race. Still, good hammock reading. (See also *Angel Death* [1981], about drug-smuggling in the Caribbean.)

WILLIAMS, David. *Treasure Up in Smoke* (GB & NY, 1978). Mark Treasure, banker and amateur sleuth, is sent by his employer to take care of some business on the tiny island of King Charles. Named after the decapitated monarch, and nominally British, the island has been owned and operated since the seventeenth century by the O'Hara family. The current O'Hara, "Uncle Joe," is a most benevolent despot, but like the martyred king, he is destined to lose his head in a plot involving rival developers, a black chief minister with silent ambitions, a Wodehouse-style young idiot named Peregrine, and some silly goings-on with a stoned pig and a single-gauge railroad. There's also an order of cigar-making nuns who lace their wares with marijuana. The tone is uncertain, the pace slow.

YORK, Andrew. *Tallant for Disaster* (NY, 1978). James Munroe Tallant, a former international cricket star, is the commissioner of police for the Flamingo Islands, a scruffy little ex-British colony a thousand miles south of Jamaica. In this second Tallant adventure, he has his hands full: a conference of Caribbean ministers is meeting on Grand Flamingo, an American tourist and her local gigolo have been murdered after finding a sunken Spanish galleon, and a hurricane is on the way. Tallant, who is black and from Guyana, is imposing, resourceful, and generally disliked by the inbred mixed-blood Flamingans. York has invented a history, politics, and a prime minister for the Flamingos. They are both instructive and very funny. First rate. (See also *Tallant for Trouble,* 1977.)

NOTED BUT NOT REVIEWED

ANDERSON, J. R. L. *Death in the Caribbean* (London, 1977). "The Dick Francis of boating" finds trouble for his hero, Col. Peter North, on the former British colony of "Nueva" in the Lesser Antilles.

DUNNETT, Dorothy. *Operation Nassau* (a.k.a. *Dolly and the Doctor Bird* [London, 1971, 1993]). Another outing for Johnson Johnson, artist, yachtsman, and sleuth.

EASTABROOK, Barry. *Bahama Heat* (NY, 1991). The minister of an impoverished mission finds a fortune in cocaine.

GRANT-ADAMSON, Lesley. *Dangerous Games* ([GB, 1994]; NY, 1995). On "St. Elena": a charming American rogue, a clique of rich British twits, and a perilous search for sunken treasure.

GREENE, Graham. *The Comedians* (London & NY, 1966). Neither mystery nor spy novel in any conventional sense, but this brilliant portrayal of Papa Doc Duvalier's Haiti should not be missed.

HUNT, E. Howard [a.k.a. Gordon Davis]. *Where Murder Waits* (Ct., 1965, 1973). "Washington intrigue and Cuban violence," says the cover.

TERMAN, Douglas. *Shell Game* (NY, 1985, 1986). The Cuban Missile Crisis finds two brothers—one a CIA agent, one a KGB recruit—playing for the highest stakes.

ZIMMERMAN, Bruce. *Thicker Than Water* (NY, 1991). A California comic inherits a Jamaican estate . . . and trouble.

XXI

CENTRAL AND SOUTH AMERICA

I thought of a labyrinth of labyrinths, of one sinuous spreading labyrinth that would encompass the past and the future and in some way involve the stars. (Jorge Luis Borges, "The Garden of Forking Paths")

BELIZE: *The sun rose out of the Caribbean, pouring blue on the black water, lighter blue on the great vaulted dome of sky. The islands awoke, palm trees nodding good morning, all the way from Trinidad and Tobago in the south up to Anguilla and Sint Maarten in the north. The sudden tropic dawn moved westward toward Jamaica and beyond, out over the flexing waters, winking next at the tiny dots of the Cayman Islands. Hundreds of miles of open sea awoke with yawning mouths until the sun reached the great barrier reef along the Central American coast; nearly 200 north/south miles of coral reef and tiny islands called cayes, just off shore from Belize. Hurrying to that coast, in a rush to get inland and raise the great green hulks of the Maya Mountains, the sun met a tiny plane coming the other way.* (Donald E. Westlake, High Adventure)

BRAZIL: *At street corners to the right and left of where they sat drummed samba bands. Boys, men, from fourteen years of age to whenever, beat on drums of various sizes, various tones, as if this were their last chance to do so, ever . . . Immediately around each band, pedestrians stayed to give in totally to the samba awhile, dancing on the sidewalk, up and down the curb, among the cars parked pridefully anywhere . . . businessmen dressed only in shorts and sandals, sometimes shirts, carrying briefcases, women in bikinis lugging bags of groceries, barefoot children running with a soccer ball, walked, lugged, ran, keeping the beat of the drums in their feet, their legs, their hips, their shoulders.* (Gregory Mcdonald, Carioca Fletch)

PERU: *There it was: immense, mysterious, gray-green, poverty-stricken, wealthy, ancient, hermetic. Peru was this lunar landscape and the impassive, copper-colored faces of the women and men who surrounded them. Impenetrable, really. Very different from the faces they had seen in Lima, the whites, blacks, mestizos with whom they had managed, however badly, to communicate. But something impenetrable separated him from the mountain people.* (Mario Vargas Llosa, *Death in the Andes*)

Into the Labyrinth

I T'S NOT UNUSUAL anywhere in the world for "serious" writers to dabble in mystery or spy fiction. In the United States, one immediately thinks of Joyce Carol Oates, William Faulkner, Thomas Berger, Paul Auster; in England, of the sublime Graham Greene. In much of Latin America, however, the practice goes beyond dabbling: the mystery genre seems almost to have been co-opted by the literati. Argentinians Jorge Luis Borges, Manuel Puig, and Osvaldo Soriano, Carlos Fuentes of Mexico, Mario Vargas Llosa of Peru, Colombia's Gabriel García Márquez, Cuba's Alejo Carpentier, the Brazilians Jorge Amado and Rubem Fonseca—many of the leading writers of the Latin American "boom" and beyond have tried their hands at a crime novel or two, adapting the conventions of the genre to their own aesthetic purposes.

Meanwhile, according to literary historian Amelia S. Simpson, Latin American crime novelists of a less literary bent, especially in Argentina and Brazil, have been unable to compete in popularity with foreign imports—even when they have gone so far as to use American or British settings and pseudonyms. Readers interested in the history of the detective novel in Latin America are referred to Simpson's excellent, if somewhat jargony, study, *Detective Fiction from Latin America* (Cranbury, NJ, 1990), which focuses on the four biggest Latin American producers of crime fiction: Argentina, Brazil, Cuba, and Mexico.

Simpson traces how the great Borges's interest in the detective novel gave the genre cachet in Argentina in the forties, making it respectable reading for the educated and the sophisticated. Borges also contributed to a trend of using the genre as a vehicle for attacking the populist politicism of the Peronists, which threatened the old way of life of Argentina's upper class.

But though Argentine writers in the forties favored classic English-style puzzles, history had no intention of leaving them to such genteel pursuits. Heading toward Latin America in fiction as well as fact were any number of scruffy CIA agents, Interpol officers, ex-Green Berets, directors of United Fruit, soldiers of fortune—all eager to intervene in local politics—plus Nazis and other nasties seeking refuge. Already on the scene were tinpot dictators, terrorist guerrillas, corrupt cops, and brutal army officers. And, of course, Cuban Communists—a Cold War obsession. "Cuban agents were filtering all through Latin America like woodworms in a piece of furniture," writes Desmond Bagley in *High Citadel*.

In the late forties, the North American hard-boiled mystery was introduced into Argentina and embraced by some young intellectuals. By the seventies, according to Simpson, the *novela dura* was fully entrenched in Argentina, and detective fiction was no longer the preserve of the conservative elite. In the sixties and seventies, the hard-boiled mystery was used by Argentine writers such as Rodolfo Walsh as a vehicle of leftist social protest. (Walsh's outspoken criticism of the ruling junta led to his abduction and murder in 1977.)

In Brazil, unlike Argentina, mystery fiction was initially held in low regard, with most native writers following English and American formulas. In 1977, Brazilian writer Moacir Amâncio commented on the inappropriateness of such foreign models: "those people [i.e., the English and Americans] are very different from us. Over there someone can actually admire the law. Here the law is feared and, whenever possible, violated. . . . We're born with fear of the police, fear of the powerful. . . . We live in a police state. We breathe and sweat repression." More recently, talented Brazilian writers such as Rubem Fonseca have used the mystery to explore the violence, alienation, degrading poverty, and official corruption of urban Brazil.

READING LIST

Argentina

BORGES, Jorge Luis. "Death and the Compass" and "The Garden of Forking Paths" in *Labyrinths: Selected Stories and Other Writings*, edited by Donald A. Yates and James E. Irby (NY, 1964). These are the two most celebrated Borges stories to make use of the conventions of the mystery. "Death and the Compass" is the mystery turned metaphysical. The superrational detective follows a series of clues in Talmudic lore to solve a symmetrical series of murders, only to find himself caught in a trap: the hunter is really the hunted. The story upends expectations; in Simpson's words, it expresses "not affirmation of order but instead doubt and menace." Similarly, "The Garden of Forking Paths" overturns the conventions of the Buchanesque spy novel. The central image of modern Latin American literature, the labyrinth, informs both stories.

BORGES, Jorge Luis, and BIOY-CASARES, Adolfo. *Six Problems for Don Isidro Parodi* [Buenos Aires, 1942], translated by Norman Thomas di Giovanni (NY, 1981); originally published under the pseudonym H. Bustos Domecq. Don Parodi is the ultimate sedentary sleuth, "the first detective to be a jailbird." A former barber framed for murder in a political plot, Parodi holds court in cell 273 of the state penitentiary in Buenos Aires, solving a series of linked mysteries brought to him by a variety of Argentine types. As the detective's name indicates, there is a strong parodic element in the book, which targets such conventions and clichés of the detective genre as the armchair detective, the "Purloined Letter" motif, the murder on a train, etc.

At the same time, the Parodi tales also satirize what the authors see as the degradation of Argentine society. Elitists and traditionalists, Borges and Bioy-Casares loathed the populist Peronist movement, the lower-class types that it empowered, and the narrow nationalism that it encouraged. But a good deal of this satire is inaccessible to those unfamiliar with the Argentine equivalents of "U" and "non-U" taste and behavior. For most nonspecialists, in fact, these stories are heavy going—without the intellectual agility, the sheer brilliance of Borges's solo works.

GREENE, Graham. *The Honorary Consul* (NY, 1973, 1974). Though Greene does not name the peaceful Argentine town where this powerful novel is set, he has written elsewhere that it is modeled on Corrientes, an old city on the Paraná River near the Argentine border with Paraguay. The novel's central character, the half-English Dr. Plarr, has been persuaded to help a group of rebels from his native Paraguay. Their scheme is to kidnap the American ambassador to Argentina and to barter his life for the release of political prisoners held by Paraguay's real-life nasty dictator, General Stroessner. (Plarr believes that one of those prisoners may be his father, whom he has not seen in twenty years.) By mistake, however, the rebels kidnap the powerless and pathetic Charley Fortnum, the honorary British consul of the title. Fortnum's value as a hostage is nil. He is also a drunk and a local joke for having married a whore. Even worse, Fortnum, who regards the emotionally frozen Plarr as his friend, is unaware that Plarr is his wife's lover and the father of the child she is carrying.

This is a story about fathers and sons—and about Father and Son; about religion and politics and the limits of both; about *machismo* and the meaning of love. Only by stretching the term to its limits can one call it a "thriller," but it's worth the stretch. (See also Greene's 1969 novel, *Travels with My Aunt,* which describes a four-day riverboat journey from Buenos Aires via Corrientes to Asunción, the capital of Paraguay.)

HOUGAN, Carolyn. *Blood Relative* (NY, 1992). Rolando, an Argentine naval officer whose wife and daughter were among the "disappeared" during Argentina's horrific Dirty War of the seventies, has become obsessed, crazed, with the desire for revenge. The target of his obsession is his niece, last seen at age four, who he believes may have survived the horrors. Indeed she has. Maria is now Mariah, a bright, pretty American teenager who knows nothing of her origins or even that she is adopted. The novel shifts back and forth between Mariah in Wisconsin and Rolando in Buenos Aires. Then Mariah is in Alexandria, Virginia. And so are Rolando and a hired thug . . . in hot pursuit. The book has problems with tone: the early Mariah chapters read like a young adult novel. But this is a real page-turner—with a social conscience.

PUIG, Manuel. *The Buenos Aires Affair: A Detective Novel,* translated by Suzanne Jill Levine ([1974]; NY, 1976, 1980). Puig *(Kiss of the Spider Woman, Betrayed by Rita Hayworth)* is one of the stars of the modern Latin American novel, known in particular for his literary uses of popular culture. In this novel about a desperately single artist and a sexually troubled art critic, unappealing characters both, Puig plays with the techniques and conventions of the thriller—as well as those of B-movies, magazine interviews, case histories, and police reports. The reader becomes the detective, seeking answers to such questions as Who was the murder victim? Did a murder even take place? And, ultimately, I'm afraid—Who cares?

SORIANO, Osvaldo. *Winter Quarters* [Barcelona, 1982], translated by Nick Caistor (London and Columbia, La., 1989). Soriano's work has been described as "Argentine Noir"—which seems to mean hard-boiled with a glaze of surrealism. Certainly everything in this short novel is slightly heightened—the bright brighter, the dark darker—as in a Magritte painting. The story takes place in Colonia Vela, a small, army-controlled town in the pampas during the Dirty War of the seventies. Colonia Vela was also the setting for Soriano's *A Funny Dirty Little War* (1986), in which most of the inhabitants were massacred.

In this second installment of the town's history, two burnt-out enter-tainers, a tango singer and a punchy boxer, are brought in to open a town festival. As a friendship develops between the unlikely pair, it becomes clear that the army and/or the town officials have sinister plans for them. Not much of a mystery, this short novel is a powerful evocation of the horrors of Argentina's recent history and a poignant portrayal of male friendship. (See also Soriano's *Shadows* [1993].)

Belize

COX, George. *With Intent to Kill* (NY, 1965). Pursued by a vengeful millionaire who blames him for his brother's accidental death, architect Barry Sanford has fled New York and gone to ground in Belize City (then the capital of British Honduras). The murderous millionaire tracks him down there—and gets murdered himself. Flat characters and a dopey plot quite unrelated to the setting. The description of Belize City when it was still recovering from a disastrous 1961 hurricane is probably accurate but it's lifeless.

*WESTLAKE, Donald F. *High Adventure* (NY, 1985). Donald West-lake's wry, wisecracking style is perfectly suited to the raffish little nation of Belize, which, happily, has thus far avoided the tragedies of its Cen-tral American neighbors. The plot revolves around American pilot Kirby Galway's scheme to smuggle purportedly ancient Mayan artifacts, inge-niously concealed in a cargo of marijuana, to some unscrupulous deal-ers and museums in the United States. Other characters include a high-minded lady archeologist, the Mayan residents of a jungle village known as South Abilene (including two hipsters who have spent time in the United States and who remind Kirby of "a couple of Marx Brothers wandering through a Robert Flaherty documentary"), a nasty Guatemalan colonel, Gurkha soldiers in the British army, and an engagingly corrupt government official named Innocent St. Michael: "His hair was African,

vault le voyage (see page 4).

his mocha skin Mayan, his courage Irish, and the deviousness of his brain was all Spanish."

This very funny book also includes some fine descriptive passages, and Westlake painlessly conveys a lot of history and background information. Not to be missed if you're going to Belize. Or if the idea of a lost Mayan temple, Lava Sxir Yt, being named after *La vache qui rit* cheese makes you smile.

Brazil

FISH, Robert L. *Brazilian Sleigh Ride* (NY, 1965; Woodstock, Vt., 1988). Fish, an American who died in 1981, wrote ten novels starring Captain José Da Silva, the Brazilian police's liaison with Interpol, a tall, mustachioed, dashing character whose best friend and sidekick is a nondescript little man named Wilson, a CIA agent whose cover is a routine embassy job. The series is formulaic in the extreme. The pair always meet to drink quantities of cognac, exchange gibes, and eat bad food at the mezzanine restaurant in Rio's Santos Dumont airport. Da Silva is irresistible to women, Wilson quite otherwise. Their barbs and jokes seem anachronistic, more forties or fifties than sixties. The formula, however, makes good use of Rio's fabulous scenery and lively culture.

This episode begins with Wilson at the airport awaiting the arrival of an old army buddy. He runs into his pal Da Silva, who is there to arrest an embezzler. Of course, it turns out they're waiting for the same man; his failure to appear ultimately takes them to the beaches of Recife and to New York City, where Da Silva tangles with American gangsters.

————. *Always Kill a Stranger* (NY, 1967; Woodstock, Vt., 1988). Da Silva plays cat and mouse with a professional assassin who Da Silva believes is targeting the Argentine head of state, in Rio for an OAS meeting. Da Silva also believes the CIA is behind the scheme, which puts him at odds with friend Wilson. Eventually the two resolve their differences in an adventure that includes vivid scenes of the cliffside *favelas* (shantytowns) of Rio and its sleaziest suburban beaches.

FONSECA, Rubem. *High Art* [Brazil, 1983], translated from Portuguese by Ellen Watson (NY, 1986). Of all the serious Latin American novelists who have tried their hand at detective fiction, Fonseca seems the most comfortable with the genre, with both its strengths and its limitations. *High Art* works on several levels—first, as a mystery (actually, a series of mysteries) to be solved: Who killed two prostitutes and carved the letter *P* on their cheeks, and what do their deaths have to do with a missing videotape that belongs to a very rich man named Mitry? And why is somebody trying to knock off Fonseca's detective, a criminal lawyer and "avid seducer of women" named Mandrake?

On another level, the novel is a powerful depiction of a rotten and corrupt society, where violence is endemic and comes as easily to the "good-guy" Mandrake as it does to his various nefarious assailants. Then, in its second half, *High Art* turns to the past—particularly to the decadent demimonde of the Argentine upper classes in the late nineteenth century. In that past, Fonseca finds both the sources of contemporary evils and contrasting standards against which they can be judged.

Fonseca is also good at depicting the edgy hubbub of modern Rio, as well as the timeless view of "infinite green plains" seen from the window of a slow train from Rio to Corumbà on the Bolivian border. *High Art* is a tough, relentless book that deserves to be better known in the English-reading world. (See also Fonseca's *Bufo & Spallanzani* [Brazil, 1985], translated by Clifford E. Landers [NY, 1990].)

McDONALD, Gregory. *Carioca Fletch* (NY, 1984). Sometime journalist Fletch, Mcdonald's series character, finds himself in Rio for Carnival, enchanted by a country that seems to move to a samba beat. He also finds himself accused of being the reincarnation of a murdered Brazilian, and since the murderer apparently believes this, Fletch is in danger of being the killer's second victim. Mcdonald's dialogue is crisp and amusing. He gets good mileage out of his Brazilian scenes, and he is sympathetic to the plight of the very poor, the *favela*-dwellers, who have few pleasures in life outside of samba, the sun, theft, and sex.

Chile

BRESLIN, Patrick. *Interventions* (NY, 1980). Published only seven years after the events it describes, this novel makes up in passion for what it may lack in historical perspective. It's 1973 in Santiago de Chile, and the socialist government of Salvador Allende is taking a lot of heat for the country's economic woes. Allende's enemies—especially the military—are getting a lot of help from the CIA, which is deeply antagonistic to the first freely elected Marxist government in history.

The novel's protagonist is Paul Steward, a burnt-out CIA agent, whose assignment to Santiago is his last chance to salvage his career. There, however, he encounters Marisa, a Chilean woman he loved in his idealistic youth, and the flame is briefly rekindled. Marisa, however, is increasingly involved in radical politics and with leftist journalist Felipe. When the CIA-backed coup against Allende takes place, Paul finds he has been unwittingly responsible for putting Marisa on an army list of political suspects and in mortal danger. Though the writing never excites, the novel is full of details about Chilean life and culture—descriptions of meals, for example, of streets and routes, and such local color as an evening at the Peña de los Parra, the nightclub owned by Chile's first family of the revived folk music known as *nueva canción*.

Colombia

CLIFFORD, Francis. *Amigo, Amigo* ([1973]; Chicago, 1985). Intrepid American reporter Anthony Lorrimer treks deep into the western highlands of Guatemala in search of a former administrator of Auschwitz, who's reinvented himself as the dentist and all-purpose *curandero* in a remote Indian village. Intrepid but dumb reporter. Not only does he screw the Nazi dentist's girlfriend, he also opens his mouth for the dentist's drill without benefit of anesthesia. Anyhow, in an unexpected twist, reporter, girlfriend, and Nazi are taken hostage by bandits, who use them to extract money from the villagers and to help in their getaway. A pretentious tale of interdependence and moral ambiguity.

LEWIS, Norman. *Flight from a Dark Equator* (NY, 1972). An unusually intelligent and illuminating political thriller about the various foreign interests seeking to intervene in Colombia on the brink of a revolution. The United States and the provincial governor of "Los Remedios," Colombia, make a deal: helicopters and "advisers" to support the governor's bid for his nation's presidency in exchange for U.S. controlling interest in a tin mine. Meanwhile, the novel's protagonist, who works for an international relief organization, finds his agency to be helpless in the face of suffering caused by political turmoil (as opposed to natural disaster). Lewis is especially good on the ambiguous role played by Protestant missionaries among the rural poor of Latin America.

LINDSEY, David L. *Body of Truth* (NY, 1992, 1993). Houston homicide detective Stuart Haydon, in search of the missing daughter of a prominent local family, makes a semiofficial trip to "Guate-god-damnedmala" (as his chief puts it) and is instantly immersed in Third

World horrors: grinding poverty, pervasive corruption, brutality and greed and violence. Seen through Haydon's eyes, Guatemala City is a City of Dreadful Night, under a miasma of pollution that (literally) stinks of death.

Though Lindsey's prose tends to be overwrought, his description of the city is full of information about real hotels, streets, and neighborhoods, and such sharply observed details as the ubiquity of auto-parts stores in Latin American capitals and the discordant spread of evangelical Protestantism among Guatemala's Indians. The book also includes a good bit of recent Guatemalan history, in which the CIA usually plays a sinister role. The complicated and very violent plot does not allow Haydon to leave Guatemala City for more scenic parts of the country until page 388, but in any case this is not a book likely to encourage tourism.

MANRIQUE, Jaime. *Colombian Gold: A Novel of Power and Corruption,* translated by Sara Nelson and Jaime Manrique (NY, 1983). The illegitimate son of a Colombian enriched by bananas and marijuana, Alvaro Villalba revenges himself on his cruelly neglectful father, getting to him shortly before the Grim Reaper arrives. It's Carnival time in Barranquilla, but nobody's having fun yet. Nor is the reader likely to start having fun unless he or she has a weakness for stories about patricide, incest, the homosexual rape of one's father-in-law, and a pharmacopoeia of illicit drugs. Manrique is a talented writer but this book verges on the repulsive.

MÁRQUEZ, Gabriel García. *Chronicle of a Death Foretold* [Bogota, 1981], translated by Gregory Rabassa (NY, 1982; 1989). Everyone in town on a certain February morning in the early fifties knows that San tiago Nasar is going to be killed that day by the Vicario brothers for having seduced their sister. Colombian Nobel Prize Winner Gabriel García Márquez has written a murder mystery in which all the crucial details— the victim, the villains, the method, the motive—are known from the novel's start. But the mystery of why no one does anything to stop it remains to haunt the reader, as well as the narrator, who twenty-seven years later attempts to reconstruct the day's events. A small classic of Latin American literature.

OMANG, Joanne. *Incident at Akabal* (NY, 1992). Akabal is a little Indian village in the highlands of an unnamed country easily recognized as Guatemala. The "incident" begins when one of the village's residents, a young revolutionary named Miguel, tosses a bomb into an army barracks. The army pursues Miguel to Akabal, where he is hidden by his compatriots. But the army officer gives the villagers an ultimatum: Turn over the guilty one or be massacred. Written by a former Latin American correspondent for *The Washington Post,* this striking first novel is notable for its powerful suspense and for the authority and lack of condescension with which Omang portrays the Indian villagers from within.

Peru

BUCKLEY, Christopher. *Wet Work* (NY, 1991, 1993). When self-made billionaire Charley Becker's beloved granddaughter dies of an overdose of cocaine, the engaging but ruthless billionaire turns vigilante, determined to track the coke to its source and to kill everyone involved along the way. The bloody trail leads from Manhattan to Miami to the Huallaga Valley of Peru and up the Amazon, where Charley's high-tech weaponry meets that of a sophisticated drug lord/Sendero Luminoso sympathizer known as El Niño, who shares Charley's passion for great art. Other perils include Indian blowguns and some nasty local fauna. Watching all this with growing alarm are various recognizable government officials, whose principal concern is to cover their own asses and whose jargon is often hilarious:

" 'It's like, I don't know what it's like, a combination tar baby and can of worms.'

" 'Right. It resonates that way for me, too.' "

Buckley clearly had fun writing this. There are lots of in-jokes (Charley's top aides are called McNamara, Bundy, and Rostow), but even readers far out of the loop will be amused by Buckley's Ross Thomas–like outrageousness.

STOUT, Rex. *Under the Andes* (NY, 1914, 1994). Twenty years before the first appearance of Nero Wolfe, Stout published this "lost race" story, which owes something to Jules Verne and Edgar Rice Burroughs, among others. Harry and Paul Lamar are brothers persuaded by a beautiful dancer named Desirée Le Mire to set off on an expedition from Cerro de Pasco in Peru in search of Inca gold. Instead they find a troll-like race of cave-dwellers, the descendants of the Incas, misshapen from generations of living underground. Piffle, as Nero Wolfe would say.

VARGAS LLOSA, Mario. *Who Killed Palomino Molero?* [1987], translated by Alfred Mac Adam (NY, 1987, 1988). When a young soldier from the

Talara air base is found impaled and grossly mutilated, Lieutenant Silva and Officer Lituma of a nearby Peruvian Guardia Civil post must investigate. The victim's name is Palomino Molero; he's a soft-soken, light-skinned *criollo,* a gifted bolero singer who suffers from "an impossible love." Things get murkier when Silva and Lituma learn that the "impossible love" object is the daughter of the base commander.

The book's spare realism is a fit vehicle for Vargas Llosa's social concerns: corruption both systemic and individual; exploitative gringos and their Peruvian accomplices; pervasive racism and classism. Lituma is an honest youth with a curiosity both intellectual and moral. His boss also is an exemplary character, despite his semicomic passion for a plump café proprietress.

————. *Death in the Andes* [1993], translated by Edith Grossman (NY, 1996). Lituma is now a corporal, in charge of a dangerous and wretched two-man Guardia post in a remote Andean settlement called Naccos, whose only reason for being is a camp of workers building a road (to where is not clear). His colleague is a sweet young man named Tomás, who in their lonely nights in the Andes unwinds the complicated story of his great love for Mercedes, a woman of dubious character.

Lituma has his own obsession: his search for the truth in the case of three Naccos men who have mysteriously disappeared. Are they the victims of the *terrucos,* the Sendero Luminoso terrorists whose presence is felt all around? Or have they met a more sinister fate, hinted at by the lewd and bibulous cantina-keeper, Dionisio, and his witch wife, who speak of spirits of the Andes who must be placated by human sacrifice for the road-workers' disturbance of the mountains?

Other stories unfold simultaneously in this technically tricky novel, in which the shift from one narrative to another can take place in the middle of a sentence. There are the individual histories of the three disappeared men, village legends of fat-sucking Indian vampires called *pishtacos,* accounts of the Senderistas' various victims—including a herd of silky vicuñas slaughtered to make an ideological point. And there are, inevitably, references to the brutal history of Incas and conquistadores . . . the beautifully evoked landscape seems awash in blood. The baroque quality of this novel contrasts with the more straightforward style of *Palomino* and suggests the more complicated political vision of the older author.

Generic Latin America

JUDD, Alan. *Tango* (GB & NY, 1990). Though the title points to Buenos Aires, the unnamed city that is the setting of this engaging novel sounds like a cross between Montevideo, Uruguay, and Santiago de Chile—with a view of the sea thrown in for good measure. William Wooding, recently arrived in South America to manage a British bookstore, falls in love with Theresa, a beautiful dancer (and prostitute) at Maria's Tango Club. Theresa has also caught the eye of the country's new president, an old schoolmate of William's. The president recruits William to act as his go-between with Theresa; William is also recruited as a spy by a ludicrous little man named Box, an agent of the newly "privatised" British Secret Service, who is fretting about a growing Cuban/Russian presence in the country. Meanwhile, William's wife has taken up with a CIA agent. The antecedents for this seriocomic tale of innocents abroad include Evelyn Waugh, William Boyd, and—especially—the Graham Greene of *Our Man in Havana.*

THOMAS, Ross. *Missionary Stew* (NY, 1983, 1984). This vintage Thomas thriller begins in the dungeons of an African ruler who sounds a lot like Idi Amin, moves on to examine the exercise of political power in the United States, and reaches a climax with a public execution in a Central American hellhole. As always, Thomas is a funny and caustic observer of political shenanigans and other peculiarities of the human condition. Treats for Thomas fans: the heroine's name is Velveeta Keats, and the title refers not to the maker of the stew but its chief ingredient.

NOTED BUT NOT REVIEWED

BAGLEY, Desmond. *High Citadel* (NY, 1965, 1972). When their small plane is sabotaged and crashes high in the Andes in the country of "Cordillera," a disparate group of survivors must battle the harsh environment as well as Communist guerrillas.

BENNETT, Ronan. *Overthrown by Strangers* (London, 1992). Three fugitives from a Los Angeles murder scene head for Latin America, each on a private quest.

BUCHAN, John. *The Courts of the Morning* (Boston & NY, 1929). A handful of Richard Hannay's old gang from *Greenmantle* (see Chapter X)—Sandy Arbuthnot, Archie Roylance, the inimitable John S. Blenkiron—are reunited in the South American country of "Olifa," where trouble is brewing for the United States.

CARPENTIER, Alejo. *The Chase* [1956], translated by Alfred Mac Adam (NY, 1989, 1990). A Cuban classic about a man in flight from political assassins.

DEIGHTON, Len. *MAMista* (GB, 1991, 1992). Set in the jungles of "Spanish Guiana," this adventure involves some idealistic foreign recruits of the guerrilla organization of the title, the *Movimiento de Acción Marxista.*

GOLDMAN, Francisco. *The Long Night of White Chickens* (NY, 1992). This densely written thriller (a finalist for the PEN/Faulkner fiction award) concerns the Guatemalan-American narrator's search for the truth about the murder of his adoptive sister, who is accused of trafficking in stolen babies.

HAGGARD, William. *Closed Circuit* (GB, 1960; Baltimore, 1963). The setting is the republic of "Candoro," in which English settlers have a huge stake. Francis Mason is the heir to a large *estancia,* but his property is threatened by a new dictator with a grudge.

LE CARRÉ, John. *The Tailor of Panama* (London & NY, 1996). In which the title character becomes an unlikely spy.

MASON, F. Van Wyck. *Maracaibo Mission* (NY, 1965). One of the last of Mason's twenty-six Colonel Hugh North adventures, this outing sends the Army Intelligence troubleshooter to the Maracaibo oil fields in Venezuela. The Russkies, and their Caribbean pals *("Los Barbudos—the Bearded Ones")* have developed a secret weapon to destroy the U.S. oil refineries.

RENICK, Jeane. *Trust Me* (NY, 1992). Set in Belize and Guatemala, this romance charts the growing passion between two volunteers on an archeological dig. In the jungle they meet new challenges: jaguars, drug smugglers, scorpions, heavy breathing.

SEYMOUR, Gerald. *The Fighting Man* (NY & GB, 1993). Three Mayan Indians from Guatemala journey to Scotland to seek the help of Fighting Man Gord Brown, who's having a sort of mercenary's midlife crisis.

SOUZA, Marcio. *Death Squeeze* [Rio de Janeiro, 1984], translated by Ellen Watson (NY, 1992). The protagonist is a former Brazilian army captain, who quit the military because of its repressive role. A murder close to home drags him back into a world of brutal politics.

SZULC, Tad. *Diplomatic Immunity* (NY, 1981). The new ambassador to the Central American nation of "Malagua" (Nicaragua under the Somozas?) has a mind of her own, which gets her into trouble.

CLOSE-UP

If You Read Spanish

By José Latour (a.k.a. Javier Morán)

SHAPED BY A long history of dictatorships, corruption, and rock-bottom poverty, to which recent years have added political terrorism, drug trafficking, and money laundering, the contemporary crime novel in Latin America is far removed from the classic mystery on the genteel English model.

The social inequalities at the root of most plots beget judgments and moral verdicts, sometimes harshly black-and-white, other times subtly nuanced in shades of gray. Perhaps the belated influence of Hammett and Chandler can be found in recent stories depicting violence, state crimes, and human-rights abuses in a realistic fashion. Forensic medicine is crude, police procedurals almost nonexistent. Powerless or corrupt courts of law have not produced an attractive literature of litigation.

On the bright side, the Latin propensity for love, music, sports, and wry humor supply an appealing atmosphere in many books.

Among the good Latin American crime writers not yet translated into English, the following are especially recommended.

In Argentina

Born in 1943, **Ricardo Piglia,** who is also known as a critic and editor, wrote his first mystery in 1967. *Respiración artificial* ("Artificial Respiration"), *Prisión perpetua* ("Life Imprisonment"), and *La ciudad ausente* ("The Missing City") are three of his best-known books. A close observer of human motivations and the propensity for violence, Piglia describes the darkest pits of Argentina's cities in a painstakingly polished Spanish loaded with complex meanings and multiple interpretations.

Argentine soccer, gambling, and nightlife are portrayed in the early work of **Juan Sasturaín,** born in 1945. *Manual de perdedores, Volúmenes I y II* ("The Loser's Handbook, vols. 1 and 2") is a good example. Sasturaín now lives in Spain. His 1991 *Los sentidos del agua* ("The Courses of

Water") is an irreverent story that deals with illegal Latin American immigrants printing pulp fiction with coded messages for subversives from Barcelona.

José Pablo Feinmann published *Ultimos días de la victima* ("Last Days of the Victim") in 1979 when he was thirty-six. This novel about a professional killer has a Borgesian metaphysical twist. Feinmann's other crime novels include *Ni el tiro del final* ("Not Even the Last Shot") in 1982 and *El ejército de ceniza* ("Army of Ashes") in 1986.

In Mexico

Argentinian **Rolo Diez** began writing while exiled in Mexico in 1981; he was forty-one. After three books set in his country of birth during the bloody dictatorship of the late seventies and two more mixing Argentine and Mexican characters and situations, his *Luna de escarlata* ("Scarlet Moon") won the 1995 Hammett prize for the best crime fiction book in Spanish. The plot unfolds in overpopulated Mexico City and concerns social climbers engaged in shady deals, drugs, and sex, among uniformed criminals on the loose.

In Chile

Now sixty, **Poli Délano,** who teaches English at the university in Santiago de Chile, has written several books blending crime fiction and Chilean political history. *Como si no muriera nadie* ("As If Nobody Died") and *En este lugar sagrado* ("At This Sacred Place") are considered two of his best. Délano's work is critical of Chilean middle-class values and the American way of life.

In Cuba

Uruguayan **Daniel Chavarría,** who has lived in Cuba for twenty-seven years, published his first book, *Joy,* a spy novel, in 1977, when he was a forty-four-year-old university professor of Greek. Among his eight books, two purely Latin American thrillers stand out: *La sexta isla* ("The Sixth Island") in 1984 and *Allá ellos* ("It's Up to Them") in 1991—the winner of that year's Hammett. Chavarría revives the tradition of the Spanish picaresque, with lovable rogues, shady deals, and hidden treasures interspersed with present-day laser beams and hallucinogens.

In Uruguay

Juan Grompone, a computer engineer born in 1939, is one of the few Latin American crime writers whose plots and styles remind readers of the classic mystery. He published *Ciao! Napolitano* ("Goodbye, Neapolitan!") in 1991 and *Asesinato en el Hotel de Baños* ("Murder at the Seaside Hotel") in 1992. In the latter, the logician members of the Leibniz Society try to find the culprit in a murder committed sixty-one years before their meeting.

A Note to the Reader

In putting together this guide, inevitably we have overlooked many worthy titles and authors. If you know of mysteries with foreign settings that should be included in any future edition of *Crimes of the Scene*, please write Nina Knig, c/o St. Martin's Press, 175 Fifth Avenue, New York, NY 10010-7848.

Index

The Contributors

NINA KING is the editor of *Book World,* the literary supplement of *The Washington Post.*

ROBIN W. WINKS, chairman of the History Department at Yale University, is the author of *Modus Operandi: An Excursion into Detective Fiction* and *Cloak and Gown: Scholars in the Secret War.*

HELGA ANDERLE, Austrian journalist and fiction writer, is the editor of the first international anthology of women crime writers.

VICKI BARKER, a radio and TV journalist based in London, covered the Gulf War and has traveled widely in the Mideast.

DENNIS DRABELLE is a Washington-based writer and editor.

CARMEN IARRERA, who lives in Rome, is the author of two crime novels, *Guantanamera* and *Jihad 1999.*

REINHARD JAHN, a German novelist and journalist, has coauthored two crime novels under the pen name H. P. Karr. The most recent, *Rattensommer,* won the Glauser Award for best German crime novel published in 1995.

JOSÉ LATOUR of Havana has published three crime novels under the pseudonym Javier Morán: *Preludio a la noche* ("Prelude to the Night"), *Medianoche Enemiga* ("Enemy's Midnight"), and *Fauna Nocturna* ("Nocturnal Fauna").

JIM LEHRER, host of PBS's *NewsHour with Jim Lehrer,* is the author of nine novels, two memoirs, and three plays.

RICHARD LIPEZ, who served in the Peace Corps in Ethiopia, writes detective novels as Richard Stevenson.

ANTHONY OLCOTT, who teaches Russian history at Cornell University, is the author of two mysteries with Russian settings, *Murder at the Red October* and *May Day in Magadan.*

MARK I. PINSKY, a former staff writer for the *Los Angeles Times,* now covers religion for the *Orlando Sentinel.* In 1982–83, he worked as an editorial adviser to the Xinhua (New China) News Agency in Beijing.

THOMAS PRZYBILKA, German bookseller and bibliographer, is the founder of BoKAS (Bonner Krimi Archiv Sekundärliteratur).

REGULA VENSKE is the author of three crime novels set in Hamburg. The most recent, *Rent a Russian* (1995), won a Deutscher Krimi Preis.